Waterfronts Revisited

Waterfronts Revisited addresses the historical evolution of the relationship between port and city and re-examines waterfront development by looking at the urban territory and historical city in their complexity and entirety.

By identifying guiding values, urban patterns and typologies, and local needs and experiences, cities can break the isolation of the harbour by reconnecting it to the urban structure—its functions, spaces and forms. Using the UNESCO recommendation for the 'Historic Urban Landscape' as the guiding concept and a tool for managing urban preservation and change, this collection of essays illustrates solutions to issues of globalization, commercialization of space and commoditization of culture in waterfront development. Through sixteen selected case studies, editors Heleni Porfyriou and Marichela Sepe offer planners and urban designers a broad spectrum of alternative solutions to waterfront regeneration interventions and redevelopments, addressing sustainability, regional cultural diversity, and the debate between conservation and transformation.

Heleni Porfyriou is Senior Researcher in charge of the Rome Unit of the Institute for the Conservation and Enhancement of Cultural Heritage of the National Research Council of Italy—CNR. She has taught and published extensively on urban and town planning history in Italy and the Nordic countries. Her current research interests concern urban conservation, enhancement and management of historic cities in Europe and China.

Marichela Sepe is a researcher with the IRISS of the CNR of Naples. Since 2003, she has been a member of the Research Doctorate Committee and a Contract Professor for the DiARC, University of Naples Federico II. Her research interests include the contemporary urban landscape, urban design, territorial and environmental planning, and creative urban regeneration. On these topics, she has published several scientific articles and books and won awards. Sepe is on the Steering Committee of INU and EURA, and a member of the UDG.

Routledge Research in Planning and Urban Design
Series editor:
Peter Ache
Radboud University, Nijmegen, Netherlands

Routledge Research in Planning and Urban Design is a series of academic monographs for scholars working in these disciplines and the overlaps between them. Building on Routledge's history of academic rigour and cutting-edge research, the series contributes to the rapidly expanding literature in all areas of planning and urban design.

Waterfronts Revisited

European ports in a historic and
global perspective

**Edited by Heleni Porfyriou
and Marichela Sepe**

Routledge
Taylor & Francis Group

NEW YORK AND LONDON

First published 2017
by Routledge
711 Third Avenue, New York, NY 10017

and by Routledge
2 Park Square, Milton Park, Abingdon, Oxon OX14 4RN

First issued in paperback 2018

Routledge is an imprint of the Taylor & Francis Group, an informa business

Library of Congress Cataloging-in-Publication Data
Names: Porfyriou, Heleni, 1956– editor. | Sepe, Marichela, editor.
Title: Waterfronts revisited : European ports in a historic and
    global perspective / Edited by Heleni Porfyriou and
    Marichela Sepe.
Description: New York : Routledge, 2016. | Includes index.
Identifiers: LCCN 2016008903 (print) | LCCN 2016009669 (ebook) |
    ISBN 9781138638433 (hardback) | ISBN 9781315637815 (ebook)
Subjects: LCSH: Waterfronts—Planning—Case studies. | City planning—
    Case studies. | Cultural landscapes—Conservation and restoration—
    Case studies.
Classification: LCC NA9053.W38 W38 2016 (print) | LCC NA9053.
    W38 (ebook) | DDC 711/.4—dc23
LC record available at http://lccn.loc.gov/2016008903

ISBN 13: 978-1-138-59509-5 (pbk)
ISBN 13: 978-1-138-63843-3 (hbk)

Typeset in Sabon
by Apex CoVantage, LLC

To our families

Contents

Acknowledgements

We would like to thank all the authors who have contributed to this volume, offering promising new opportunities for cultural exchange on the topic of waterfronts.

We would also like to thank the publisher, Routledge, the referees and team for their support, useful comments and suggestions towards improving the book. Our special thanks go to Elizabeth Brooks for her creative editing and work to make the chapters flow in her mother tongue.

Figures

Contributors

Donatella Calabi is Professor Emeritus of Urban History at the University IUAV of Venice. She has been a Visiting Professor in Europe, South America and Japan. She worked on Town Planning History between the nineteenth and the twentieth centuries and on the European city of early modern times (on market spaces and buildings, minorities and their districts in great commercial cities). Some of her essays have been translated into English, French, German, Greek, Dutch, Spanish, Portuguese and Japanese.

Francesco Gastaldi is Associate Professor in Town Planning at the University IUAV of Venice. He achieved a degree in Architecture at the University of Genova, and a PhD in Territorial Planning and Local Development at the Polytechnic University of Turin. He has written extensively on urban regeneration in Italy.

Oriana Giovinazzi is an architect with a PhD in Urban Planning and Public Policies from the University IUAV of Venice. She is a journalist and the Managing Director and Editorial Coordinator of *PORTUS—Port City Relationship and Urban Waterfront Redevelopment* and *PORTUSplus*. She has spoken at conferences and has been a scientific coordinator of conventions and exhibitions. Giovinazzi has published articles in journal and monographs, and she has directed several research projects.

Vilma Hastaoglou-Martinidis is Professor Emeritus of the School of Architecture, Aristotle University of Thessaloniki, Greece. She has published on Greek and Eastern Mediterranean cities in the late nineteenth and the twentieth centuries. Her research interests include planning history, urban modernization and heritage preservation.

Carola Hein is Professor and Head, Chair of History of Architecture and Urban Planning at Delft University of Technology. She has published and lectured widely on topics in contemporary and historical architectural and urban planning—notably in Europe and Japan—and has authored several articles and books on capital city issues in Brussels, Strasbourg, Luxembourg, Berlin and Tokyo.

Felicitas Hillmann is head of the Regeneration of Cities and Towns research unit at the Leibniz-Institute for Society and Space (IRS) and is Professor of Urban Transformation in International Perspective at the Technical University in Berlin. Her research interests focus on questions of migration and urban transformation. She has published widely in the fields of international migration and labour market integration, and on the dynamics of migrant entrepreneurship. Recent work includes the question of development and fragmentation, e.g. the emergence of new regional formations and the emblematic role of new mobilities in port cities.

Hidenobu Jinnai was born in Fukuoka, Japan, and earned a B.Sc. of Engineering from the University of Tokyo. He studied at the University IUAV of Venice on an Italian government scholarship (1973–1975) and at ICCROM (1975–1976). He has been a Professor at Hosei University since 1990. His awards include Onorificenza di Ufficiale of Repubblica Italiana, 2002; Laurea honoris causa in Architettura, Sapienza Università di Roma, 2007; Premio Architettura Sardegna, 2008; La Federazione degli Architetti, Pianificatori, Paesaggisti e Conservatori della Sardegna, 2008; and the cittadinanza onoraria di Amalfi, 2011.

Dimitrios M. Kontogeorgis is Adjunct Lecturer in History at the International Hellenic University. He was awarded his Doctor of Philosophy degree by the University of Athens. His research interests focus on Modern Greek and Balkan political and intellectual history, the Greek diaspora, as well as the economic and social history of South-eastern Europe. He has published various studies in journals and collective volumes.

Cristina Pallini is Senior Researcher at DABC, Politecnico di Milano, and teaches Architectural Design at the local faculty of Architecture. She holds a PhD in Architectural Composition (IUAV, 2001). Her research has been supported by scholarships from the Italian CNR, the Greek IKY and Ministry of Education, AKPIA@MIT, and the Onassis Foundation.

Rosario Pavia is Professor of Theory of Urbanism at the Faculty of Architecture, University of Pescara. He is also the director of *Piano Progetto Città, LiST.* He has published extensively, including *L'idea di città* (Franco Angeli, 1994), *Paesaggi elettrici* (Marsilio, 1998), *Babele* (Meltemi, 2002), *Le paure dell'urbanistica* (Meltemi, 2005), *Waterfront* (LiSTLab, 2012), *Il Passo della città* (Donzelli, 2015). He is an international recognized expert in waterfront planning. In Italy he designed numerous waterfront projects, such as the waterfront of Naples, Taranto, Marina di Carrara, Pescara and Corigliano Calabro.

John Pendlebury is a town planner and urban conservationist. He is Head of School of Architecture Planning and Landscape, Newcastle University. His principal publications include *Conservation in the Age of Consensus*

(Routledge, 2009) as well as the edited collections *Valuing Historic Environments* (Ashgate, 2009, with Lisanne Gibson) and *Alternative Visions of Post-War Reconstruction: Creating the Modern Townscape* (Routledge, 2015, with Erdem Erten and Peter Larkham).

Marcela Pizzi Kirschbaum earned her Master of Architecture at Washington University. She is Professor of Architecture and Urbanism at the University of Chile and at present acts as Dean of Faculty. She teaches studio and architectural history as well as research on industrial architectural heritage, and she has published extensively.

Heleni Porfyriou is Senior Researcher in charge of the Rome Unit of the Institute for the Conservation and Enhancement of Cultural Heritage of the National Research Council of Italy—CNR. She has taught and published extensively on urban and town planning history in Italy and the Nordic countries. Her current research interests concern urban conservation, enhancement and management of historic cities in Europe and China.

Michelangelo Savino has been Associate Professor of Urban Techniques and Planning since 2003. After a period of teaching at the Faculty of Engineering at the University of Messina, he joined the Department of Civil, Environmental Engineering and Architecture at the University of Padua in 2013. Since 2007 he has been co-editor of the international journal *Archivio di Studi Urbani e Regionali*. He has a PhD in Regional and Town Planning from the University IUAV of Venice.

Dirk Schubert is Professor for Urban Planning, Comparative Planning History, Housing and Urban Renewal at HafenCity University in Hamburg. His research focuses on urban planning history and he studies the revitalization of harbour and waterfront areas in seaport regions and city/port interface areas. His latest books are *Contemporary Perspectives on Jane Jacobs: Reassessing the Impacts of an Urban Visionary* (Routledge, 2014), and *Jane Jacobs und die Stadt. Diskurse—Perspektiven—Paradigmenwechsel* (Franz Steiner Verlag, 2014). He is elected President of the International Planning History Society.

Marichela Sepe is a researcher with the IRISS of the CNR of Naples. Since 2003, she has been a member of the Research Doctorate Committee and a Contract Professor for the DiARC, University of Naples Federico II. Her research interests include the contemporary urban landscape, urban design, territorial and environmental planning, creative urban regeneration. On these topics, she has published several scientific articles and books and won awards. Sepe is on the Steering Committee of INU and EURA, and a member of the UDG.

Hicran Topçu is an architect and holds a PhD in Restoration. She taught in the Middle East Technical University of Ankara and worked in the

Development Agency of Izmir. She carried out part of her postgraduate studies in Italy and attended courses at the ICCROM and ILO on cultural heritage management and development.

Stephen V. Ward is Professor of Planning History at Oxford Brookes University, UK. He is a past President of the International Planning History Society and former Editor of *Planning Perspectives*. He has published very extensively on many aspects of planning history, and has authored many articles and book chapters, along with several well-known books. His current work focuses on the international circulation of planning ideas, the British garden city and new town movements.

Chen Yu is an Architect and Urban Historian, and is Assistant Professor in the Department of Architecture, National University of Singapore, JSPS. She is a Visiting Scholar in the Department of Architecture, Hosei University (Japan). Her research focuses on history of treaty ports in China, Chinese overseas architecture in South-east Asia and urban regeneration in Asia.

Introduction

Port Cities and Waterfront Developments: From the Re-actualization of History to a New City Image

Heleni Porfyriou and Marichela Sepe

This introduction sets out by presenting the purpose and outline of the book, explaining the division of its chapters into parts and sections, and framing the chapters that follow by tracing the steps through which the waterfront area has become disconnected from its urban context, and through a range of international case studies, reconnecting the waterfront with its proper historical and urban moorings. The second part of the introduction then brings together various cultural, social and environmental elements of contemporary waterfront schemes, highlighting the way culture is deployed to shape consumable experiences and new marketing strategies for contemporary waterfront developments, and exploring more holistic strategies that might embrace the complexity of developing city-port-waterfronts.

Purpose and Outline of the Book

Water cities, in pre-industrial societies, represented a predominant urban form. From ancient times, the foundation of a city has been linked to the choice of a site close to water, usually a river or a natural harbour. Rivers, canals and harbours have determined the birth and the growth of many cities in Mediterranean, European and American or Asian countries up to the nineteenth century.

Ports in this long history of cities, worldwide, were integral parts of city building and development and were often closely related to regional economies. At times, places of a cosmopolitan and multicultural character, of intense exchanges of goods and ideas, they were considered as maritime gateways, international showcases and spaces for promoting economies, that always developed according to natural topography and in close relationship to local history and traditions.

With the advent of industrialization, technical innovations regarding both the means of transportation and the handling of goods greatly affected the spatial configuration of port cities, often introducing a rigid separation or stratification (physical, functional and social) between the harbour and the city itself.

Since the 1960s, however, deindustrialization has resulted in the abandonment of a large number of harbour sites. To confront the urban and social decay of these areas a new approach aiming at their revitalization, known as *waterfront development*, has appeared and gradually grown. In their early phases, these interventions treated the waterfront as a separate part of the city, detached from the surrounding urban fabric and its characteristics, and introduced new functions (leisure, commercial and green areas). The 'festival market' approach, together with mixed public-private partnerships and the strategy of 'returning the shoreline to the people', became inseparable ingredients of the model, which can be said to have originated in Baltimore.

Although this model was criticized in its European incarnation in the London Docklands (1980s), it persisted and evolved with the introduction of international events organized to take place in waterfront developments, as in the cases of Barcelona and Genova—developing as a global myth, which was even cited in the recent redevelopment schemes for Singapore and Shanghai.

The focus of this book is the evolution of historic port cities, and it aims to revisit *waterfront development* in the context of the urban territory and the historical city in their complexity and entirety, undoing the isolation of the harbour and reconnecting it with the urban structure, its functions, spaces and forms. Considering the waterfront development approach—as codified in what has become known as the Baltimore-Boston-Barcelona model—as congruent with the growing level of competition between cities, the increased demands of the tourist industry and market-driven urban developments, but alien to local economic and cultural needs and historic conditions, this collection of essays revisits waterfronts, hoping to discover lessons from the past that can help to deal with the contemporary issues of globalization, commercialization of space and commoditization of culture. The intention is, in other words, to raise awareness among the various stakeholders in waterfront cities, so that future projects might make space for re-actualizing the past, through the identification of guiding values related to the city-waterfront relationship in history, and for urban conservation, rather than simply re-enacting the entrepreneurial blueprints promoted by a global market.

In this context a number of case studies are presented that offer a broad spectrum of alternative solutions to waterfront regeneration interventions and redevelopments worldwide, that address issues of sustainability, regional cultural diversity and of conservation versus transformation, while introducing the concept and tool of the Historic Urban Landscape as a way of simultaneously managing urban preservation and change.

Waterfronts in a Historical Perspective

Since the appearance of the Baltimore model, a large body of literature has grown up around waterfront developments, from a range of disciplinary perspectives; while port cities and their history have also been the topic of various interdisciplinary research studies. So what contributions can this volume make, on such a broadly researched subject?

Making a critical assessment, the simplest answer is that it addresses both the concept of *waterfront* and the different transformations that the *waterfront development* approach has undergone up to the present. In this sense, the book focuses on the relationship throughout history of the port with the city and investigates in what ways planning, conservation, urban design and management tools (such as the recent UNESCO recommendation on the Historic Urban Landscape) have tried to address this connection in recent regeneration projects. The intention is to increase awareness of the nature and extent of city-port interactions, in historic European cities both in the past and today and to contribute to more responsive planning and design policies worldwide, relative to environmental, heritage and identity issues. Such a critical assessment is principally based on this volume's historical perspective and comparative approach.

One of the book's foundational positions is that the 1960s waterfront development approach introduced a new model for urban regeneration and, most importantly, it *affirmed a distinction between the waterfront and the city, which had never previously existed.* Ports—as the two chapters of Part I, dedicated to urban history and the development of European sea and river ports in early modern and modern times, describe—have always been founded, developed and transformed as a whole and in close relationship with larger territorial demands and opportunities. It is only with the advent of industrialization that in port cities—similarly to all other urban agglomerations—a zoning approach to industrial functions was introduced, that gradually evolved a more fragmented and distinct development which isolates port functions from the city. But even then, the port and the city were parts of a single whole, although at times physically separated.

In fact, harbours with their daily productive functions, as well as their notorious districts and dangerous night life, feature equally in the chronicles of early modern times and of nineteenth-century romances, as well as in the 1950s descriptions of London or Genova—and belong to a single urban literature on port cities. However, with the 1960s waterfront development approach this unity of perception is broken down. The harbour, or more specifically its liminal waterfront area, is detached from its context (in geographical and historical terms) and considered as a separate element with respect to the city area, one where new development can be introduced.

Of course, by the time the harbour and its related functions had changed, becoming obsolete, these areas were abandoned and these parts of the city often belonged to a maritime or port authority, which was distinct from the municipal authority. In many cases docks, arsenals or other port services were separated from the rest of the city with walls. In other cases, railway lines and other partition structures divided the city from its port. Still, port cities were a unique, entangled whole. With the interventions of the 1960s, however, a new era was opened up. The regeneration of abandoned harbour areas introduced the concept, which had never previously existed, of the 'waterfront' and consequently the new fiction that thanks to 'waterfront development' citizens would be able to regain their lost contact with the sea(!). In other words, the waterfront development approach introduces implicitly, or even involuntarily, a separation in the perception of port cities, between the city and the port and more specifically between the city and the waterfront.

The book investigates that new perception and narrative through different case studies. In this sense it 'revisits' waterfront developments. It does so by introducing a historical perspective and by analyzing the impact of the 'waterfront approach' model. In Part I it reaffirms what really took place in the historical development of a number of European port cities, ranging from medieval Venice to Renaissance Le Havre or Livorno, up to the eighteenth and nineteenth century Danubian port cities or the Black Sea port of Constanţa. As is clearly shown by Calabi and Kontogeorgis in the two chapters that make up Part I of the book, independently of the different historic and geographic connotations and developments of the multiple case studies they discuss, the two facets of the port city (that is the city and its harbour) have always been closely interlinked.

In Part II follow a few examples showing the development of Eastern Mediterranean port cities, that, historically speaking, represent the most stratified cases. Cases such as Istanbul, Thessalonica, Izmir, Beirut or Alexandria are presented through the double lens of their historical development. On the one hand these cases show how the harbours' conversion in the nineteenth century maintained a unity of perception between the port and the city; and on the other they highlight how contemporary projects, introduced since the 1990s, exclusively address the waterfront area along the lines of the 1960s approach.

These chapters illustrate how the regeneration of old harbour sites, aiming at the creation of a culture-led service sector, could be a powerful tool for re-establishing these important cultural ensembles as major points of innovation, at both local and global levels. However, the practical outcomes of these redevelopment processes show, as revealed in Hastaoglou-Martinidis's chapter, that historic waterfronts are more likely to be restructured in a way that overturns their traditional character, as opposed to enhancing it. The loss of cities' individuality and ultimately of essential features of their history is closely related not only to the use of globalized models, but also to the aims and objectives of the developers (and corporate capital) involved. In this sense the marketing slogan for Beirut's new waterfront—proposed by the site's developer, Solidere, in the early twenty-first century—'Beirut, an ancient city for the future' (which replaced the initial motto they had proposed in the 1990s: 'Beirut, the Hong Kong of the Mediterranean') speaks volumes. It suggests evidence for the contention that real estate capital, with the advent of the new century, has understood that global regeneration models are better marketed using culture rather than simply through notions of 'free-ports' consumerism. Furthermore, it represents a misuse of the idea of culture, particularly in light of the treatment meted out to the rich archaeological findings discovered during the rehabilitation project, which were barely preserved, some even being removed. Closely following these lines of development is the situation in Istanbul, where the Galataport Project—for a cruise port, a recreation area and a social-cultural facility in the Karaköy-Salıpazarı quarter—seriously threatens the integrity of the historic peninsula.

Part III, revisiting waterfront developments, represents the core of the volume, covering eleven chapters split into two sections. In the first section, Stephen Ward's chapter critically presents the birth of waterfront regeneration as a global phenomenon and highlights the way the redevelopment process of derelict docks and abandoned or obsolete port areas has been promoted since the 1960s. The model role played by the Boston-Baltimore cases was initially characterized by a festival market idea centred on the leisure-tourism-tertiary functions of a joint venture intervention. When it began to be emulated in Europe, this model was enriched by the impact of major events and star-architect interventions, both of which represented clear investments in marketing the city's image. Notwithstanding the negative criticisms made of the London Docklands (in relation to planning deregulation and gentrification) the approach taken by the London Docklands Development Corporation to introducing housing in environmentally qualified conditions, alongside new tertiary activities, gave further impetus to waterfront developments. So, from a simple model—exported and disseminated by its original authors (such as Rouse and Thompson) as Ward's chapter suggests—it evolved into a global approach, the first such to take advantage of the globalisation of financial markets.

The chapters that follow, through diverse case studies chosen from across the world, exemplify how the waterfront development model was copied or emulated and its impacts on different local contexts. They illustrate "differences in cause, procedure, results and planning tradition", stressing that "transformation and reclamation is not simply a matter of architectural design but also depends on a complex set of planning, institutional, political, client-related, economic, ecological, legal and financial issues" as Dirk Shubert puts it in Chapter 14. Thus, the case of Italy is presented through different lenses, with both success and failure stories, such as those relayed in the chapters on Genova and Messina respectively. The development of Italian historic port cities in the nineteenth century is identified by Rosario Pavia in Chapter 10 as the principal cause for the lack of substantial experimentation with the waterfront development model in Italy. However, it's difficult to avoid noticing—as the cases of Marseille or HafenCity show (discussed in Chapters 15 and 14 respectively)—that the real obstacle in Italy's waterfront regeneration projects is the lack of management capacities and strategic decision making by central government.

These cases show that, due to the 'successful' outcomes from waterfront developments since the 1960s, derelict harbour areas are now considered 'attractive waterfront locations', based on the high returns promised by their regeneration. If initially, with the Boston-Baltimore model, these locations were valued mainly as sites for leisure-tourist functions, soon afterwards, with the London Docklands introduction of housing and tertiary sector facilities, so as to develop in the direction of a 'financial yuppie city', waterfronts' proximity to rivers or the sea has also been appreciated for its environmental benefits—an idea immediately taken up by the markets through the image of 'world-class city quarters' (e.g. Dublin). Nowadays in most waterfront developments a new, added-value aspect has been identified (one that was largely missing in the early years): namely, heritage assets and cultural value. This is mainly due to the importance assumed by cultural tourism as a major industry worldwide, promoting the equal profitability of culture-led with property-led regeneration. This trend has developed gradually since the late 1980s and has gone hand in hand with the major events industry (Culture Capital Cities, Expo, Olympic Games, etc.). The chapter dedicated to Genova is in this sense representative as a success story, while the story of Valparaiso discussed in Chapter 11 raises opposing considerations. By contrast, in Chapter 13 Tokyo is discussed as a 'city on the water', addressing the issue from an ecological viewpoint.

Different dynamics follow the transformation of urban waterfronts in China. As Chapter 12 illustrates these areas, often representing a colonial heritage, had an ambivalent role: posing identity issues and acting as a stimulus to city development in the post-reform era. Their social and cultural values were therefore reinterpreted to bolster city image and to increase place competiveness in a global context.

Heritage- and Culture-Led Regeneration

The kinds of features initially considered in the light of heritage assets included the architecture of old industrial buildings, their spatial sequences and typologies. But as Shaw (2001) identified, the context of the post-1990s worldwide economic recession was an important factor, leading cities to rethink their use of resources. Thus, since the 1990s, in some of the old stratified cities, the historic core, or the shoreline itself when endangered by land reclamation, are also recognized as heritage assets, together with the city's traditional profile, mixed-use harbour milieu and the archaeological discoveries made when excavations for port expansions are undertaken (such as in Istanbul, Beirut and Alexandria).

These heritage values, found in most old harbour areas, are, however, at times misused rather than enhanced by the new cultural functions assigned to old docks or warehouses (such as exhibition halls, museums, libraries, marketplaces, etc.). The imposition of star architects further contributes to this 'cultural' upgrading and successful marketing of old waterfront derelict areas as first-class tourist destinations. While, on occasion, the whole process has promoted appropriate preservation interventions that have culminated with the sites being included in the World Heritage Sites (WHS) list (e.g. Liverpool 2004, Genova and HafenCity), at the reverse end of the spectrum, some sites have consequently been added to the UNESCO 'in danger list' (Liverpool Waters 2013). Nonetheless, as John Pendlebury shows in his chapter on Liverpool, even these value judgements are not univocal.

In other words, the various case studies show how waterfront regenerations—whether property led (as in the 1960s), housing led (as in the 1980s), or environmentally and culturally led (since the advent respectively of the green and culture-tourism economies)—remain, above all, market-led regenerations, unless mitigated by a more complex, conscious approach that reintroduces waterfronts in their historic and geographical context. This book shows how each place grows and is transformed in relation to its own reality and local forces, and not exclusively in response to global market conditions. Through its comparative and historical perspective, the book is able to identify tendencies, reveal missteps, and recognize success stories and negative outcomes, with the hope of providing a useful overview and concrete insights that promote and re-establish the complexity of city-port-waterfronts for future developments.

Considering that the development of historic waterfronts can act as a catalyst for economic regeneration, two aspects should be kept in mind to support comprehensive and long-term sustainable interventions: the port's relationship with the city (both in infrastructural, functional and urban design/physical terms) and with its built and intangible heritage. It needs to be borne in mind that the transformation from a working port to a new post-industrial space can often be socially painful and politically contentious (Ward 2011). Economic regeneration has the potential to be socially exclusive and culturally selective: market dynamics do not always change the image of the city, but often generate fragmentation in the affected urban areas, as well as problems of social cohesion (Soja 2000). This is particularly the case now that tourist development and global marketing dictate what is successful, and where local identity has often being exchanged for star-architect flagship projects, branded as symbols of a new waterfront image. What can better exemplify this tendency than the tradition initiated with Cesar Pelli's Canary Wharf Tower in London Docklands (1990), Frank Gehry's Guggenheim Museum in Bilbao (1997) and the contemporary icon of the booming port of HafenCity in Hamburg: Herzog & de Meuron's Elbphilharmonie?

The second section of Part III, which begins with Chapter 14, is dedicated to recent tendencies in waterfront development based on sustainable planning solutions developed in relation to local cultures and history—such as the case of Marseille, based on a 'Euroméditerranée' project, and of a number of north-western European cities. Among these latter, Hamburg's HafenCity stands out as one of the most promising recent port city transformations.

It is in fact one of the largest redevelopment projects in Europe, halfway through its planned construction, and represents the best application of the lessons learned from the last forty years of waterfront revitalization, while encompassing all the standard ingredients. It reconnects the river and the city centre, giving a new direction to urban growth; it is plan-led, mixed-use, environmentally and socially sustainable, with good public infrastructure, and a warehouse/office district that is to be inscribed to the WHS list. It is managed by a quasi autonomous non-governmental organization that owns most of the land on the site, and in a nutshell, represents a blueprint for the development of a city on the waterfront.

However, HafenCity is also one of the major ports for the cruise industry, which in the eyes of many scholars represents a debatable and risky solution for waterfront revitalization in as much as it accentuates social and spatial fragmentation on urban waterfronts, as Hein and Hillmann's chapter discusses.

Thus, although contemporary waterfront development is shown to be increasingly organized around the marketing of cultural experiences, this book suggests that much still remains to be done in order to re-establish the complexity of city-port-waterfronts, in the interests of more integrated, sustainable, historically aware and context-sensitive future developments.

Culture and Consumption

The next part of this introduction looks more closely at the interconnections between culture and consumption in waterfront development, aiming to better contextualize how contemporary projects deploy place identity and branding in their search for a new city image. Before reviewing the extent to which these waterfront rebrandings are able to consider wider social and environmental concerns, this part discusses how culture is increasingly transformed into a consumable through the creation of a user or visitor 'experience'.

Smith and Garcia Ferrari (2012) highlight that, during the post-war period—by contrast with the periods that preceded it—many changes became evident, in particular depending on the use and meaning of places no longer devoted to production but utilized as spaces for consumption and (in some cases) rapid consumption. Thus the production of goods and services was replaced by the consumption of culture, food and events of various kinds (Couch *et al.* 2003; Urry 1995).

In contemporary projects, culture itself becomes an object of consumption through the creation of a marketable ensemble of sensory experiences, tied together through place-specific and historical narratives. The senses are part of people's everyday life, and sensory experience strongly shapes their memories (positive or otherwise) of the place (Lefebvre 1991). Urban environments, such as waterfronts, are nowadays designed to be distinctive in the attempt to create memorable sensory experiences for the people who use them. Urban studies agree on the fact that the goal of project interventions in urban space is increasingly to alter the experience of that space for its residents. Even people who visit ordinary urban centres can undergo a series of emotional experiences (perceived through the five senses) and descriptions of these experiences can vary from one place to another. Furthermore, the experience can differ depending on the means of transport available or pedestrian use of a place.

The term 'experiential' was introduced in 1982:

> as an approach that focuses on the symbolic, aesthetic and hedonistic nature of consumption, and which is based on the conception of the experience of consumption as an activity aimed at searching for amusements and sensations.
>
> (Holbrook and Hirschman 1982 in Capitello et al. 2012)

Later, it was shown that rational and emotional components can coexist and influence the degree of satisfaction, immersing the consumer in an experiential vision. In the product design process, the recognition of the importance of variables such as consumer emotions—in particular, feelings of pleasure—becomes critical. Since the beginning of the twenty-first century, market research has proposed a holistic product experience to the effect that every moment of the process of knowledge acquisition related to the product can be perceived satisfactorily (Falk and Campbell 1997; Menon and Kahn 2002; Rieunier 2002). This approach on the one hand affords a significant competitive advantage to the company which offers the product (such as those selling cruise trips) while on the other hand it necessitates a more accurate study of the offer in terms of experience. It also requires that the company achieve differentiated offerings in order to meet different needs, leading to 'customization' and an increase in terms of time and costs compared to the standard design. Besides the quality and reputation of the proposed product, determining factors in this regard are the attractiveness of the place and the functionality of its services, and intangible values such as tradition and the hospitality of the local population (Capitello et al. 2012). Profound knowledge of the place becomes an integral part of the product experience and, in that sense, the overall 'package' does not entail only a single product but also a system where one or more undertakings, local initiatives and entertainment activities promote a new image of the area.

The experience of the cruise in all its parts has taken on this direction. The growing number of tourists constitutes an important stimulus to undertake waterfront enhancements, creating a total experience of the place, its heritage and products (Hein 2011). Depending on the time devoted to the visit, the experience may be related to limited or larger parts of the city. In any case, everything has to be experienced in a short time. This has improved the design of innovative public spaces, buildings realized by international firms of architects, old factory renovation, food quality districts and so on, aimed at attracting people arriving from cruise ships to make a longer visit.

The sensory experience is used for the spectacularization of the place and its commercialization, as in the case of 'brandscapes' (Klingman 2007). In this case it is important to avoid widespread cloning of places because they might not fully engage the people who move into them (Lehtovuori 2010).

To complete the experience of a place and its urban environment, you need, as Seremetakis (1994) claimed, to recall previous memories of that area. Remembering how such a place was different in the past both relates its history back to the environment in its current form and also revives the memory of the way it looked in the past. Alternatively, recognizing that a historic part of a city is just like other old town centres leads it to be defined as a 'type' rather than a unique urban environment. "As sustained by Eizenberg (2010), the continual remembrance of other places and previous surveys in the same place, whether a person assimilates in place both experienced and constantly refers to other places elsewhere" (Degen and Rose 2012).

Branding and Creativity

The increasingly important role of experience in the urban regeneration process—both for cruise passengers and for visitors in general—is leading cities to be involved in constructing suitable images and symbols of their transformed areas in order to meet new trends. As Jensen (2007) asserts: "The idea is understood to involve selective storytelling, or attempts to re-imagine the city" (in Eckstein and Throgmorton 2003). It has to do with coining concepts and articulating difference and identity. Seen in this light, urban branding is evocative storytelling aimed at educating its recipients to 'see the city in a particular way'. However, branding for identity construction also means branding for alterity construction (Czarniawska 2002).

In determining the new representation of the city, the role of communication—both that deriving from media and from participation processes—is important. It is also vital to comprehend the previous and coexisting images of the city. As Greenberg (2000: 230) observes:

> the branding strategy, in a complex manner, bears witness to the way in which the 'world city' is overlaying the 'built city'. In a dynamic process of socio-spatial dialectics (Richardson and Jensen 2003), the city becomes the frame upon which its physical surface is inscribed with new ways of playing the global competitive game. At the same time the city is represented in images, texts and logos and is thus embedded in a certain logic specific to the urban intervention.

In line with this approach, creativity is an important factor in the operations of waterfront regeneration (Sepe 2009). The main aim of the creative operation of transformation is to promote urban areas owing their competitiveness to distinctive local features with 'symbol-city' value, devoting special attention to opportunities in order to guide the evolution of urban systems (Florida 2002).

Examples of creative cities show us two types of creative cluster (Carta 2007). The first is the cultural cluster, which is created around activities such as fine arts, music, cinema, architectural works and design, and whose initiation is encouraged and planned by the local administration. The second is the event cluster, which develops out of the organization of great events or different kinds of recreational and cultural manifestations. Public support for the cultural cluster is necessary in the start-up phase as it provides credibility for cultural investment in the project and allows visibility at the international level. In this case, territorial policies should be devoted to creating the social and economic conditions necessary to develop an urban environment that attracts actors interested in the cultural arena. At the same time, these policies should be devoted to promoting those cultural activities which already exist, organizing events and cultural manifestations or building the infrastructure necessary to link the new image of the place to them. The Ciudad of Valencia, HafenCity in Hamburg (Sepe 2014), the Baltic on the Newcastle-Gateshead quayside, the Albert Docks and the Tate Liverpool are pertinent examples, which, together with the Cities of Art, represent extensive cultural clusters. In contrast, event clusters include the Expos (Zaragoza in 2008, Shanghai in 2010, etc.), the Venice Biennale, the European Capital of Culture (Genova in 2004, Helsinki in 2000, Marseille in 2013 etc.) and the Olympic Games (Athens in 2008, London in 2012, etc.). Such gatherings are based on activities which are related to leisure and are bound together by the importance that the city gains in connection to these events. Indeed, the organization and realization of these events bring together firms, sponsors, users and tourists, which in turn influence the city brand. The manufacturing and services 'machine' built around the event stays active throughout the year, while the event itself is of limited duration.

To enable a cluster of urban creativity, a system of governance must be created to support the network of players who cooperate with the objective both of enhancing the new and pre-existing resources, and contributing to embedding the results in the territory. This averts the danger of losing the positive impacts which these operations contribute throughout the year by the conclusion of the event. Thus, the cluster should serve to transform the intangible energies connected to culture, art and leisure into financial, productive and social resources both for the host city and the surrounding area (Anholt 2007; Landry 2000).

Towards a Sustainable Complexity

The increase in cruises all over the world, with the related rise in numbers of passengers, represents a new development in the relationship between the port and city which from one point of view is a stimulus for the enhancement of an area, but from another perspective represents a danger to the environment. Another environmental threat comes from climate change, with an interesting development in many countries being (as in the case of Tokyo) design projects arising from the need to increase the resilience of cities near coasts.

An all-inclusive approach comes from the EU Commission report *Cities of Tomorrow. Challenges, Visions, Ways Forward* (2011), which reports that a more holistic model for the sustainable development of the city is needed. In particular, one section of the document suggests that to develop a green, healthy and attractive city, a holistic approach must be adopted towards the environmental and energy-related sphere. To achieve this, there has to be a balanced and innovative territorial development that safeguards identity-giving features and connects economic growth with the sustainable use of natural resources. Global competiveness has to be inclusive and to favour the local economy—adopting an integrated approach to urban planning and development—and to involve social, economic, environmental and territorial dimensions of urban development.

This approach should be combined with a strong and clear strategic vision of the city, and, especially, a shared one—at all levels—in order to avoid unsatisfactory results that will not last. Diversification is also important. As Bruttomesso (2001: 42) asserts:

> On observing the main waterfront projects in detail, it is clear that one of the essential elements is the co-presence of numerous activities which, combined in different percentage depending on the case, give life to new pieces of cities marked by an interesting feature entailing complexity.

The diverse activities in the waterfront area need to be integrated into urban life cycles. The area should house public buildings such as universities, museums and so on. This allows its continuous use and full integration into the city, with a consequent increase in satisfaction for residents, visitors and tourists.

Urban development based merely on physical and material aspects, disregarding intangible culture, threatens to produce cloned places that could easily become consumed by globalization. To support local identities and enhance the distinctiveness of a place, the emphasis must be placed on art and culture.

Even though the process of urban transformation of waterfronts is typically the result of appropriate public-private negotiations between partners, problems often arise due to difficulties with involving local communities at all stages. This can be observed both during the process of transformation and in the new city areas created (Smith and Garcia Ferrari 2012). For successful long-term urban and cultural renewal that benefits all who frequent the area, it is important to constantly involve the population and consolidate place identity (Lynch 1960), while taking care to ensure the economic, social and environmental sustainability of the project.

The more value is given to local cultural distinctiveness—such as cultural heritage and place identity—the more the operation of urban regeneration may be embedded within the local fabric and be attractive for both residents and visitors (Richards and Wilson 2006).

This second part of the introduction has looked at how waterfront development in its many incarnations might be understood and, at the same time, steered towards more positive trajectories. Not all the chapters in this book have chosen to explore all aspects of a successful waterfront development—some are more focused on the way culture and history are used in the waterfront image and experience, others broaden out to explore economic factors, and the issues around social inclusion and environmental impacts. But it is hoped that, collectively, these contributions succeed in engaging a new and critical conversation between waterfront stakeholders and interpreters that seeks to open out the discussion and raise ambitions for the future.

Bibliography

Anholt, S. (2007), *Competitive Identity: The New Brand Management for Nations, Cities and Regions*, Houndmills and New York: Palgrave MacMillan.

Bruttomesso, R. (2001), 'Complexity on the Urban Waterfront', R. Marshall (ed.) *Waterfront in post-industrial cities*, London and New York: Spon Press.

Carta, M. (2007), *Creative City*, Barcelona: LISt.

Capitello, R., Castellani, P., Rossato, C. (2012), 'Territorio, impresa e consumatore: percorsi esperienziali nelle imprese vitivinicole', *XXIV Congresso annuale di sinergie*, Lecce: Università di Salento.

Couch, C., Fraser, C., Percy, S. (2003), *Urban Regeneration in Europe*, Oxford, UK: Blackwell Science Ltd.

Crang, M. (1998), *Cultural Geography*, London: Routledge.

Czarniawska, B. (2002), *A Tale of Three Cities: Or the Glocalization of City Management*, Oxford: Oxford University Press.

Degen, M., Rose, G. (2012), 'The Sensory Experiencing of Urban Design: The Role of Walking and Perceptual Memory', *Urban Studies*, 49(15): 3271–3287.

DETR/CABE (2000), *By Design: Urban Design and the Planning System: Towards Better Practice*, London: DETR.

Eckstein, B. J., Throgmorton, J.A. (2003), *Story and Sustainability: Planning, Practice, and Possibility for American Cities*, Cambridge, MA: MIT Press.

Eizenberg, E. (2010), 'Remembering Forgotten Landscapes: Community Gardens in New York City and the Reconstruction of Cultural Diversity', Fenster, T., Yacobi, H. (eds) *Remembering, and Forgetting City Builders*, Farnham: Ashgate.

EU Commission Report (2011), *Cities of Tomorrow. Challenges, Visions, Ways Forward*, www.ec.europa.eu

Falk N., (undated), *Turning the Tide*, www.urbed.com

Falk P., Campbell, C. (1997), *The Shopping Experience*, London: Sage.

Florida, R. (2002), *The Rise of the Creative Class. And How It's Transforming Work, Leisure, Community and Everyday Life*, New York: Basic Books.

Gordon, D.L.A. (1996), 'Planning, Design and Managing Change in Urban Waterfront Redevelopment', *The Town Planning Review*, 67(3), 261–290.

Graham, B. (Ed.) (1998), *Modern Europe - Place, Culture, Identity*, London: Arnold.

Greenberg, M. (2000), 'Branding Cities. A Social History of the Urban Lifestyle Magazine', *Urban Affairs Review*, 36(2), 230.

Hein, C. (ed.) (2011), *Port Cities: Dynamic Landscapes and Global Networks*, London: Routledge.

Klingman, A. (2007), *Brandscapes: Architecture in the Experience Economy*, Cambridge, MA: MIT Press.

Kolb, D.A. (1984), *Experiential Learning: Experience as the Source of Learning and Development*. Upper Saddle River, NJ: Prentice-Hall.

Jensen, O. B. (2007), 'Understanding Cultural Urban Branding', *Planning Theory*, 6

Landry, C. (2000), *The Creative City: A Toolkit for Urban Innovators*, London: Earthscan.

Landry, C. (2006), *The Art of City Making*, London: Earthscan.

Landry C. (2008), 'The Creative City: Its Origins and Futures', *Urban Design Journal*, 106.

Lefebvre, H. (1991), *The Production of Space*, Oxford, UK: Blackwell.

Lehtovuori, P. (2010), *Experience and Conflict: The Production of Urban Space*, London: Ashgate.

Liverpool Waters (undated). Home page. Available at: http://www.liverpoolwaters. co.uk/content/home.php (accessed on 4 September 2013).

Lynch, K. (1960), *The Image of the City*, New York: Architectural Press.

Marshal (ed) (2001), *Waterfront in post-industrial cities*, London and New York: Spon Press.

Menon S., Kahn B. (2002), 'Cross-Category Effects of Induced Arousal and Pleasure on the Internet Shopping Experience', *Journal of Retailing*, 78.

Mommaas, H. (2004), 'Cultural Clusters and the Post-Industrial City: Towards the Remapping of Urban Cultural Policy', *Urban Studies*, 4(3): 507–532.

Moulaert, F., Swyngedouw, E., Rodriquez, A. (2003), *The Globalized City*, Oxford, UK: Oxford University Press.K

Muxi, Z. (2004), *La Arquitectura de la Ciudad Global*, Barcelona: Gustavo Gili.

Richards, G., Wilson J. (2006), 'Developing Creativity in Tourist Experiences: A Solution to the Serial Reproduction of Culture?', *Tourism Management*, 27(6).

Richardson, T., Jensen, O. B. (2003), 'Linking Discourse and Space: Towards a Cultural Sociology of Space in Analysing Spatial Policy Discourses', *Urban Studies*, 40(1), 7–22.

Rieunier, S. (ed), (2002), *Le marketing sensoriel du point de vente*, Paris: Dunod.

Scott, A. J. (2006), 'Creative Cities: Conceptual Issues and Policy Questions', *Journal of Urban Affairs*, 28(1), 1–17.

Sepe, M. (2009), "Creative Urban Regeneration between Innovation, Identity and Sustainability", in *International Journal of Sustainable development*, special issue, "Creative Urban Design and Development" L. Fusco Girard, P. Lombardi, P. Nijkamp (eds.), 12 (2–3–4): 144–159.

Sepe M. (2014), 'Urban Transformation, Socio-Economic Regeneration and Participation: Two Cases of Creative Urban Regeneration,' *International Journal of Urban Sustainable Development* 6(1): 20–41.

Sepe, M. (2013a), *Planning and Place in the City. Mapping Place Identity*, London and New York: Routledge.

Sepe M. (2013b), 'Places and Perceptions in Contemporary City', *Urban Design International*, 18(2): 111–113.

Sepe M. (2013c), 'Urban History and Cultural Resources in Urban Regeneration: A Case of Creative Waterfront Renewal,' *Planning Perspectives Journal*, 28(4): 595–613.

Sepe, M., Pitt, M. (2014), 'The Characters of Place in Urban Design', *Urban Design International*, 19(3): 215–227.

Soja, E. (2000), *Postmetropolis: Critical Studies of Cities and Regions*. Oxford: Basil Blackwell.

Seremetakis, N. (1994), *The Senses Still: Perception and Memory as Material Culture in Modernity*, Chicago: Chicago University Press.

Shaw, B. (2001), 'History at the Water's Edge', R. Marshall (ed.) *Waterfront in Post-industrial Cities*, London and New York: Spon Press.

Schubert, D., (2011), 'Waterfront Revitalizations: From a Local to a Regional Perspective in London, Barcelona, Rotterdam, and Hamburg', G. Desfor, J. Laidley, D. Schubert (eds.) *Transforming Urban Waterfronts, Fixity and Flow*, New York and London: Routledge.

Smith, H., Garcia Ferrari, M.S. (2012), *Waterfront Regeneration. Experiences in City-building*, London and New York: Routledge.

Sorkin, M. (ed.) (1999), *Variations on a Theme Park: The New American City and the End of Public Space*, New York: Hill & Wang.

Splendiani, S., Pencarelli, T., Franch, M., De Salvo, P., Calzati, V., Splendiani, S. (2013), *La valorizzazione del territorio in ottica esperienziale attraverso i percorsi del tipico: riflessioni teoriche ed evidenze empiriche in Italia*, Proceedings of Aidea, Lecce: Accademia Aidea.

Seremetakis, N. (1994), *The Senses Still: Perception and Memory as Material Culture in Modernity*. Chicago: Chicago University Press.

Urry J. (1995), *Consuming Places*, London and New York: Routledge.

Ward, S. V. (2011), 'Port Cities and the Global Exchange of Planning Ideas', C. Hein (ed.) *Port Cities: Dynamic Networks and Global Networks*, London: Routledge.

Zukin, S. (1991), *Landscape of Power: from Detroit to Disney World*, Berkeley: University of California Press.

Zukin, S. (1995), *The Culture of Cities*, Cambridge, MA: Blackwell.

Part I
Port Cities in History

1 Early Modern Port Cities
Harbouring Ships and Residential Settlement

Donatella Calabi

Introduction

As the subject is quite broad and cannot be approached in general terms, with no pretence of providing a comprehensive account, this chapter will present a range of case studies, which differ first and foremost in their physical forms and structures and secondarily in their historical trajectories. On the one hand, I will discuss port cities that have existed since the Middle Ages and subsequently underwent early modern interventions, and on the other hand, those that were built from scratch mainly between the sixteenth and seventeenth centuries.

Among the first group, Venice is quite special because of the relationship established between the city and its lagoon. There was no pre-existing sea cove in this location where arriving vessels could be accommodated, but rather a series of inlets along the coastline and series of port functions scattered inside a water basin replete with islands.

Over the centuries, La Serenissima's excise system grew more and more complex; for a start, it was fractured, with different locations reserved in different ways for different operators, beginning with a number of existing facilities that were equipped and scattered along the navigation canals. The fifteenth and sixteenth centuries saw the further development of surveillance mechanisms and of the rationale for selecting certain locations in the urban fabric. In short, the administrative organization, which clearly was partly dependent upon the operation of the market, ended up encouraging those aspects of the diffused seaport that were the most closely tied to the form and structure of the lagoon and that constituted its valuable assets.

A number of taxes were normally paid through services established at fixed, regularly supervised points, most of which were located along the Adriatic coast in ports that were of strategic importance for the Republic. But the magistrates also had an office at the Rialto that was responsible for monitoring what arrived in the city, for verifying disbursements made, for preventing fraud and for clamping down on smuggling. The establishment of a series of offices (the *Visdomini* or 'masters' of the Lombards, those of the Sea, of the Ternaria, of the Fontego dei Tedeschi and the Levant's

Ufficio delle Merci) divided up administrative tasks according to the nature and provenance of products, and structures supporting navigation spread throughout the city.

In the lagoon city and in many of the cities and towns ruled by the Republic of Venice, various sorts of *fondaci* (warehouses) were established at more or less the same time in the Middle Ages, both as operational tools and to guarantee regular relations between La Serenissima and the many local public authorities operating in its dominion. In the early modern age, the complex, pivotal role in the Republic's budget played by excise duties seems to go hand in hand with the existence of a physical location in which, in addition to warehousing goods, officials could carry out the tax collection duties assigned to them. It was not always necessary, however, to construct an entire, state-owned building for this specific purpose: The offices responsible for inspecting certain products (salt, oil, wine, fat) were characterized by their peripatetic nature.

Where a *fondaco* did exist, it functioned as a sort of island in the city, a special marketplace within the commercial centre. It always corresponded to a form of public interference in trade, through regulations intended to prevent hoarding, shortages, competition or price fluctuation. It was, in short, a mechanism for controlling economic life. To the extent to which it was identified with a particular building complex, the commercial structure became more rigid, intervening in the reception and conservation of goods.

Both the public warehouses for daily food products and those assigned to foreign 'countries' qualified as *fondaci* in the proper sense. From ancient times, flour, wheat and millet were goods that the city's denizens imported and conserved in building complexes constructed precisely for this purpose.

The system that applied to citizens was soon extended to foreigners as well: Germans, Turks, Persians, Arabs, Greeks, Armenians, Florentines and natives of Lucca who traded continuously in the Venetian market would eventually be permitted their own 'home'. Given the functions that were carried out there, given the fact they were the mandatory landing point for anyone arriving in the city from abroad and given their independent structure, these buildings can be considered among the most important 'port' facilities of the lagoon's urban landscape, in much the same way as those in the East, in particular in Byzantium and in the Islamic countries, or in Alexandria, which is to say, in those areas most widely frequented by Venetian merchants.

The Ports of the Venetian Maritime Dominion

The model adopted for the capital city was taken and readapted to the physical characteristics of the territories it ruled (Ortalli 1998).[1] In this respect, the ports on the island of Crete are significant. The maps produced by the cartography workshops which existed in Venice from the mid-sixteenth century onwards provide valuable information about the port facilities. Many a well-made maritime pilots' book was published; old wood engravings were taken up again and often reprinted with additions or changes, with the knowledge that they were intended, perhaps, not solely for navigation but for the interest of the 'amateur'. Sometimes these are only partial maps of a stretch of coastline between two capes, or a deep bay, or a small island that could protect an inlet, or a reef that might inhibit landing or make it easier to pick up supplies. They have brief geographical descriptions, a legend and a few words about the customs and traditions of the places they represent (Poleggi 1991).

Another example is Angelo degli Oddi's *Viaggio nelle provincie di mare*, drawn in 1584. In it, this native of Padua describes the Venetian, Turkish, Imperial and Ragusan settlements he had often visited and their qualities as '*lochi ameni e fruttiferi*' (pleasant and fruitful places). He records the names of every city and every inlet, the capacity and the degree of safety guaranteed by every single port; he specifies the cases in which '*ci si può far acqua e legne*' (one could obtain water and wood). All this degli Oddi recorded for the benefit of Republic, as well as for the many men who '*si dilettano di saper et veder sempre cose nove*' (who delight in knowing and seeing ever new things).[2] His curiosity was fuelled by ancient practices and by the well-known hardships of seafaring—in the knowledge, however, that Venice derived her fortune from the sea (Concina 1990).

Only a few of the forty-three plates by Francesco Basilicata (1612) are plans (Basilicata 1993). These feature the major city-fortresses (Candia, Rethymno, Souda, Chania) and provide accurate drawings of the walls, the port and its arsenals, the bastions, the gates and even the names of associated ramparts; in the case of Candia and Rethymno, there is a special legend listing these elements of the fortresses. The images that refer to Souda and Spinalonga show the new and existing public salt works that, suitably rearranged, made it possible to increase the amount of salt to be sent to Venice after the loss of a major supplier like Cyprus. They also redraw parts of the coastline and the plains.

Of equal impact is the *Historia di Corfù* (1672) by Andrea Marmora, a member of the local nobility who, wishing to report the crucial role played by Corfu's port after the tragic end of the Cretan War, alludes to the island's inevitable centrality between the East and the West through written and drawn allegories.

The events that concern the port of Zara also evolved over the long term and regard the strategic-mercantile role of that inlet with respect to other landing places on the Dalmatian coast. For almost a century a number of issues made it necessary to rely, from time to time, on expert engineers for an up-to-date survey and well-documented opinions. These issues included the gradients of the land; the problems of landfill, garbage removal, rainwater and drainage to the sea; the need to excavate; strict rules regarding the uses or settlements that were or were not permitted near the coast; maintenance of the pier; and the concern to maintain an efficient arsenal at all times.[3] This sort of tool was not only necessary in the large cities: Also on the small islands of Cythera and Zakynthos, the need to guarantee free passage to pedestrians and horses along the shore and assuring the continual traffic of an infinite number of vessels moving around the basin required a careful and systematic technical survey.[4]

Facilities and Public Buildings

Subsequent or parallel to the choices made for these port facilities is the special attention that the Venetian magistrates constantly paid to the marketplaces and their configuration: new biscuit deposits, animal fodder and flour warehouses, customs offices, the reuse of old buildings as sites for keeping stock or a series of shops and the relocation of the butchers' shops to somewhat removed, often waterfront, sites in the piazza were all operations aimed at reorganizing and freeing up space.

As such, the new facilities realized over the course of the sixteenth century deserve special attention. Comparing the views and plans of Split from before[5] and after the implementation, in 1580, of the town 'scale' (a customs house), it is evident that, on the whole, what actually underwent the most obvious change was the city's port, with the quay that closes it off (Calabi 2003). Following this intervention, the question of filling the basin arises with ever-increasing frequency, in relation to the state, shape and size of the quays, and especially to the mercantile factories that were to be built. Capitalizing on the technical know-how of a *cavacanali* (canal digger) like Carlo Silvestrini, the final project was a plan for reorganizing the port, consistent with the urban redevelopment work already under way. In just a century, the irregular shape of Split's port become much more defined.[6] In this regard, the proactive presence of Daniel Rodriguez, a Jew from Spain who lived in the Old Ghetto, was fundamental for Split and similarly influential for the Jewish community's permanence in Venice.

New Ports

The construction of new ports from scratch presents a completely different case. These ports correspond to the needs of inland cities to secure an outlet to the sea for commercial and military purposes. Here just two cases will be cited, Le Havre and Livorno, both of which bear considerable weight in the destiny of port cities, even in contemporary times.

Le Havre is one of the newly founded cities that was destined for considerable development. The importance of the site, where the Seine enters the ocean near Harfleur, is obvious. It is a port of refuge, one that was continually silting up, but remained particularly important for travel to the new world. At the beginning of the sixteenth century it was largely out of use. In 1515 the inhabitants of Rouen asked King Francis I for a 'shelter' (*havre*), that is, basins in which ships and vessels could be safely harboured, with the fortification necessary for their defence. Restoring shore access for large ships was also necessary. It was to be a 'shelter', rather than a city, because

Rouen, in the Seine valley, was sufficient to enable the High Normandy region to compete with the considerable development of the Flemish and Hanseatic ports (Lavedan et al. 1982: 18–19; Corvisier 1983: 45–55). The year after, the king delegated Admiral Bonnivet to look for a suitable location. After several explorations, Bonnivet chose a site downstream from Harfleur, and on 7 February 1517, the king granted him full power to create the so-called shelter there, in a place that had been recently founded and called 'Grace'. Five days later, however, Guyon Le Roy, who had been put in charge of overseeing the realization of these orders, immediately understood that the port could exist only if it were able to attract people. A city had to be built. The king accepted the idea, perhaps without even realizing what it entailed. In 1517 he had not been thinking about anything more than a port; by 1520, however, he quoted his own mandate with the following words: 'make, excavate, open at the named site of Grace a port and a city around it'. In order to attract new inhabitants, he granted various privileges and the right to hold two markets a week. The initial land allocation for these plans was simple: the neighbourhood of Nôtre Dame and a few rectangular plots that were juxtaposed more than they were coordinated. Only in the area near the waterfront was the ground level raised, using mud extracted from the canals and the basin, and only here was the land truly protected from heavy sea storms. Almost twenty years later, in 1541, Francis I again addressed the issue, and by giving compensation to the landowners, the city was adopted under the national dominion. This is when Gerolamo Bellarmato came into the picture. Bellarmato was an engineer from Siena who had worked in Paris. He was given the task of improving the neighbourhood of Nôtre Dame and of building a second neighbourhood (that of Saint François) to which he would add a citadel. He was granted a great deal of power, to the extent that he was able to force everyone who wanted to build in the city to comply with his orders. He also had all the buildings that interfered with his overall scheme demolished. At this point, therefore, there was a plan, a building permit and, as a sanction against anyone who broke the rules, the threat of demolition. The overall layout of the city almost doubled. It became a sort of square (in the geometric sense of the term), cut diagonally by a wide road that passed in front of the church of the same name, with a piazza located along that route. It was necessary to elevate the city's ground level to avoid flooding, to create an underground sewage system 'based on the Italian mode' and to set forth a series of 'ordonnances' or building codes that had to be observed.

A comparable case of a new port city is that of Livorno (traditionally known in English as 'Leghorn'), which evolved in a Tuscany that, over the course of the sixteenth century, was to play an important role in Europe. Without undermining their existing role as patron to the arts, the Medicis were determined to develop as an important economic and political power and, to do so, they needed access to the sea. To achieve this, it would be necessary to undertake works to reclaim the wetland area that stood in their way.

An arsenal had already been built on the coast of Livorno in 1421, reinforcing the city's defences. So, after erecting a customs house and a military hospital, Cosimo I went on to open a navigable channel to Pisa, and, in 1548, declared the city of Livorno a free port. Duke Francesco I (1574–1587) promptly continued the work of his predecessor, relying upon Buontalenti, the painter, sculptor and military engineer who had built the fortress of Terra del Sole for Cosimo. The design for the new Livorno was based on a grid located within bastioned walls that were in the form of an irregular pentagon, ten times larger than the old centre. The port, with its two basins, was located at the side. Though this original scheme was not fully implemented, two of its essential features were preserved: the perimeter and the subdivision of the land inside of it. A piazza was also added (Morini 1963). Ferdinando I (1587–1609) gave crucial impetus to the growth of the city within a regular grid form: a wide thoroughfare between two gates, and a pattern of rectangular blocks, except in the north where the neighbourhood called 'Venice' was built on canals with humpback bridges. The piazza, providing a setting for the church, was a perfectly ordered square with closed corners, and access was created at the mid-point of each side. An edict (the so-called Livornina)—issued in 1593 to provide incentives for population growth—invited merchants, fugitives and malcontents (Greeks, Armenians, Arabs, Jews) to settle in the city. Even criminals and insolvent debtors were welcome.[7] Jews, in particular, arrived in large numbers and—according to Braudel—were the real workers of its success (Lavedan *et al.* 1982: 21). The population of the city grew from 1,000 in 1530 to 10,000 in 1606, and then doubled over the course of the seventeenth century (Fasano Guarini 1978; Battilotti 2007).

Between the end of the sixteenth and the early decades of the seventeenth century, the grand dukes—through the Ufficio della Fabbrica—built houses, shops, factories and warehouses as well as the various infrastructures that were necessary for the port and military garrison. In 1590 the grand duchy owned twenty-nine shops and about twenty warehouses located in front of the fortress, at the port and at Sant'Antonio. They were reserved, in part, for use as arsenals for the galley ships, for customs and for the courts. Many others were rented to private concerns for storing alum, grains, soda and textiles.[8]

Concluding Words

In early modern times we find a great number of different ways of harbouring ships and establishing necessary relations between ports and housing. In this paper I have simply mentioned some significant case studies, but the full range is really quite extensive.

As these few case studies have made evident, there were many and varied relationships between the harbouring facilities of the ports and the core urban areas. However, in early modern times, whatever the history of the site or its development, these two facets of the port city (that is the city and its harbour) were always closely interlinked.

Notes

1 See cartography as discussed.
2 *Viaggio de le Provincie di Mare della Signioria di Venetia, . . . di Angelo degli Oddi Padovano*, in Venetia MDLXXXXIIII, BAU, Ms. 109.
3 ASV (State Archive of Venice), *Collegio, Relazioni*, b. 66, f. 9, cc. 4 v.–5r., Relazione di Lorenzo Venier provveditore generale in Dalmazia, 1 March 1616; see also M. Morcellin, *Zara rinascimentale*, thesis at the Department of History of Architecture, University IUAV, a.a. 1986/87, tutor prof. Ennio Concina.
4 ASV, *Collegio, Relazioni*, b. 87, report presented by N.H. ser Iseppo, when he returned from his office as provveditor in Cerigo, 9 April 1620; report by Francesco Loredan, 27 June1601; Senato Mare, R. 39, c. 97 r., 7 September 1569.
5 These were not completely accurate.
6 ASV, *Collegio, Relazioni*, b. 72, report of Lunardo Bollani, who came back as Count and Captain of Spalato, 3 April 1600; report of Andrea Renier; report of Paolo Trevisan; report of Cesare Dolfin Count and Captain of Spalato, 22 April 1611; Senato mare, R. 71, c. 78 v., 21 January 1612 (m.v.); Dispacci dei rettori [di Dalmazia al Senato], b. 46, report of Gio. Pietro Marchi, 23 July 1641; report of Girolamo Querini, 18 July 1641 (accompanied by a drawing of the harbour).
7 The two decrees of 6 January and 8 October 1590 were addressed to Greeks, to expert sailors, to the '*calafati*' (those who tar the boats) and to foreign manual workers; the third decree, of 1 July 1591, expanded in 1593, is the first Livornina addressed to Jewish merchants.
8 ASFi (Florence State Archive), *MP*, 2132/2.

Bibliography

Basilicata, F. (1993) *Il Regno di Candia* (reprint of the seventeenth century atlas with an introduction by Donatella Calabi), Venice: Marsilio.
Battilotti, D. (2007) 'Luoghi di commercio e produzione degli stranieri nei primi anni dell'espansione livornese (1587–1609)', *Città e storia*, 3: 45–60.
Calabi, D. (2003) 'La rappresentazione del paesaggio urbano come strumento di governo: Venezia e il suo stato da mar fra XVI e XVII secolo', in F. Bocchi and R. Smurra (eds.), *Imago Urbis*, Rome: Viella, 505–518.
Concina, E. (1990) *Navis. L'umanesimo sul mare, 1470–1740*, Turin: Einaudi.
Corvisier, A. (ed.) (1983) *Histoire du Havre et de l'estuaire de la Seine*, Toulouse: Privat.
Fasano Guarini, E. (1978) 'Esenzioni e immigrazione a Livorno tra sedicesimo e diciasettesimo secolo', in *Transactions of the Conference on 'Livorno e il Mediterraneo nell'età medicea'*, Livorno: no publisher, 56–76.
Lavedan, P., Henrat, P. and Hugueney, J. (1982) *L'urbanisme a l'époque modern, XVI–XVIII siècles*, Geneva: Droz.
Marmora, A. (1672) *Della Historia di Corfù descritta da Andrea Marmora nobile corcirese libri otto*, Venice: Presso il Curti.
Morini, M. (1963) *Atlante di storia dell'urbanistica: dalla preistoria al secolo 20*, Milano: Hoepli.
Ortalli, G. (1998) *Venezia e Creta*, Venice: Istituto Veneto di Scienze lettere ed Arti.
Poleggi, E. (1991) *Carte francesi e porti italiani del Seicento*, Genova: Sagep.

2 Romanian Danubian and Black Sea Ports during the Nineteenth Century

A Quest for Modernization

Dimitrios M. Kontogeorgis

Introduction

During the second quarter of the nineteenth century numerous Western merchants, writers, diplomats, sailors and adventurers of all sorts travelled to the Black Sea, or more specifically, to its Lower, Romanian and Ottoman, Danube and north-western shores. Taking advantage of the recently (1829) founded Austrian Danube Steamship Company (Donau-Dampfschifffahrts-Gesellschaft, henceforth DDGS), which had established a line of steam-powered riverboats from Vienna to the Danubian port of Galaţi (Galatz),[1] and travelling from there to Constantinople, usually on Austrian Lloyd liners, they experienced the peculiarities and travails of Danubian navigation, while enjoying the picturesque scenery of the two sides of the river (Ardeleanu 2009). Their accounts of the journey (Cernovodeanu and Buşă 2004–2010; Ardeleanu 2012) often referred to the ports of the region in scathingly critical terms, depicting the main Danubian ports of Brăila (Braila), Galaţi and Tulcea as squalid places, oriental in nature and insalubrious. The travellers did not, however, fail to notice these ports' flourishing commerce and navigation and their increasing economic significance. Until the early twentieth century these cities, as well as those of Sulina and Constanţa (Constantza), would still be a popular subject for travel guides, newspaper articles, diplomatic and consular reports, but the assessments would not always concur. Just like every living organism, ports bring about change and are simultaneously subject to change.

The growth of Galaţi, Brăila, Sulina and Tulcea, the main Romanian Danubian harbours accessible to sea-going vessels, and also of Constanţa, the only important Black Sea port in Dobrogea, has been presented and analyzed in a rich bibliography. Although the phases of their development have been systematically studied, in particular during recent decades,[2] many aspects remain obscure or relatively unexplored. This is because there is a frequent emphasis on a single factor, usually the role of Western states and entrepreneurs in integrating these regions into the European economy. While not unjustified, this approach is too uni-dimensional, as it tends to sideline the contributions of other agents.

This study aims therefore to investigate the dynamics of port development in the Lower Danube-North-western Black Sea region, by analyzing the way state authorities, local elites, commercial interests and foreign investors have attempted, and to a certain degree succeeded, to create a network of vibrant new ports, despite the daunting physical obstacles (Focas 1987: 119–129; and Ardeleanu 2014: 20–22 and 29–34). Inevitably, their success also generated major changes in the urban and social landscape of these city ports and their hinterland, shaping everyday life for millions of people, at least until the second half of the twentieth century. The remarkable success of these ports not only at a regional, but more broadly at a European and international level, should not overshadow the considerable friction between the various agents of change in the area, which led to the formation of different economic and urban models.

The Ports of Brăila and Galați

Until the early nineteenth century, the ports of the Lower or Maritime Danube,[3] were either directly (Brăila, Tulcea, Sulina), or indirectly (Galați in the Principality of Moldavia), under Ottoman control. Their economic activity was regulated by a complex array of treaties and agreements with the Ottoman Empire and revolved around trade with Constantinople (Istanbul).[4] The Danubian ports were of crucial importance in provisioning the Ottoman capital with wheat, barley, meat and other foodstuffs.[5] Furthermore, Tulcea and Galați provided the Ottoman ship-building yards with timber and constructed a number of vessels for the Ottoman fleet (Toderașcu 1969). This commerce, important both in volume and value, was controlled by Turkish and Greek merchants of Constantinople.

The Danube ports were relatively isolated from the rest of Europe, as their use by foreign, non-Ottoman, vessels was restricted or even outright forbidden. The Ottoman Porte had not only imposed severe limitations on trade for several products, such as wheat, but had also excluded the fleets of other nations both from the Black Sea in general and the Danube in particular (Inalcik 1979).

The gradual weakening of Ottoman control in the region permitted the strengthening of relations with the West (Cernovodeanu 1976).[6] By the end of the eighteenth century, European efforts to force the Ottoman Porte to relax its policy in the Black Sea and the Danube had begun to bear fruit. According to the Treaty of Küçük Kaynarca (1774) between the Russian and Ottoman Empires, Russian vessels were allowed to trade in the Black Sea and from 1784 until 1806 the Ottoman Porte was compelled to sign similar treaties with the United Kingdom, France and Prussia (Cernovodeanu 1986: 18–21). The Russo-Ottoman war of 1828–1829 and the Treaty of Adrianople (1829) completed this process of 'opening'. The Treaty strengthened the autonomy of Wallachia (to which it also accorded the port of Brăila) and of Moldavia vis-à-vis the Ottoman Empire. The latter could no longer control the trade of its vassal states as all kinds of restrictions were abolished, the commerce of cereals was liberalized and the entry of foreign vessels into the Danubian ports was not subject to any limitations (Focas 1987: 101–106; Ardeleanu 2014: 53–54).

The ports which were able to benefit from the new opportunities were Brăila and Galați, mainly because they were the only ones, in Wallachia and Moldavia respectively, that were accessible to sea-going vessels. Figure 2.1 reveals that despite fluctuations, substantial growth—which was considerably boosted in the 1840s—was sustained in the departures of sea-going vessels from the Danubian ports.[7]

The development of navigation was related to the growing demand for grain and other foodstuffs in Mediterranean ports, while Constantinople remained the most important outlet for Romanian cereals and timber. This high demand had an impact not only on trade but also on production, which led to the expansion of the area of land under cultivation. The increase in the cereal exports is presented in Figure 2.2 (Cernovodeanu and Marinescu 1979; Ardeleanu 2014: 107–114, 264–267).[8]

The location of Brăila and Galați on the margins of the Romanian Principalities deprived them of engaging actively with internal trade. Their economy was export-oriented and depended on the maintenance of close relations with the European ports. Indeed, the European governments tried to exploit the new favourable circumstances in the Lower Danube by urging their merchants to engage with this new market. They stressed that the opening of the sea routes could significantly enhance the competitiveness of their products in the Principalities. Direct access to Marseille and Great Britain

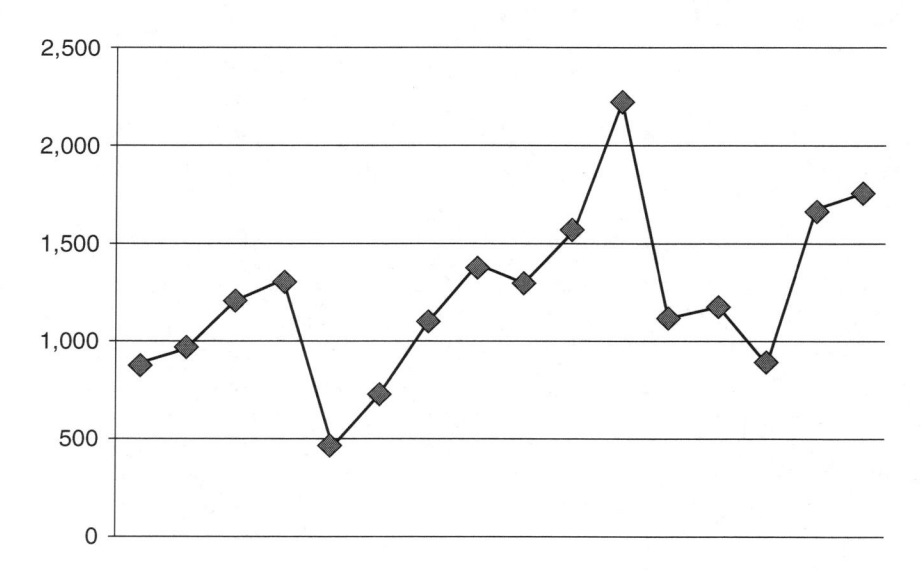

Figure 2.1 Departures of sea-going vessels from Brăila and Galați (1837–1852)

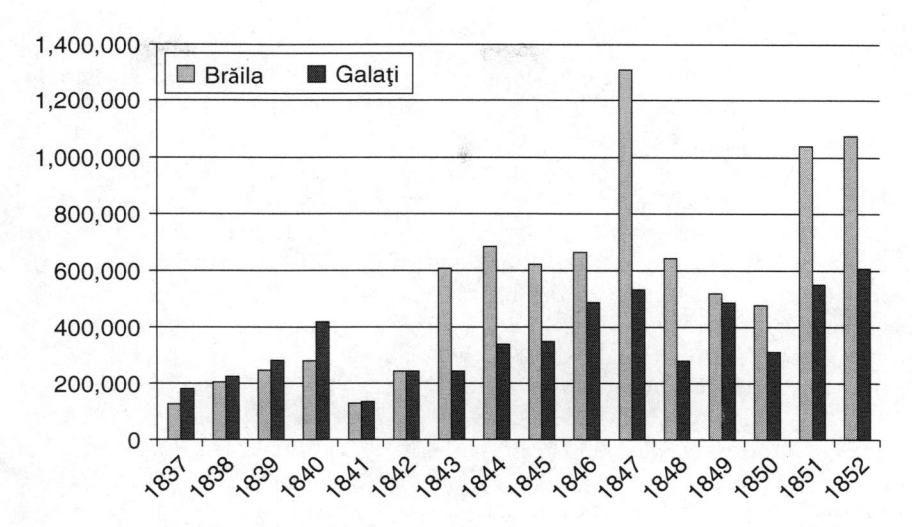

Figure 2.2 Exports of cereals (in imperial quarters) from Brăila and Galaţi (1837–1852)

could increase imports, as it bypassed the 'intermediate' and expensive (for French and English goods) markets of Vienna and Leipzig (Urquhart 1833: 163–164; Ionescu 1974: 269–271; Bardy 1994: 296–302). The literature and journalism propagating the importance of these ports for European commerce convey the impression that a new 'region' was being discovered.[9]

The Habsburg policy towards the Danube has been characterized as 'hesitant' (Lampe and Jackson 1982: 106). Nevertheless, it seems that, while not always successful, it was more systematic than that of the Western powers. The establishment of the DDGS and the expansion of the Lloyd Austriaco linked Brăila and Galaţi through regular lines not only to the Empire's river ports but also to the Mediterranean port of Trieste. Moreover, the Austrian government pressed the Russian authorities to take the necessary measures for the amelioration of navigation at the Danube Delta (see Austro-Russian convention 1840 in Focas 1987: 205–210; Ardeleanu 2014: 180–183).

The desire of the Europeans to promote the rapid and fuller integration of the Lower Danube region into the European economic system was the main stimulus for the formation of a dense consular network.[10] The British, French, Italian (Sardinian) and Austrian consuls acted not only as invaluable sources of information for their compatriots, regarding the economic prospects of the ports (cf. Callimachi and Georgescu 1964), but also exerted influence on the formulation of the Wallachian and Moldavian commercial and navigation policy. Even more significant was their impact on local cities. In Brăila, Galaţi and Tulcea the consuls were dynamic promoters of modernizing efforts in the field of commerce. It is indicative that the establishment of the first money exchange institution in the Maritime Danube, at Galaţi, was initiated and directed by the British vice-consul Charles Cunningham (Buşe 1976: 74).

The importance of the contribution of foreigners to the growth of these ports notwithstanding, one should not overlook the similar endeavours of the Wallachian and Moldavian authorities, as well as those of the local elites. Pavel D. Kiselev, the Russian governor of the Principalities (1829–1834) had stressed that Wallachia was 'ignorant of the benefits of urban centres' and envisioned the establishment of 'model cities'; Brăila would be one of them (Sturdza *et al.* 1891: 439). Indeed, from 1830 Brăila and Galaţi began to attract systematic government attention, which developed on a twofold basis. It aimed to create both a proper institutional environment for the regulation of commercial affairs, as well as the required infrastructure for the promotion of trade and navigation.

In this context, Brăila and Galaţi were declared *porto franco* in 1836 and 1837 respectively (Buşe 1976: 30–36; Mocanu 2012: 24–27). A series of commercial laws were promulgated and treaties with other countries were signed. Commercial courts were established and various other institutions, such as a Customs Office and Quarantine, were organized (Focas 1987: 131–140; Ardeleanu 2014: 67–73). In the case of Brăila the government's plan did not only focus on the improvement of the city's harbour, but also included alterations to its urban 'landscape'. Two city plans were promulgated in the early 1830s, similar to that of Odessa, which would seal Brăila's role as a significant centre of external trade and highlight its prosperity. A ring road embraced the confines of the city; squares and parks were planned; and two boulevards heading from the centre connected it with Silistria and Galaţi (Perianu 1944: 387–390; Giurescu 1968: 165–166; Stoica 2009: 14–15, 22–24, plates 4–5).

Changes in Brăila were not merely the product of government decisions. They were also attuned to and stemmed from the needs and desires of merchants. This socially dominant and multiethnic corps was the first to organize committees to support the efficiency of commercial institutions and upgrades to the urban landscape. A concrete example of the vitality and potential of commercial elites can be traced to Brăila and Galaţi, where merchants established associations in the 1830s, independently from government and local authorities.

In Brăila, the association (Deputaţia Mercantilă din Brăila/Ἐμπορικὴ Ἀντιπροσωπεία), founded in 1838, consisted mostly of foreign, large-scale merchants, mainly Greeks, Italians and Dalmatians.[11] They had consistently asked Alexandru D. Ghica (prince of Wallachia from 1834 to 1842) to permit the establishment of a voluntary, self-governing association. Using money levied as a form of dues from commercial transactions, the merchants claimed that the Deputaţia would not only cater to their needs; it would also invest in the construction of a wharf, modern warehouses and flood gates, the repair of roads and the protection of the docks.

Soon after the prince's approval, the Deputaţia emerged as a significant institution, acting as a counsellor to local and central authorities for commerce and navigation. Some of its major contributions were the standardization of weights and measures, the regulation of money exchange and the organization of a fire brigade.[12]

Roughly the same people participated in the committee for the beautification of the city (Comitet de Înfrumuseţarea). Having lived abroad, they desired to 'renovate' their urban space along the lines of European models. The public garden (Grădina Publică) and the building of a hospital are two examples of the new spirit which was infused into Wallachian society by this wealthy and multicultural element.[13]

The European Danube Commission and the Port of Sulina

The development of the Lower Danube ports was highly affected by the Crimean War (1853–1856) and its aftermath. The defeat of Russia led to the temporary withdrawal of a power which hindered efforts to facilitate navigation in the Delta, while the constitution of the European Danube Commission (Commission Européenne du Danube, henceforth CED) in 1856 fundamentally altered the political and institutional environment, offering new perspectives on the region.[14] The works of the CED in the Lower Danube were instrumental in integrating Brăila and Galaţi even further into the European network of ports. Moreover, the CED created the modern port of Sulina at the mouth of the river. Apart from the CED, in the following decades, other agents, such as the Wallachian authorities or private investors, launched modernizing projects in order to materialize their own vision for the region.

Situated in one of Danube's entrances and used by most sea-going vessels travelling to Brăila and Galaţi, Sulina had, by the early 1830s, become a junction of river and sea navigation.[15] The captains entering the river needed the services of the local pilots. Nonetheless, until the late 1850s Sulina was a port of notorious reputation. At the margins of the Russian and Ottoman empires, but also at the margins of legality, Sulina was a haven for smugglers and pirates. The majority of its inhabitants were Greeks and Maltese, with a much smaller number of Turks and Russians. Exploiting the city's isolation from land routes, this very 'special' community had created a society that was unique in the wider region.[16] Things, however, would change when the CED intervened in the affairs of the Delta.

Choosing, for reasons of convenience and economy, the regulation of the Sulina branch,[17] the CED elaborated and formulated a comprehensive programme of port development and urbanization. Sulina, practically under its administration (Zaharia 1980), would be transformed into a 'model' port. As for the harbour, the CED financed the building of wooden wharves—later replaced by stone—and established workshops for the repair of ships and river boats. For the safety of navigation and trade it stipulated rules for navigation, constructed lighthouses, set up a service of accredited pilots, imposed the policing of the river (Rosetti and Rey 1931: 261–310; Ardeleanu 2011: 73–94) and connected Sulina with the hinterland, first (1857) by telegraph and later (1903) by telephone (Zaharia 1980: 522–524).

The CED's plan exceeded the confines of the harbour. It transformed the city itself. Not only did it build one of the most imposing edifices of the city to house its own services, but it also constructed and ran two hospitals and took various sanitary measures to reduce the incidence of malaria. The local mosque and several churches and schools—of nearly all confessions and nationalities—were also supported by it; electricity was introduced and a system of running water was established in 1897 (Zaharia 1980: 524–527; Covacef 2003: 34–35).[18] The majority of the inhabitants were directly or indirectly employed by the CED. Its interference with the daily life of the city was intended to strengthen its social fabric and to create or modernize its institutions for the benefit of trade and navigation.

The Ottoman authorities restricted themselves to a role of secondary importance. The Ottoman Porte did not hinder the European efforts, sanctioned in any case by an international conference, but neither did they contribute significantly to that endeavour, apart from declaring Sulina a 'free port' in 1870 (Rosetti and Rey 1931: 311–313; Zaharia 1980: 515–517).

On the whole, the activity of the CED was extremely successful, both generally in the Lower Danube and more specifically in Sulina. Sulina remained a major port until the mid-1920s, attracting a multitude of sailors, ship-agents, ship-owners, pilots and entrepreneurs, who constituted a community that was highly diversified, both ethnically and religiously. This multiethnicity was aptly depicted in *Europolis*, a novel by Romanian former marine officer Jean Bart, published in 1933. As Figure 2.3 reveals, the majority of Sulina's inhabitants were Greeks, but the city was also home to Russians, Austrians, English and various other nationalities.[19]

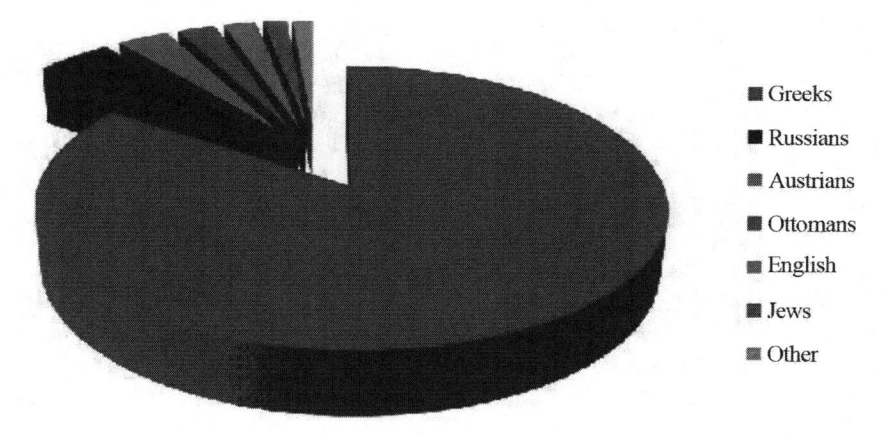

■ Greeks
■ Russians
■ Austrians
■ Ottomans
■ English
■ Jews
■ Other

Figure 2.3 Ethnic distribution of the population of Sulina in 1876

The Port of Constanţa

In comparison with Sulina and the other Danubian ports, Constanţa (Ottoman Kustendjie) constitutes a different case.[20] Like Sulina, its development was also masterminded, during the 1850s and 1860s, by 'foreigners', but in this case by a private British company (Danube and Black Sea Railway and Kustendjie Harbour Ltd.). Until the late 1850s, Constanţa had been a humble port neglected by the Ottoman authorities. Its lack of infrastructure, its exposure to fierce Black Sea winds and its location in a sparsely populated province with relatively low productivity not only disheartened potential investors but also overshadowed its unique physical privileges: Constanţa was an ice-free sea port and close both to the Danube and Constantinople.[21]

The initiative of the British company in building (1857–1860) a modern harbour in Constanţa and a railway to connect it with the cereal-producing Wallachian and Bulgarian hinterland was related to an investment frenzy which had been sweeping the Ottoman Empire since the end of the Crimean War (Jensen and Rosegger 1968: 106–109). The British company conceived the ambitious plan of challenging the dominance of Brăila as the outlet for exports of Wallachian cereals. It wished to establish a shorter route to transfer cereals from the interior to the sea, by creating 'a direct link of river and deep water port' (Jensen and Rosegger 1978: 681). Thus, it would eliminate the need to navigate the dangerous and obstacle-ridden Danube. Constanţa was situated at the shortest distance between the Black Sea and the middle Danube and could easily be linked to Constantinople. If it was connected by rail with the river port of Cernavoda, which was 65 kilometres away from it, it would alleviate merchants of the need to go to Brăila. Moreover, the plan also provided for the building of grain cleaning and storage installations, nonexistent in the Danubian ports up to that time. The plan boldly intended to transfer modern rail technology to a backward region of Europe and was immediately perceived as antagonistic to the CED's efforts in the Delta (Jensen and Rosegger 1968: 680–686). Unfortunately for the investors, the plan backfired. The execution of the railway not only took much longer than expected but it also cost much more, and the harbour constructed by the company, albeit modern, was insufficient for such an ambitious aim. Furthermore, the necessary large warehouses were not built, undermining the investment (Jensen and Rosegger 1978: 683–686).[22] In the meantime the CED continued its far-reaching works in the Delta, strengthening the position of the three Danubian ports.

The entrepreneurs' ambitions might have not been realized, but Constanţa nevertheless benefited greatly from their actions. Its population grew as many foreign merchants settled there, and imposing new buildings were built, such as the local Greek church and a mosque. The hotels and the new 'European' quarter shaped the port's modern physiognomy (Jensen and Rosegger 1968: 126; Lăpuşan *et al.* 2005: 21–22).[23]

The Ottoman Dobrogea policy

The Ottoman authorities did not remain passive onlookers with regard to the extension of British and overall European influence in the region; neither were they ignorant of Dobrogea's economic potential (Ionescu de la Brad 1850). Nevertheless, although they permitted the modernization of the Constanţa harbour and they declared Sulina as a free port, their main interest lay elsewhere. They attempted, by the 1860s, to implement a series of administrative, judicial, fiscal and economic reforms in the region, in the context of the wider Tanzimat reforms. The most tangible result of this policy was the establishment of the Danube Province (Tuna Vilayeti), in 1864. The Province included the north-western shores of the Black Sea and the majority of the Ottoman Danubian border (Petrov 2006). The Ottoman administration laid heavy stress on the modernization of agriculture—founding credit cooperatives and model farms—while it also encouraged industrial enterprises. Furthermore, the economic and urbanistic development of the provincial capital, the Danubian port of Ruse (Rusçuk), was effectively promoted and the city was linked, via a railway, with the Black Sea port of Varna, while in general the infrastructure and the communications of the Vilayet were expanded (Jensen and Rosegger 1968: 118–122; Petrov 2006: 111–159).

The changes in Dobrogea proper, albeit important, were not as comprehensive. With the purpose of promoting export trade from Tulcea and Constanţa, the government tried to transform the sparsely inhabited pastoral hinterland to an agricultural one through settling it with peasants such as Tatars or Circassians (Petrov 2006: 353–371).[24] In an effort to 'europeanize' the cities of the Vilayet, new government buildings were constructed; streets were widened and illuminated, both in Tulcea and Constanţa, as well as other urban centres (Petrov 2006: 117–123). It seems that the economic impact of these endeavours was nevertheless restricted.

There were a number of reasons for the apparent lack of interest in the Danubian ports of Tulcea and Sulina and, to an even greater extent, Constanţa. On the one hand, thanks to the resources and activity of the European Commission, Sulina was fast developing, but at the same time it was 'emancipating' from Ottoman control, because the prerogatives and privileges of Europeans in the city were exceptional. On the other hand, by the early 1860s, both the Ottomans and some European entrepreneurs seemed to have realized that the anticipated diversion of Wallachian and Moldavian cereal exports through Constanţa harbour could not materialize. The works undertaken by the CED had ameliorated navigation in the Lower Danube to such an extent that the ports of Brăila and Galaţi retained and even strengthened their predominant position in the Principalities' commercial transactions. Eager to promote the agriculture of the Danube Vilayet, one of their more fertile European provinces, the Ottomans were left with one alternative: the development of Varna and the expansion of its communications with the hinterland.[25]

The systematic efforts of the European powers to promote, through the CED, navigation in the Delta, the rival project of the British company at Constanța and even railway construction and other measures undertaken by the Ottomans at Danube Vilayet, gave rise to expectations among the merchants of Brăila and Galați but also provoked fear. Hence, they pressed energetically for the construction of modern harbours and the installation of up-to-date facilities. Even more, they lobbied the government to invest in the creation of a dense railway network, so as to link their ports more closely to the hinterland (Ardeleanu 2006: 46–48).[26] Although a few of these proposals were accepted (Mocanu 2012: 49–72), in the early 1870s the Romanian authorities succeeded in establishing an adequate railway system (Mănescu 1906; Lampe and Jackson 1982: 209–211).[27]

The Transformation of Constanța

Romania gained its independence in 1878, but its politicians claimed that economic independence was still a goal to be achieved. The penetration of foreign capital into the country—and above all, the predominance of the CED in its commercial life—would collide with emerging Romanian nationalism. Romania needed space to create, to profit, but also to boost its national self-esteem. Her harbours were the appropriate place for this. As most of these were under the sway of the CED, the only promising alternative left was the port of Constanța (Jensen and Rosegger 1978: 686–688).

The Romanian government therefore undertook the ambitious and challenging task of transforming Constanța into its major centre for exports by creating a passage across the Danube. It constructed a huge railway bridge, the second largest in the world, to connect the two banks of the river and to link the railway line of Bucarest-Fetești to that of Cernavoda-Constanța. Lavish government funds were invested for upgrading the port, increasing its traffic capacity, and constructing an inner and outer harbour. As regards inland communications, apart from widening the roads, the government purchased the Cernavoda-Constanța line from the British company, funded the construction of double rail tracks, and improved the line's course by undertaking a tunnel project.

As regards technique and modernity, the Constanța scheme was exceptional (Cioriceanu 1928:44–49; Covacef 2004). Nonetheless, it also seems to have exceeded Romania's commercial needs. It absorbed immense amounts of money, took approximately two decades to finish (1895–1910), and could be said to have circumvented the established traditions and commercial trends of the country. Although the dominance of Brăila and Galați in the cereal trade had been put into question by the Constanța plan, as their merchants certainly feared (Budeanu 1887; Memoriu 1906), it was never shattered. It was only in the interwar period that Constanța finally overtook the Danubian ports. Romanian oil exports alone were from the outset a 'prerogative' of Constanța (Jensen and Rosegger 1978: 695–698).

The nineteenth-century scheme for the waterfront at Constanța seems to have functioned more as a flagship for Romanian nationalism. According to the Romanian prime minister, Ion C. Brătianu, it would be the proof 'that we are a powerful nation' (Iordachi 2010: 171). The city, which had greatly benefited from this underlying antagonism, assumed a symbolic importance. Its Romanian character was fostered by, for example, the decoration of its squares with statues of Ovid and the construction of a huge Romanian church. Constanța was also designated as a major Romanian tourist resort, often visited by the king himself during vacations (Lăpușan *et al.* 2005:40–55).

Conclusion

The nineteenth century constitutes an important chapter in the history of Romania's city ports. This did not simply concern the upgrading of their infrastructure. Their development was a complex procedure which either altered their physiognomy, as in the case of Constanța, or boosted and modernized their traditional role in commerce, as in the case of Brăila and Galați. Either way, during that period, the fate of the cities was inextricably linked to that of their ports. The integration of the Danubian ports into the European economy brought about multiethnicity and Europeanization in the cities. This significant change was not the achievement of only one agent but of a variety, extending from international committees and governments to private capital or local associations.

Notes

1 For the *DDGS* see Paskaleva (1976). The names of ports are given in their modern (Romanian) form. At first mention, the most common English form is also given.
2 See amongst others Cernovodeanu (1986); Harlaftis (1996); Ardeleanu (2008); Ardeleanu (2014).
3 Maritime Danube is that part of the Danube, stretching approximately from Brăila in Wallachia to the mouth of the river, which is accessible to sea-going vessels.
4 Here after the term *Constantinople* is used, as it appears in most of the nineteenth-century western European and Balkan sources
5 For the provisioning of Constantinople, see Güçer (1980: 26–31); Inalcik and Quataert (1994: 719–721). For the 'Romanian' aspect see Alexandrescu-Dersca (1957).
6 For Galați in particular, see Păltănea (1970).
7 For data on the navigation of the Lower Danube during the second quarter of the nineteenth century see Vacalopoulos (1980); Ardeleanu (2014: 37–41 and 259–264). For the case of Brăila see Κοντογεώργης (2012: 333–339).
8 For Brăila see Κοντογεώργης (2012: 325–332); Mocanu (2012: 147–157).
9 The books by Urquhart (1833) and by Colson (1839) were very important.
10 For the consulates, see Kammerhofer (1996: 7–35); Ionescu (1974: 270–272); Cernovodeanu (1986: 51–52, 58–62). For Galați, see Bușe (1976: 41–42).

11 For the ethnic composition of Braila's mercantile elite, see Vârtosu (1939: 17–56); Mocanu (2012: 119–133).
12 The activity of the Deputaţia is analyzed in Κοντογεώργης (2012: 38–43) and Mocanu (2012: 44–45, 50, 58–59). For a similar organization in Galaţi, see Buşe (1976: 82).
13 Stoica (2009: 155–163). See also Direcţia Judeţeană a Arhivelor Naţionale Brăila/ Primăria oraşului Brăila, dos. 17/1834, f. 1r–5r.
14 The literature on the *CED* is abundant. See amongst others Rosetti and Rey (1931); Focas (1987: 253–422); and the many studies by Constantin Ardeleanu, in particular Ardeleanu (2008).
15 Ardeleanu (2014: 131–252).
16 For the early history of Sulina, see Focas (1987: 179–190); *Covacef (2003)*.
17 For the work of the CED until 1930 see Rosetti and Rey (1931: 185–250).
18 In general for the CED's sanitary policy see Rosetti and Rey (1931: 334–341) and for its help towards the city of Sulina, see Rosetti and Rey (1931: 342–349). Although the hospitals were intended for sailors, pilots and the CED's personnel, they were open for all the inhabitants of the city.
19 There is some uncertainty around the data on the number and ethnic distribution of Sulina's population. The port's inhabitants, however, doubled when commercial activity was at its peak. See Foreign Office/Commercial Reports 9 (Sulina-Tulcea 1867): 265–267.
20 For the history of Constanţa, see Lăpuşan *et al.* (2005), amongst others.
21 See the characteristic book by Forester (1857).
22 Cf. also the comments of the British vice-consul, Foreign Office (1867: 332).
23 See also Foreign Office (1867: 332–333).
24 The Tatars' crucial role in the expansion of agriculture in Dobrogea was acknowledged by the foreign consuls, too. See *Recueil Consulaire Belgique*, VIII (1862): 251.
25 Varna's port was better than Constanţa's in terms of 'size and exposure'. See Turnock (2001: 149).
26 See also *Recueil Consulaire Belgique*, XI (1865): 19.
27 For the railway at the Danubian ports, see Foreign Office (1874: 688–699).

Bibliography

Alexandrescu-Dersca, M.-M. (1957) 'Contribution à l'étude de l'approvisionnement en blé de Constantinople au XVIIIe siècle', *Studia et Acta Orientalia*, I: 13–37.
Ardeleanu, C. (2006) 'Efectele construirii căii ferate Cernavodă-Constanţa asupra navigaţiei dunărene (1859–1860)', *Analele Universităţii'Ovidius' Constanţa-seria Istoria-Ştiinţe Politice-Relaţii Internaţionale şi Studii Europene, Studii de Securitate*, 3: 41–54.
Ardeleanu, C. (2008) *Evoluţia intereselor economice şi politice britanice la gurile Dunării (1829–1914)*, Brăila: Muzeul Brăilei, Editura Istros.
Ardeleanu, C. (2009) 'From Vienna to Constantinople on Board the Vessels of the Austrian Danube Steam-Navigation Company (1834–1842)', *Historical Yearbook*, 6: 187–202.
Ardeleanu, C. (2011) 'The European Commission of the Danube and the Result of Its Technical and Administrative Activity on the Safety of Navigation, 1856–1914', *International Journal of Maritime History*, XXIII(1): 73–94.
Ardeleanu, C. (2012) *Gurile Dunării—o problemă europeană. Comerţ şi navigaţie la Dunărea de Jos în surse contemporane (1829–1853)*, Brăila: Muzeul Brăilei, Editura Istros.

Ardeleanu, C. (2014) *International Trade and Diplomacy at the Lower Danube: The Sulina Question and the Economic Premises of the Crimean War (1829–1853)*, Brăila: Muzeul Brăilei, Editura Istros.

Bardy, G.M.P.A. (1994) 'Deux rapports français inédits du début des années 1830 sur l'état et les perspectives des liens commerciaux Franco-Roumains', *Revue Roumaine d' Histoire*, XXXIII(3–4): 293–306.

Budeanu, C.S. (1887) *Un podu existent pe Dunăre la Brăila*, Brăila: Tipo-Litografia Pericle M. Pestemalgioglu.

Buşe, C. (1976) *Comerţul prin Galaţi sub regimul de port franc (1838–1883)*, Bucureşti: Editura Academiei Republicii Socialiste România.

Callimachi, S. and Georgescu, V. (1964) 'Une source anglaise relative au commerce sur le Danube (1837–1838)', *Revue Roumaine d'Histoire*, III(2): 255–276.

Cernovodeanu, P. (1976) 'British Economic Interests in the Lower Danube and the Balkan Shore of the Black Sea Between 1803 and 1829', *Journal of European Economic History*, V(1): 105–120.

Cernovodeanu, P. (1977) 'An Unpublished British Source Concerning the International Trade Through Galatz and Braila Between 1837 and 1848', *Revue Roumaine d'Histoire*, XVI(3): 517–531.

Cernovodeanu, P. (1986) *Relaţiile comerciale româno-engleze în contextul politicii orientale a Marii Britanii (1803–1878)*, Cluj-Napoca: Dacia.

Cernovodeanu, P. and Buşă, D. (eds.) (2004–2010) *Călători străini despre Ţările Române în secolul al XIX-lea*, serie nouă, vol. I–VI, Bucureşti: Editura Academiei Române.

Cernovodeanu, P. and Marinescu, B. (1979) 'British Trade in the Danubian Ports of Galatz and Braila Between 1837 and 1853', *Journal of European Economic History*, VIII(3): 707–742.

Cioriceanu, G.D. (1928) *Les grands ports de Roumanie*, Paris: M. Giard.

Colson, F. (1839) *De l'état présent et de l'avenir des Principautés de Moldavie et de Valachie*, Paris: A. Pougin.

Covacef, P. (2003) *Cimitirul viu de la Sulina*, Constanţa: Ex Ponto.

Covacef, P. (2004) *Portul Constanţa. Portul lui Anghel Saligny*, Constanţa: Ex Ponto.

Focas, S.G. (1987) *The Lower Danube River in the Southeastern European Political and Economic Complex from Antiquity to the Conference of Belgrade of 1948*, Boulder, CO: Columbia University Press.

Foreign Office (1867) 'Report by Mr. Vice-Consul Dupuis on the Trade of Sulina and Toultcha for the year 1866', *Commercial Reports*, 9: 265–268.

Foreign Office (1867) 'Report by Mr. Vice-Consul F. F. Sankey for the year 1866', *Commercial Reports*, 10: 332–333.

Foreign Office (1874) 'Lower Danube, Report by Consul Ward', *Commercial Reports*, 20: 688–699.

Forester, T. (1857) *The Danube and the Black Sea. Memoir on Their Junction by a Railway Between Tchernavoda and a Freeport at Kustendjie*, London: E. Stanford.

Giurescu, C.C. (1968) *Istoricul oraşului Brăila din cele mai vechi timpuri până astăzi*, Bucureşti: Editura ştiinţifică.

Güçer, L. (1980) 'Grain Supply of Istanbul in the Eighteenth Century', in C. Issawi (ed.), *The Economic History of Turkey, 1800–1914*, Chicago: University of Chicago Press, 26–31.

Harlaftis, G. (1996) *History of Greek-Owned Shipping: The Making of an International Tramp Fleet, 1830 to the Present Day*, London: Routledge.

Inalcik, H. (1979) 'The Question of the Closing of the Black Sea Under the Ottomans', *Αρχείον Πόντου*, 35, 74–110.

Inalcik, H. and Quataert, D. (eds.) (1994) *An Economic and Social History of the Ottoman Empire, 1300–1914*, Cambridge: Cambridge University Press.

Ionescu, T. (1974) 'L' échange maritime de marchandises entre les Principautés Danubiennes et la France durant la période 1829–1848', *Revue Roumaine d'Histoire*, XII(2): 269–284.

Ionescu de la Brad, I. (1850) *Excursion agricole dans la plaine de Dobroudja*, Constantinople: publisher unidentified.

Iordachi, C. (2010) 'Global Networks, Regional Hegemony, and Seaport Modernization on the Lower Danube', in B. Kolluoğlu and M. Toksöz (eds.), *Cities of the Mediterranean from the Ottomans to the Present Day*, London, New York: I.B. Tauris, 157–182.

Jensen, J.H. and Rosegger, G. (1968) 'British Railway Builders Along the Lower Danube, 1856–1869', *Slavonic and East European Review*, 46: 105–128.

Jensen, J.H. and Rosegger, G. (1978) 'Transferring Technology to a Peripheral Economy: The Case of Lower Danube Transport Development, 1856–1928', *Technology and Culture*, 19(4): 675–702.

Kammerhofer, L. (1996) 'Das Konsularwesen der Habsburgermonarchie (1752–1918): Ein Überblick mit Schwerpunkt auf Südosteuropa', in H. Heppner (ed.), *Der Weg führt über Österreich zur Geschichte des Verkehrs—und Nachrichtenwesens von und nach Südosteuropa (18.Jahrhundert bis zur Gegenwart)*, Wien: Böhlau, 7–35.

Κοντογεώργης, Δ. Μ. (2012) 'Η ελληνική διασπορά στη Ρουμανία. Η περίπτωση της ελληνικής παροικίας της Βραΐλας (αρχές 19ου αι.–1914)', unpublished doctoral thesis, University of Athens, Αθήνα.

Lampe, J.R. and Jackson, M.R. (1982) *Balkan Economic History, 1550–1950, from Imperial Borderlands to Developing Nations*, Bloomington, IN: Indiana University Press.

Lăpuşan, A., Lăpuşan, S. and Stănescu, G. (2005) *Constanţa File de Album*, Constanţa: Dobrogea.

Mănescu, C.C. (1906) *Istoricul Căilor fierate din România*, vol. 1, Bucureşti: Editura Direcţiunii Generale a Căilor Fierate Române.

Memoriu relativ la cauzele decăderei portului Brăila şi remediile propuse spre a i reda activitatea din trecut (1906), Brăila: Tipografia Artistică.

Mocanu, E.O. (2012) *Portul Brăila de la regimul de porto-franco la primul război mondial (1836–1914)*, Brăila: Muzeul Brăilei, Editura Istros.

Păltănea, P. (1970) 'Comerţul Moldovei cu Apusul Europei prin Galaţi în a două jumătate a secolului al XVIII-lea', *Danubius*, IV, 197–218.

Paskaleva, V. (1976) 'Le rôle de la navigation à vapeur sur le bas Danube dans l'établissement de liens entre l'Europe Centrale et Constantinople jusqu' à la guerre de Crimée', *Bulgarian Historical Review*, 4(1): 64–74.

Perianu, R. (1944) 'Planul oraşului Brăila din 10 Mai 1830', in C. Giurescu and C. Marinescu, *În amintirea lui Constantin Giurescu*, Bucureşti: publisher unidentified.

Petrov, M.V. (2006) 'Tanzimat for the Countryside: Midhat Paşa and the Vilayet of Danube 1864–1868', unpublished doctoral dissertation, Princeton University, Princeton.

Recueilj Consulaire Belge (1865), XI, Bruxelles: H. Tarlier.

Rosetti, C. and Rey, F. (1931) *La Commission Européenne du Danube et son œuvre de 1856 à 1931*, Paris: Imprimerie Nationale.

Stoica, M. (2009) *Brăila. Memoria orașului-Imaginea unui oraș românesc din secolul al XIX-lea*, Brăila: Muzeul Brăilei, Editura Istros.

Sturdza, D.A., Sturdza, D.C. and Lugoșianu, O. (eds.) (1891) *Colecția Hurmuzaki, Documente privitoare la Istoria Românilor, 1802–1849*, IV/Suplementul 1, București: Socec.

Toderașcu, I. (1969) 'Construcții navale la șanțierul din Galați în ultimul sfert al secolului al XVIII-lea', *Danubius*, II–III: 95–109.

Turnock, D. (2001) *Eastern Europe, an Historical Geography, 1814–1945*, London: Routledge.

Urquhart, D. (1833) *Turkey and Its Resources: Its Municipal Organization and Free Trade: The State and Prospects of English Commerce in the East*, London: Saunders and Otley.

Vacalopoulos, C.A. (1980) 'Données statistiques sur la prédominance du potentiel hellénique dans la navigation et le commerce au Bas-Danube (1837–1858)', *Balkan Studies*, 21: 107–116.

Vârtosu, I. (1939) 'Trei catagrafii pentru Brăila anului 1837', *Analele Brăilei*, 11(2–3): 17–56.

Zaharia, P. (1980) 'Sulina-Porto-Franc (1870–1939)', *Peuce*, VIII: 515–529.

Part II

The Transformations of Historic Ports in Eastern Mediterranean Cities

3 The Historic Harbours of Eastern Mediterranean Cities
The Challenges of Enhancement

Vilma Hastaoglou-Martinidis

Introduction

The sites of historic harbours are outstanding landscapes of architectural and technical culture that embody tangible memories of exchange and entrepreneurship, trade and labour. They constitute predominant features of both the specific and generic identity of Mediterranean cities. The activation of this rich cultural heritage, along with the mobilization of the natural advantages of the region, is a recent trend for these cities that strive to attract tourism and capital, and seek to implement innovative projects to bring about a coveted urban physiognomy.

The idea of regenerating obsolete harbour sites, which has been diffused across North America and Europe since the 1970s, began to surface in Mediterranean cities in the 1990s. Within a globalized and competitive context, a burgeoning urban agenda tried to address the decline of previous economic activities, focusing on the rehabilitation of large sections of historic waterfront and aiming at the creation of a modern service sector. Large projects were initiated for the enhancement and reuse of old port sites in Barcelona, Genova, Valletta and currently Marseille, providing evidence that development linked to major international attractions—such as the Olympic Games, the Anniversary of Columbus or the European Cultural Capital nomination—could substantiate the quest for a renewed cityscape and the replacement of old port functions by post-industrial, culture-led, spaces of consumption.

While an extensive literature offers a comprehensive account of the kinds of projects just described, less is known about waterfront regeneration schemes in Eastern Mediterranean cities. This chapter will attempt an overview of urban and architectural projects undertaken during the last two decades on the seafronts of Beirut, Istanbul and Thessaloniki, emphasizing the significance of this strategy as a step towards the aspired-to identity of these cities for the twenty-first century.

Eastern Mediterranean cities have benefited from the legacies of the *longue durée*, which still mark their present aspect. Legendary port cities that have been in existence for millennia, capitals of empires that have played a leading role in the history of the Mediterranean, they are the heirs of an exceptionally rich and multilayered heritage, shaped in the course of successive transfigurations. These cities are Alexandria, original creation of the Hellenistic world, revived by Mohamed Ali in the early nineteenth century, and turned into the symbol of Cosmopolitan Diaspora; Beirut, port of the Phoenician sea-realm, Roman, Byzantine and Ottoman bridgehead, celebrated up to the 1960s as the 'Paris of the Middle East'; Istanbul, the colony of Megara destined to be the capital of three consecutive empires—Eastern Roman, Byzantine and Ottoman—and grown to become a multicultural world city; Izmir, contemporary with the first city of Troy, re-founded by Alexander the Great, outstanding centre of the Roman Republic and Byzantine Empire, declining through Ottoman times only to be reborn as the cosmopolitan 'pearl of the Aegean' in the nineteenth century; Thessaloniki, major centre of the Macedonian kingdom, and in turn regional capital of the Roman, Byzantine and Ottoman empires, famed as the 'Jerusalem of the Balkans', up to the early twentieth century (Abulafia 2011).

The Legacies of the Past

Historic harbour sites in these cities date back mainly to the late nineteenth century. Built upon centuries-old urban seafronts, they have been gateways for various innovations—social, urban and technical—and each major urban transformation has left its own particular imprint on the waterfronts and entailed the drastic restructuring of the cities' relationship with the sea. The landscapes of these harbours represent the last layer of the Mediterranean urban palimpsest, landmarks of the integration of the port cities into the world's economy.

A brief overview of the main steps in the creation of historic harbours and their subsequent evolution up to the present day is essential in order to appreciate the importance of this precious urban and architectural heritage for contemporary strategies of urban regeneration.

First Step: The Cosmopolitan Heritage

After 1850, with the opening of the Suez Canal and growing international trade, coastal towns became the theatre of spectacular changes triggered by the construction of modern ports and railways. Between 1868 and 1910 harbour works were implemented in all major port cities of the region, such as Alexandria, Beirut, Izmir, Istanbul and Thessaloniki, and were soon followed by port building in minor coastal towns such as Patras, Chios, Hermoupolis, Alexandretta and Haifa, amongst others. Harbour works reshaped the commercial map of the Eastern Mediterranean and they had great impact on the economic and demographic growth of coastal cities. After long centuries of enclosure, the cities burst the limits of their medieval walls to spread beyond their traditional nuclei (Figure 3.1). Modern quays restructured the inherited traditional urban patterns and reordered urban functions. The building of new docks signalled the ties of these cities to modernity and wealth, and attracted new inhabitants of the Mediterranean diaspora. The rise of the late-nineteenth-century cosmopolitan city is the outcome of this process (Hastaoglou-Martinidis 2010).

The harbour of Izmir was built between 1869 and 1875 by Joseph and Élie Dussaud Frères, a French contracting company with extensive experience in France and abroad. It included a quay 3.5 kilometres in length along the old seafront, where regular urban blocks were laid out, accommodating commercial premises, public buildings and residences, and drastically reshaping the profile of the city. In Beirut, a concession for modern harbour facilities was issued in 1888 to a society set up by the French shareholders of the Beirut–Damascus road company. The construction of modern docks was completed in 1895 with a 1-kilometre long dock, with the medieval core behind it, which swept away the picturesque marine fortress dating from the Crusader era (Figure 3.2). In Istanbul, harbour works were begun

Figure 3.1 The banks of the historic Istanbul peninsula in 1890 as filled in during the Ottoman centuries

in 1891 and completed by 1900 by the French company of Marius Michel Pasha, the empire's General Administrator of Lighthouses. The new docks, equipped with modern shipping and trade facilities, were distributed along 1.16 kilometres on either side of the Golden Horn, in front of the city's traditional markets. In Thessaloniki, after the sea wall was demolished, harbour works started in 1869, with the construction of a linear quay along the old seafront, signalling the modernization of the city. However, this quay rapidly proved inadequate and the construction of a proper harbour was undertaken between 1896 and 1904 by the company of Edmond Bartissol, public works contractor and former Member of Parliament from Paris (Figure 3.3).

Second Step: The Refashioning of the City and Reordering of the Seafront, 1920–1940

In the turbulent interwar period, the new political and economic conjuncture—namely the territorial expansion of Greece (1912–1919), the emergence of republican Turkey (1923), the establishment of the French and British Mandate in the Middle East (1920), and the independence of Egypt from British colonization (1919–1923)—triggered the overall modernization, or Westernization, of cities. European architects were called upon to create a nationally meaningful city image that radically reordered the previous cosmopolitan image. The waterfront, and its refashioning, once again became the theatre of operations.

Beirut was remodelled in 1932 along French lines by Réné & Raymond Danger with monumental breakthroughs in the historical core and carefully designed residential extensions at the perimeter; a seaside boulevard was fashioned (the Corniche) and the harbour zone was extended. In Izmir the fire of 1922 destroyed the greater part of the historic city (all the non-Muslim quarters), while the violent expulsion of all Christian residents that followed eradicated the cosmopolitan character of the city and led to its nationalization. The 1924 plan, by R. and R. Danger and Henri Prost, radically reshaped the burnt-out area, created a new commercial port at the

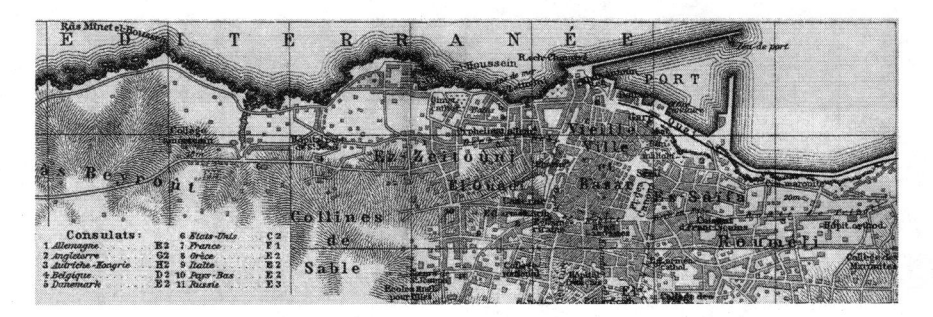

Figure 3.2 Beirut seafront in the 1900s

point of Alsancak, and extended the city along the coast with new commercial and residential districts (Figure 3.4). In Istanbul the master plan of 1937 by Henri Prost emphasized the creation of traffic arteries along the coasts and the extension of urban space along the Bosporus. Specially designed parks and squares—Eminönü Square in the old city and Karaköy Square on the European side—opened up the historic fabric and were to transform the seaside image drastically when implemented in the next decades. In Thessaloniki, after the destruction by fire of the historic core, the replanning of the city in 1918 by Ernest Hébrard created a modern European city stretched along the seafront, with a port extension and industrial areas on the west coast. The old ethnic topography and urban patterns were completely ignored and refashioned along French Beaux-Arts lines (Hastaoglou-Martinidis 2011a).

Third Step: Urban Explosion and the Misuses of the Waterfront, 1950–1890; the Purging of the Past

In the post-war years, an uncontrolled urbanization had severe repercussions for the inherited seafronts. The cities encountered the anonymous and aggressive face of modernity with renewal projects that sacrificed historic locations to traffic imperatives. Fragmentary urban plans attempted to control an unprecedented urban growth, while intense building activity swept away old districts, occupied the coasts and downgraded the natural environment. For this state of exponential growth, the past did not exist. Transport infrastructure works were usually arranged on the seafronts, which also offered the grounds for large extensions of harbour zones, industrial and other heavy uses, with no concern for the environment and the historic heritage of the city.

Beirut was severely tried by civil strife and the Arab–Israeli war (1967–1990), which thinned out its previously broad multicultural population structure and ruined its architectural physiognomy; the historic core with the old port was founded precisely on the war line and suffered extended destruction. In Izmir, the master plans drawn up in the 1950s by Aru, Özdeş and Canpolat, and A. Bodmer failed to control an intense post-war urbanization, which caused the sprawl of the city around the gulf, with both authorized and illegal extensions, the uncontrolled positioning of productive facilities, and requiring important transport works that disrupted the continuity of the urban fabric. Istanbul at this time saw the most violent and anarchic urban extension in its history and occupied the shores of the Bosporus as a result of massive internal migration; at the same time, the city lost its centuries-long multicultural population, together with a big part of its historic waterfront, which was sacrificed to the opening up of coastal highways. Thessaloniki spread out rapidly in every direction and witnessed an intense burst of building activity, while aggressive modernist projects giving priority to traffic imperatives were to eliminate the inherited profile of the eastern shore, with its mansions, from the cosmopolitan phase (Hastaoglou-Martinidis 2001).

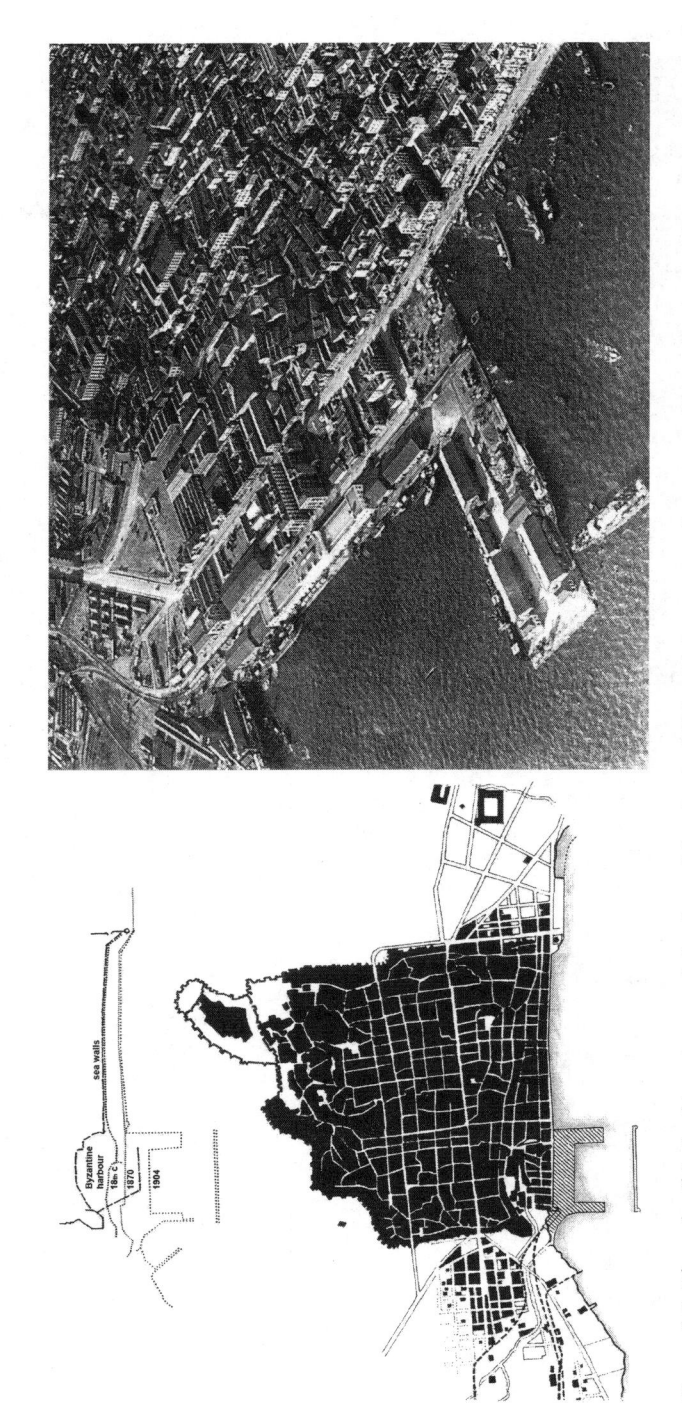

Figure 3.3 Thessaloniki, the historic port: left, plan of the city in 1902 with successive alterations of the coastline; right, aerial photograph of the port in 1917

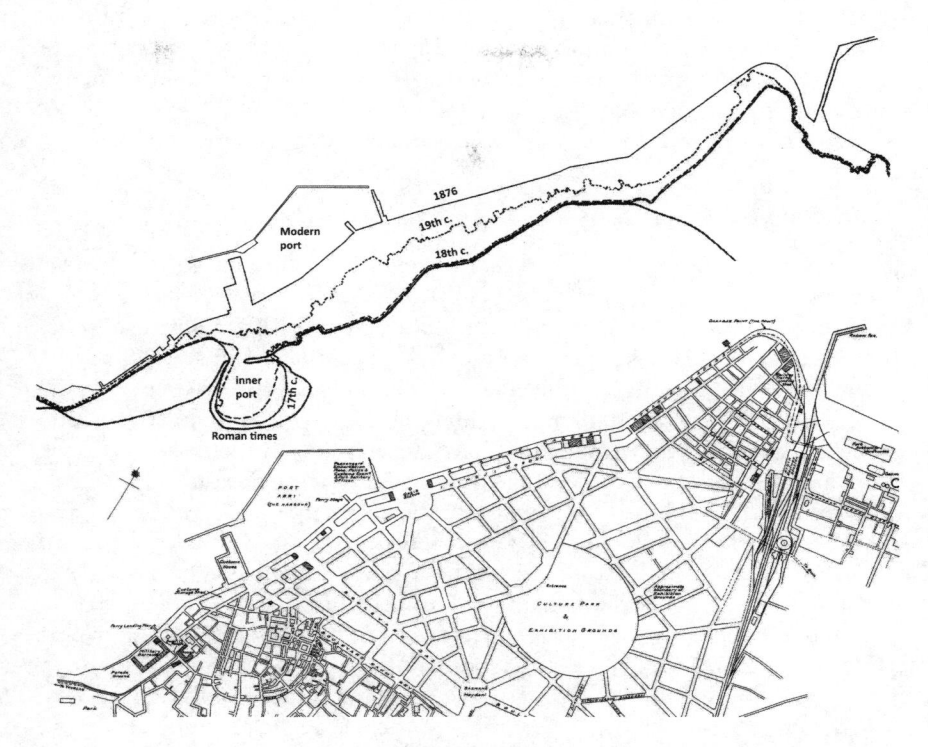

Figure 3.4 Izmir, successive alterations of the coastline as projected against the 1941 city layout

Retrieving the Past for Staging the Future: The Enhancement of Historic Harbour Sites

In the last few decades, the harbours' previous relationship with urban activities has reached a breaking point. The city has been enlarged and rearranged, engulfing the historic port. Furthermore, changes in loading and unloading technology and the dynamic growth of passenger traffic have contributed to pressure for a reorganization of the port areas: the old harbours are mostly left to coastal transport and passenger traffic, while freight activities are being transferred to new zones (Istanbul, Izmir) or in specially arranged extensions (Thessaloniki, Beirut, Alexandria).

Out of such developments, a valuable stock of inactive sites and buildings has emerged on the seafront of the historic city centre. Furthering their functional obsolescence, historic port sites were more and more exposed to the risk of demolition, extensive alterations and non-reversible interventions, such as the opening up of seaside traffic arteries and so on. In recent years the importance of this valuable heritage became obvious and efforts to remove the signs of previous depredations and to re-integrate important sites and buildings into city life were increasingly adopted by many cities in order to attract economic and tourist activities within the context of an intense global antagonism. However, this process is not unobstructed, and controversies and challenges are surfacing in the implementation of wished-for corporate schemes that correspond with the global agenda.

Thessaloniki: The Enhancement of the Old Port

The rehabilitation of the historic harbour of Thessaloniki, with a surface area equal to 5% of the urban core, is the most important regeneration project in the city in recent years. It was initiated by the 1997 Cultural Capital (CC) agency in order to create new cultural facilities of metropolitan relevance and has been the leading effort to rehabilitate a historic harbour site in Greece. The city, with 1 million inhabitants, two large universities and an extensive industrial zone, has a harbour zone of 155 hectares, running 3.6 kilometres along the western shore. Today, with the development of passenger traffic and the construction of the new container pier, the old harbour has lost its commercial use. Thus a valuable stock of obsolete sites and buildings with great historic and aesthetic value has emerged. These sites and buildings survived the fire of 1917 intact; this fact made their protection and enhancement highly significant for a city that lost the greater part of its architectural heritage. The harbour was designated as a historic site in 1994 and a number of its buildings were listed for conservation (Figure 3.5).

In 1995, in view of the CC celebrations, the CC agency intended to house some of its events in the old harbour, and the project was commissioned jointly with the Ministry of Public Works in order to prepare the intervention. The initial scheme concerned the integration into the city of the entire historic harbour, an area of 5.5 hectares containing old buildings with a surface area of 13,500 square metres. Its aim went beyond the urgent provision of venues for cultural events and sought to upgrade the entire city centre. The rehabilitation proposal assigned new urban uses of a public and cultural character to the site, provided for the restoration of the historic layout and landscape, and prohibited any demolition of the surviving historic premises. However, before the study was approved, implementation started under pressure of the urgent need for cultural venues. It was funded by the Ministry of Public Works (to the tune of €16,129,000) and comprised the enhancement of the first pier (2.9 hectares) alone, and the renovation-reuse of five dock sheds (6,700 square metres). This inversion of priorities has not been without problems. The works were entrusted to private contractors who were responsible for both the definitive architectural study and the renovation work on the old structures. This entailed a significant change to the preliminary architectural studies, which led to a 'façadist' treatment of the old structures. Furthermore, while the works were under way, the Port Authority changed the previously agreed reuse plans for two warehouses in favour of more lucrative recreational uses.

Figure 3.5 The old port of Thessaloniki: above, the 1997 conservation plan; below, views of the renovated warehouses

Today, the rehabilitated part of the harbour has developed into a popular cultural and leisure destination in the city. It hosts major events, such as the International Film Festival, exhibitions, conferences and various other activities. However, the reputation of this project is unsettled by the fact that the site is still not incorporated into the town plan and remains under the jurisdiction of the Port Authority (transformed into a private company since 1999). The effects of a latent tendency towards privatization are obvious in the way that this site is run, while similar preoccupations have so far hindered the enhancement of the rest of port's historic premises (Hastaoglou-Martinidis 2011b).

Recently, a soft-impact project intended to enrich the relationship between the sea and the city was implemented along the 4-kilometre strip of the waterfront stretching to the south-east shore of the city. This sequence of thematic parks, completed between 2006 and 2013, rendered the waterfront accessible to the citizens (Nikiforidis and Cuomo 2011).

Istanbul: Controversies and Challenges of an Outstanding Waterfront Heritage

In Istanbul, the two major harbour installations dating from the early twentieth century—the docks of Sirkedji and Karaköy (at the entrance of the Golden Horn)—have lost their primary function as commercial uses have moved elsewhere. Currently, the area of Sirkedji serves a very dense coastal navigation, crucial for this mega-city that has reached a population of 15 million residents. In the 1960s the Sirkedji docks and the neo-renaissance customhouse (1907) were sacrificed to open up the seaside boulevard; yet, in the rear area a significant part of the original urban fabric and buildings (khans, warehouses, shops etc.) survive, though in poor condition, next to the ornate railway station (1890). On the Galata side, in Karaköy, a large part of the harbour heritage—fabric and buildings—is preserved. The dock serves intense cruise-ship traffic and remains a busy place that brings together commercial and recreational uses as it is undergoing gradual gentrification.

Initial action was taken in 2004 with Istanbul Modern, the first contemporary art museum in the city, housed in renovated Warehouse Number 4 on the Karaköy dock. This is one of the four warehouses erected in 1958 on the location of the old Tophane Barracks, right after the opening up of the coastal boulevard and the arrangement of Tophane Square by the prominent architect Sadad Hakki Eldem. However, what followed reflects the clear priority given by the authorities to privatization and the lucrative redevelopment of historic sites, in an urban economy fuelled by intensive construction activity. In October 2012 Turkey's High Privatization Board approved the plan for the so-called Galataport project, comprising a cruise port, a recreation area and a social-cultural facility in the Karaköy-Salipazarı quarter. The trajectory of this politically troubled privatization project, which has been on the table since 2005, came to a close in May 2013, when Doğuş Holdings beat off the competition with the highest offer, a $702 million bid that won them the right to operate the port area for thirty years. The 2010 development plan by IMM and the Beyoğlu Municipality Headquarters defines the project area of circa 11 hectares, stretching for more than 1.2 kilometres along the coastline. The scheme includes the construction and operation of a cruise port, five-star hotels, shopping malls, cinemas, entertainment facilities, restaurants, cafés and underground car parks. To accommodate the development, Warehouse Number 4, which presently accommodates

Istanbul Modern museum, as well as the three similar buildings nearby, will be demolished (Köksal 2012).

In July 2013 another part of the Golden Horn coastline came on offer to private tender, namely the former shipyards, originally set up by Sultan Mehmed II in 1455. The new project, entitled Haliçport, with a surface area of around 22.5 hectares from Kasımpaşa to Hasköy, includes two yacht marinas, two five-star hotels, a shopping mall, a 1,000-person mosque, and spaces for restaurants, cinemas and a cultural centre. The majority of structures in the area will be pulled down, preserving only the Aynalikavak Pavilion, the Corlulu Ali Pasa Mosque, and the Naval Administration building as historic landmarks to be refurbished as museums (Erimtan 2012).

Galataport and Haliçport are only links in the chain of super mega-projects that have been promoted in the last decade, aspiring to shape the image of the New Turkey; combining political ambition and economic expedience, this global-flavoured policy gravely threatens the natural and cultural landscape of Istanbul and is hardly justifiable in the era of sustainable cities. Projects include the doubtful Metro crossing bridge (2005–2013), the largest structure in the Golden Horn; the controversial third Bosporus Bridge, founded in May 2013; and the projected Third Airport, with a 150-million passenger capacity, the world's largest airport in the Black Sea region. The most audacious scheme of this kind has been dubbed the 'second Bosporus' and consists of a 40-kilometre canal that would divert shipping and turn the built-up area of the European side of Istanbul into an artificial island; first announced in the AKP's 2011 electoral campaign and scheduled for 2023, the centenary of the Republic of Turkey, it is in a preliminary stage at the time of this writing (Perouse 2013).

In the context of these accounts, the Marmaray Railway, a mega-engineering project for an undersea rail tunnel that connects the European and the Asian sides of the Bosporus, is of special interest. Excavations for the construction of the central interchange station for a railway, a light train and a new metro line in the Yenikapı area, under way since 2004, unearthed the Byzantine harbour of the Emperor Theodosius on the Sea of Marmara, in use between the fifth and the eleventh centuries, and filled in during the Ottoman epoch. The Yenikapı excavation is the largest archaeological dig in Turkey, both because of its size (a 5.8-hectare site) and the number of shipwrecks found—a total of thirty-six sunken ships. Successive layers of the city's history that include prehistoric, Roman, Byzantine and Ottoman remains have been brought to light: a section of the first city walls of Constantinople, an early Byzantine church, and relics of a Neolithic settlement are among the most impressive finds (Zan *et al.* 2013) (Figure 3.6).

The confluence of the excavation size, duration, conservation difficulties and the transport mega-projects at Yenikapı caused repeated delays and ambiguity in the management plan of this outstanding heritage site. The initial idea, advanced by the Istanbul Metropolitan Municipality (IMM) in

Figure 3.6 The Yenikapı excavation site in 2010

2005, was that a museum would exhibit the archaeological finds inside the future Metro; in 2011, a new and ambitious vision was adopted, advancing to the concept of a 'transfer point and archaeon-park', which would be designed by a well-known architect and become a symbol of the city. In June 2011 the 'Yenikapı Transfer Point and Archaeon-Park International Preliminary Architecture Project' was announced, showcasing architecture over archaeology. The project area extends for 27.7 hectares around the excavation site, from Samatya Sea Wall Gate to Yenikapı Ferry Terminal and Aksaray Square to the north. It required the elaboration of an urban scale master plan, design studies for public spaces, the rehabilitation of two historic neighbourhoods, and an architectural preliminary project for the new buildings. The three finalist designs, by Eisenmann Architects & Aytaç Architects; Atelye 70 & Francesco Cellini & Insula Architettura e Ingegneria; and Cafer Bozkurt Architects & Mecanoo Architects were chosen in April 2012; although the projects were publicized in the media, their actual status was not made clear (Bustler.net 2012).

In July 2012, however, the affair took a different turn. The IMM announced a new plan at Yenikapı for an assembly ground for political rallies and outdoor fairs. The 'Yenikapı Assembly Ground' project provides a controlled

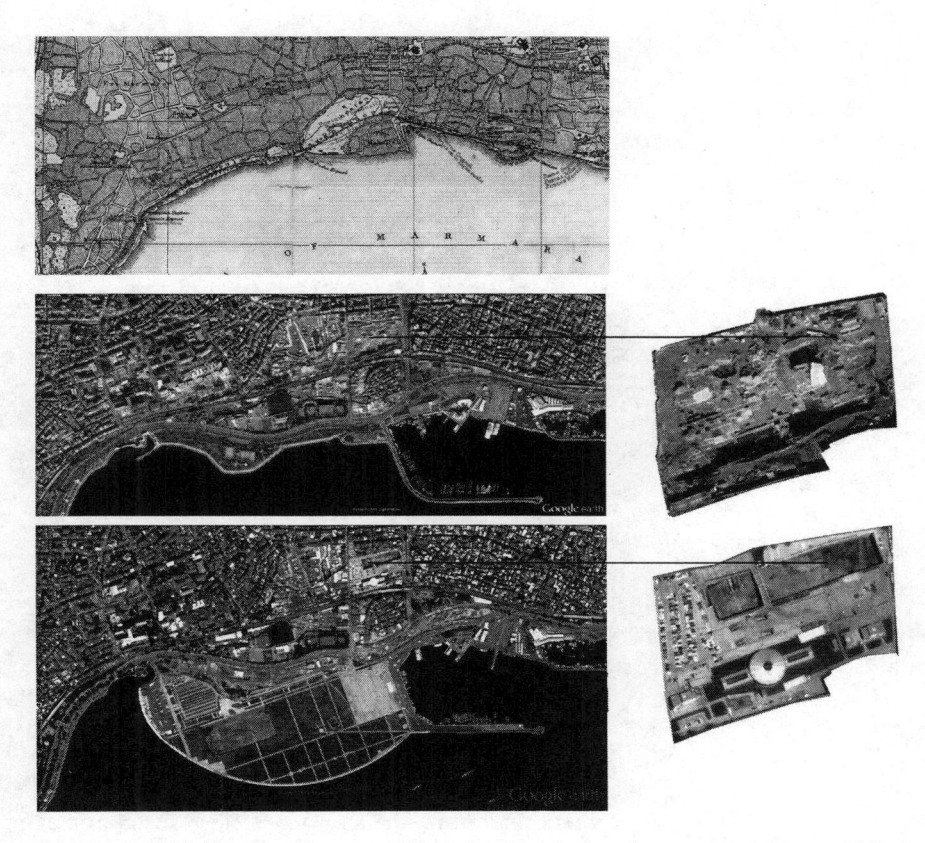

Figure 3.7 The Yenikapı area transformations: above, the area in 1900; middle, the area in 2007 and a detail of the excavation site (right); below, the Yenikapı Assembly Ground landfill in 2014 and the present-day archaeological site (right)

demonstration area that allows gatherings of up to 1 million people to take place away from the city centre. It offers an enormous sea embankment of some 58 hectares off Yenikapı, between the Ferry Terminal and the site of Samatya Gate (the only spot where Byzantine sea walls now meet the sea). The project was approved on September 2012 by the Ministry of Environment and Urbanism, and the landfill construction of the platform was entrusted to the Nuhoğlu Construction firm (Nuhoğlu 2013). The prosecution of such a scheme in an area of vast archaeological significance raised a lot of criticism and serious concerns within the heritage milieu (the Cultural Assets Conservation Council, UNESCO and ICOMOS); stress was placed on the unprecedented status in the city's long history of the creation of a gigantic reclaimed area outside the sea wall, which will ravage the shape of the historic peninsula and its silhouette (UNESCO 2013). Reclamation works started in September 2012 and were already complete by December 2013 (Figure 3.7).

The Bosporus tunnel was officially opened on 29 October 2013 on the Turkish Republic's ninetieth anniversary. Presently, in the place of the former Yenikapı excavation site, a concrete slab serves the entrance to the massive underground station, and the 'Archaeon-Park' is reduced into an uninspired rectangular ditch.

Beirut: A New Global Waterfront and a Contested Heritage Project

The reconstruction of Beirut after a lengthy period of civil war (1975–1990) may be considered as the latest phase in a centuries-long sequence of transfigurations, giving this city the character of an urban chameleon. The war caused the loss of a large part of the city's historic core and the old port. The reconstruction programme for the Central District is undoubtedly the prime global project in the Eastern Mediterranean region, and resulted in the radical reshaping of the historic city centre and notably the waterfront (Sandes 2013).

The reconstruction of Beirut was initiated in 1977 with President Elias Sarkis' plan; this was followed by Amin Gemayel's plan of 1982. The recovery of the Central District was at the heart of those schemes and the sole component to be implemented exclusively by Solidere, the private development company founded in 1994 by President Rafik Hariri (Larkin 2009). The thirty-year master plan for the city (1994–2024) focuses on reconstructing Beirut as a global tourist commercial centre; it covers 191 hectares, out of which 73 hectares is reclaimed land along the shoreline. New development such as offices, residences, marinas, hotels and global commerce is allocated 73 hectares, while of Beirut's original urban fabric, only 22 hectares (including 265 key buildings), has been retained (Solidere 2002–2013a).

A mass of literature has been produced on the subject, including both scholarly literature and items in the media (Davie 1997; Rowe and Sarkis 1998; Khalaf 2006; Nasr and Verdeil 2008). Solidere's project has faced considerable public debate, academic criticism and civic activism, which has challenged the adopted models of global urbanism and sought to reclaim Beirut's lost and endangered heritage.

In the early 1990s, Solidere cleared the way for its ambitious master plan by removing the war-damaged urban fabric and creating a *tabula rasa* in place of what used to be the old downtown area. Critiques suggest that by 1993, about 80% of all structures in the centre of town were damaged beyond repair, yet only a third of this destruction had been inflicted by the war (Makdisi 2006). However, criticism and protest are credited with the readjustment of the initial plan so as to integrate the city's multilayered past. Though eminently selective, the preservation approach managed to incorporate the conservation of all properties owned by religious communities and to designate certain zones as conservation areas (Sandes 2010).

The costly restoration and rebuilding of Etoile Square (a French Mandate legacy), Maarad Street and Foch-Allenby District have led to these areas being upgraded as the prime destination for nightlife and retail. The redevelopment of the damaged Martyrs' Square (the famous Place des Canons), the finds dated to various historic periods such as the Roman baths, the Cardo and Decumanus Maximus, and the Canaanite Tell, are displayed together with mosques, churches and Ottoman buildings along a Heritage Trail that runs through the centre (Alkantar 2012). Consequently, Solidere promoted its new marketing slogan 'Beirut, an ancient city for the future', which replaced its initial motto of 'Beirut, the Hong Kong of the Mediterranean' (Schmid 2006).

The brand image of Beirut's reconstruction is the New Waterfront, a globalized landscape that replaced the picturesque rocky seafront with the old harbour and the interwar corniche promenade—the Avenue des Français. It is arranged on 73 hectares of reclaimed land north of the old seashore and

Figure 3.8 Beirut's Central District: aerial photo showing the medieval (I) and the Ottoman (II) coastlines; the sites of the Phoenician port (1), the Roman Hippodrome (2), the Old Shoreline Walk (3) and the Garden of Forgiveness (4)

provides an uninterrupted 3.5-kilometre extension of the city's shoreline. It contains the Waterfront District flanked by the West and East Marinas, a waterside city park, corniche and promenades, with 29 hectares of new waterside development land (Figure 3.8).

The Waterfront District, previously known as the Normandy Landfill, is a huge area of about 36 hectares jutting from the mainland into the sea for 600 metres beyond the original shoreline. It was created as a dumping ground in the Mediterranean Sea, initially for municipal and later for other kinds of waste (including the landfill's namesake Normandy Hotel) during the fifteen years of civil unrest. The original site consisted of a small picturesque bay that used to cut 200 metres into the mainland and that housed a small marina and the legendary Saint Georges Hotel. The landfill treatment and land reclamation were completed by 2012, and the grid layout plan was finalized. Chris Blandford Associates (UK) have been assigned the landscape design.

The 2005 master plan for the new waterfront recognizes Beirut as a prime tourist destination and aims to turn the district into a mixed leisure, residential and commercial area. It is based on a 2001 planning study by a consortium of US firms including Skidmore Owings & Merrill (SOM). The development, criticized as 'Solidere's final frontier', is a major real estate project open to private investors and designed by international and local architects (Sadek and El-Fadel 2000).

Adjacent to the Normandy Landfill, the West Marina or Zaitunay Bay, opened in 2012, was designed by the British architect Steven Holl as a new urban beach, with a series of overlapping platforms varying in width from 45 to 110 metres, which provide outdoor spaces and new developments for a yachting club, restaurants, stores, the luxurious Marina Towers (the biggest residential project in the Mediterranean, designed by the US firm Kohn Pedersen Fox Associates) and public facilities. It is flanked to the west by the Hotel District, which assembles the city's suite of new luxurious hotels (Solidere 2002–2013b). The East Marina is an anchor project of the Waterfront District. The site north of the port's first basin will be developed as a private luxury urban beach resort, accommodating a hotel, serviced condominiums, low-rise residences and quayside retail. The implementation of the 7.8-hectare Waterside Park along the new sea cornice is scheduled to take place next; the ambition for the development, currently under design by COWI (Denmark), is to create a recreational attraction for the city and its metropolitan area.

Buried under a dumping ground, the lost shoreline of Beirut has been the object of a project intended to trace the memory of the historic coastline. The 'Old Shoreline Walk' was designed in 2003 by Gustafson Porter's UK firm as a sequence of open spaces. It runs between the original rocky shoreline corniche with its avenues of palms and cafés in front of the medieval street layout of the old city, and the new waterfront landfill, in an effort to re-establish the east-west connection in this part of the city that was once created by the celebrated Avenue des Français. The project includes five landscaped squares and gardens—Harbour Square, All Saints Square, Shoreline Gardens, Zeytouneh Square and Santiyeh Garden—linked in a circuitous walk, with each of the spaces revealing remnants of the character of pre-war Beirut that had been forgotten or destroyed (Spens 2007).

Closing Remarks

As everywhere else in the globalized world, Eastern Mediterranean port cities have tried since the 1990s to confront fierce international competition and foster economic growth. For the first time in the post-war years, they undertook to redeploy and rehabilitate large parts of their waterfronts, aiming at the creation of a culture-led service sector.

This chapter has revealed that the regeneration of old harbour sites could be a powerful tool for re-establishing these important cultural ensembles as major points of innovation, at both local and global levels. At a local level, the activation of harbour heritage for the creation of renewed spaces of metropolitan compass can decisively contribute to the upgrading of densely built historic centres, making up for serious deficiencies in the provision of public space and qualitative services. Furthermore, at a regional level, it emerges that they have the potential to act as strong points in a cultural network which will encourage maritime communication, tourist development and finally a new cosmopolitanism based on the synergy of cities.

However the practical outcomes of this trend, as so far registered, do not always follow this reasoning. It is obvious that increasing privatization and the pronounced leaning towards globalized models would result in the opposite effect; that is, the loss of cities' individuality and eventually of essential features of their history. Historic waterfronts are witnessing a profound alteration; their refashioning upon their original sites is more likely to be structured so as to overturn their traditional character, and far less frequently in order to enhance it. Historic waterfronts thus become the theatre of a complicated encounter of the local with the global, which involves different and conflicting stakeholders, while enhancement projects are marked by controversies and challenges.

The absence of corporate involvement in the case of the Thessaloniki rehabilitation schemes allowed the local to prevail against the global thus far, although there are signs for privatization that cannot be ignored. In Istanbul the emphasis on the local—apparent in regeneration projects prior to 2000—proved less 'persuasive' after 2004 and was eventually systematically pushed aside, giving way to ambitious and aggressive mega-schemes. The case of Beirut reveals the major flaws in the new concept and configuration promoted for the waterfront, and the challenges and threats inherent in such a globally oriented choice.

This is evident in the cases where the legacies of previous eras that inadvertently come to the surface during rehabilitation projects are barely preserved, some even being removed, as happened in Istanbul and Beirut. In this respect, the growing role of criticism and protests in bringing about the readjustment of historically insensitive schemes should also be underlined. The challenging of the adopted models of global urbanism and the reclaiming of cities' endangered heritage highlight a counter-demand for sustainable development and a bridge between the present and the past that would allow cities to strengthen their natural and cultural identity for the present advantage and the future benefit of their inhabitants.

Bibliography

Abulafia, D. (2011) *The Great Sea: A Human History of the Mediterranean*, New York: Oxford University Press.

Alkantar, B. (2012) 'Minister of Culture "Dismantles" Beirut's Roman Hippodrome', *Al-akhbar*, 13 March 2012. Available at: http://english.al-akhbar.com/content/minister-culture-dismantles-beiruts-roman-hippodrome

Battah, H. (2013) 'Activists Fight to Preserve Beirut's Roman Heritage', *BBC News, Middle East*, 25 September 2013. Available at: www.bbc.com/news/world-middle-east-24222755

Bustler.net (2012) 'Three Entries Share First Prize in Istanbul's Yenikapı Design Competition'. Available at: www.bustler.net/index.php/article/three_entries_share_first_prize_in_istanbuls_yenikapi_design_competition/

Caldwell, L. (2011) 'Solidere's Final Frontier?', *Al-akhbar*, December 2011. Available at: http://english.al-akhbar.com/node/2913

Davie, M.F. (ed.) (1997) *Beyrouth, regards croisés*, Tours: Urbama.

Erimtan, C. (2013) 'Galataport & Haliçport: Privatization in Overdrive?' Available at: http://istanbulgazette.com/galataport-halicport-privatization-in-overdrive/2013/07/04/

Hastaoglou-Martinidis, V. (2001) 'Towns and Settlements Network in the Mediterranean', M. Modinos (ed.), *The Eco-Geography of the Mediterranean* [in Greek], Athens: Interdisciplinary Institute of Environmental Studies, 61–92.

Hastaoglou-Martinidis, V. (2010) 'The Cartography of Harbour Construction in Eastern Mediterranean Cities: Technical and Urban Modernization in the Late Nineteenth Century', in B. Kolluoğlu and M. Toksöz (eds.), *Cities of the Mediterranean*, London: I.B. Tauris, 78–99.

Hastaoglou-Martinidis, V. (2011a) 'Urban Aesthetics and National Identity: The Refashioning of Eastern Mediterranean Cities Between 1900 and 1940', *Planning Perspectives*, 26(2): 153–182.

Hastaoglou-Martinidis, V. (2011b) 'Rehabilitation of Historic Sites in Thessaloniki: Protection, New Building and Re-Use', in D. Babalis (ed.), *Chronocity. Sensitive Interventions in Historic Environment*, Florence: Alinea editrice, 15–17.

Khalaf, S. (2006) *The Heart of Beirut-Reclaiming the Bourj*, London: Saqi.

Larkin, C. (2009) 'Reconstructing and Deconstructing Beirut: Space, Memory and Lebanese Youth'. Available at: in www.conflictincities.org/workingpapers.html

Makdisi, S. (2006) 'Reconstructing History in Central Beirut', *Middle East Research and Information Project*. Available at: www.merip.org/mer/mer203/reconstructing-history-central-beirut

Köksal, G. (2012) 'Galataport Projesi Üstüne Tartışma: Salıpazarı Rıhtımı Nasıl Biçimlenmeli?', *Mimar.ist*, 12(46): 55–62.

Nasr, J. and Verdeil, E. (2008) 'The Reconstructions of Beirut', in S. Jayyusi, R. Holod, A. Petruccioli and A. Raymond (eds.), *The City in the Islamic World*, Leiden: Brill, 1116–1141.

Nikiforidis, P. and Cuomo, B. (2011) 'Redevelopment of the New Coast of Thessaloniki', in Technical Chamber of Greece (ed.), *Public City*, Thessaloniki: Ianos, 53–54.

Nuhoğlu Insaat (2013) 'Yenikapı Rally Square Project'. Available at: www.nuhogluinsaat.com.tr/projeler.asp?id=33&lng=en

Perouse, J.-F. (2013) 'Hybristanbul. Les grands projets d'aménagement urbain en Turquie', 24 Septembre 2013. Available at: www.laviedesidees.fr/IMG/pdf/20130924_turquie.pdf

Rowe, P. and Sarkis, H. (eds.) (1998) *Projecting Beirut: Episodes in the Construction and Reconstruction of a Modern City*, New York: Prestel Publishing.

Sadek, S. and El-Fadel, M. (2000) 'The Normandy Landfill: A Case Study in Solid Waste Management', *Journal of Natural Resources and Life Sciences Education*, 29: 155–156.

Sandes, C. (2010) *Archeology, Conservation and the City: Post-Conflict Redevelopment in London, Berlin and Beirut*, British Archaeological Report S2159. Oxford: Archaeopress, 95–97.

Sandes, C. (2013) 'Urban Cultural Heritage and Armed Conflict: The Case of Beirut Central District', in J. Kila and J. Zeidler (eds.), *Cultural Heritage in the Crosshairs: Protecting Cultural Property during Conflict*, Leiden: Brill, 287–314.

Schmid, H. (2006) 'Privatized Urbanity or Politicized Society? Reconstruction in Beirut After the Civil War', *European Planning Studies*, 14(3): 375.

Solidere (2002–2013a) 'Master Plan'. Available at: www.solidere.com/city-center/urban-overview/master-plan

Solidere (2002–2013b) 'Districts & Main Axis'. Available at: www.solidere.com/city-center/urban-overview/districts-main-axes/waterfront

Spens, M. (2007) 'Deep Explorations into Site/Non-Site: The Work of Gustafson Porter', *Landscape Architecture: Site/Non-Site*, 77(2): 69–75.

UNESCO World Heritage Committee (2013) *Historic Areas of Istanbul*, 37 Session, May 2013: 33–37.

Zan, L., Bonini Baraldi, S. and Shoup, D. (2013) 'Mega Engineering Projects and Archaeological Discovery: Institutional Context, Organisation Challenges and professional Issues at Yenikapı, Istanbul'. Available at: www.aidea2013.it/docs/102_aidea2013_public-management.pdf

4 The Transformation Process of the Galata Port in Istanbul

Reflections on the Impacts of the Galataport Project

Hicran Topçu

Introduction

Waterfront areas in historic port cities are usually considered as having the potential to boost the city's tourist appeal, and, in many cases, are subjected to extensive transformation projects. In view of the fact that reconciling the goals of conservation and development has become a requisite for the sustainability of both, change in historic areas is acceptable up to a certain extent, so long as the urban integrity is respected as 'the result of the historic layering of cultural and natural values and attributes'.[1]

The question of waterfront development is even more challenging in the case of a city like Istanbul, where the water is the main source of its unique urban image as a bridge between different continents, seas and cultures. It is due to this unique image that Istanbul has always attracted people from everywhere. On one hand, it is also the main reason for its overpopulation, leading to rapid development and urban degradation, air pollution, poor life quality, and the increasing loss and decay of cultural and historic values. On the other hand, instead of aiming to reverse this situation, and focusing on the sustainability of cultural values and improvement of life quality, the urban politics regarding the city's future still seem to point at strengthening the iconic image of Istanbul as a 'world city' through mega-scale infrastructure and urban regeneration projects. Galataport is one of these projects, promoted by the Turkish government as 'the main international sea gate of Istanbul' and 'one of the best cruise ports in the world'. Since it was first introduced in 2005, the project has given rise to several discussions and objections regarding its possible impacts not only on the historic identity of Galata but on the wider urban context of Istanbul. However, the project has received great political support on the part of the Turkish government and it is apparently steaming ahead in spite of all the ongoing complaints and legal actions.

Several aspects of the project management process deserve to be discussed from the perspective of the principles of integrated planning and participatory decision-making. For instance, though being part of a historic context and the container of several historic buildings, the project area, disjointedly from the conservation area planning boundaries, has been designated as a 'tourism centre' under the control of the National Privatization Administration. This division constitutes a threat for the physical integrity of the historic urban context, resulting in a 'conservation area' disconnected from its front and its main access, and a 'waterfront area' planned apart from its background. Nevertheless, the discussion in this chapter will be limited to the impacts of the port project on the visual and functional integrity of the site, with particular reference to the historic continuity of the city.

Galata and Its Port through the Ages

The quarter of Galata is situated on the opposite side of the historic peninsula of Istanbul, on the northern part of the Golden Horn (called *Haliç* in Turkish), the 8-kilometre-long inlet of the Bosphorus that divides the European side of the city into two parts. Due to its corridor-like shape and considerable depth at both sides, permitting the access of ships almost right up to the land, and the geographical location protected from the strong winds affecting the city, historically the Golden Horn was the main port of Istanbul. In fact, since the Byzantine period, and all through the Ottoman period, the entire waterfront area of the Golden Horn was considered as a single port (Müller-Wiener 1998) divided into several small docks or quays (called *iskele* in Turkish, deriving from the word *scala* in Italian, recalling the presence of Italian colonies in the city) aligned in a row along the sea.

Galata originated as a distinct centre within Byzantine Constantinople. However, its privileged position in a city at the intersection of all the historic routes made Galata one of the most important ports in the Mediterranean maritime trade. Indeed, it is its relationship with the sea that is the main source of its unique urban image, noted and expressed by numerous travellers and painters in all ages as the most heterogeneous, multicultural, multiethnic, chaotic and lively quarter of Istanbul.

The historical sources highlight that Galata (initially called *Sykai*) was already a settlement area surrounded by defence walls during the reign of Constantine I (324–337). The *Notitia Urbis Constantinopolitanae* (c. 447) reported that Sykai, as the thirteenth Regio of Constantinople, had 431 houses, an avenue with portico, two churches, baths of Honorius, a theatre, five private baths, a public mill and an arsenal called *Navalia* (Eyice 1969; Freely 2000). However, the golden era of Galata began in the fourteenth century when it was conceded for use by the Genoese colony. At that time, there were also other Italian communities (Amalfians, Venetians and Pisans) living in the city, each having a privileged area with several docks reserved for their use (Müller-Wiener 1998). However, it is the Genoese quarter of Galata that we have more accurate information on, thanks to the presence of several official documents such as treaties and decrees regulating the social and commercial life of the Genoese population within the Byzantine capital.

The decree of 1303 gives a detailed description of the first area of concession, referring to many important buildings of the period, such as the Vetus Tersana (the Byzantine arsenal, probably situated at the same location as the Ottoman arsenal), and Kastellion tou Galatou, the sixth-century Byzantine fort in the south where the legendary chain closing off the Golden Horn was anchored. The documents reveal that although the Byzantine fortifications were demolished at the time of concession, in spite of all restrictions imposed by the empire, in a short time the Genoese community reconstructed the walls and enlarged their quarter (Eyice 1969).

From the time of concession until Ottoman rule, Galata was a typical Genoese fortified harbour town with towers and gates, set out in a grid-iron pattern, with streets parallel and perpendicular to the shoreline. The main public buildings, such as the Podesta (assigned by Genova to the governor of the colony and the ambassador in the Byzantine capital), the marketplace, the loggia (the traders' meeting point), the hospital and the main churches (San Domenico and San Paolo, San Michele and San Pietro) were all concentrated along the main perpendicular axis, connecting the port to the Galata Tower at the highest point of settlement.

Fourteenth- and fifteenth-century travellers were impressed by the intensive commercial traffic and the social life in Galata. Ibn Battuta (1335) described the district as 'one of the largest ports in the world with hundreds of galleys, large and small ships' and people from all nations (Freely 2000). Similarly, the fifteenth-century Spanish ambassador, Ruy Gonzales de Clavijo, reported a small but a very populous township with excellent houses and numerous shops, ateliers and warehouses. He described the waterfront area as a narrow band of land extending between the city walls and the sea with several timber docks (Müller-Wiener 1998; Freely 2000).

The earliest view of Istanbul, *Urbis Constantinopolitanae Delineato* by Cristoforo Buondelmonti (1422), illustrates the state of Galata just before the Ottoman period. In the image, Galata is differentiated from the rest of the city with its densely built urban fabric composed of masonry houses and churches. The Galata Tower and Kastellion on the waterfront stand out clearly as the two most important landmarks of the time.

The port of Galata kept its commercial capacity as an international port in the Ottoman period. Along the waterfront area of Galata, there were forty-seven quays, each dedicated to certain types of goods or ships coming from certain regions (Müller-Wiener 1998). These quays were named after the type of traded good or the closest city gate providing access to the city. In fact, the entire urban system was determined according to the network of functional relationships between the waterfront and the inner settlement. Behind each dock, there was a cluster of port-related functions: warehouses, ateliers and shops, as well as social services for the artisans and traders.

In his book *Die Häfen von Byzantion, Konstantinupolis, Istanbul*,[2] the German historian Wolfgang Müller-Wiener presents a very detailed topographical analysis of the Istanbul port during the Ottoman period. The western end of the Galata waterfront was marked by the imperial arsenal, while the docks closer to this area were predominantly used for public transportation of the arsenal workers as well as the residents of the surrounding quarters. Behind the waterfront, there was a concentration of functions related with the arsenal, such as ateliers and shops for the production and trading of equipment (such as oars and anchors) for vessels and ships, restaurants for the artisans and warehouses for the construction materials.

The central part of the waterfront (including the Yagkapani oil market and Balikpazari fish market docks) constituted one of the most important ports in Istanbul for ships coming from Europe. The Karaköy quay on its east, which was later the connection point for the Galata Bridge, was predominantly used for public transportation, and was famous for the taverns behind it.

The eastern end of the waterfront, Tophane, where the Galataport project is planned today, was historically known as the most spacious and lively area of Galata. This was the main port of departure for the Ottoman navy and for the ambassadors of Pera to come into the presence of the Ottoman sultan. Tophane Square behind the port, with its central fountain, lined with coffeehouses and taverns, was the main meeting point for local people and travellers. Horse carriages waiting for people from the ships, and *caiques*, to take people for a trip along the Bosphorus, were typical elements of the port, illustrated widely by painters and photographers of the nineteenth and twentieth centuries.

Regarding the Ottoman period, we can talk about two distinct stages in the urban transformation of Galata. The first stage refers to the transformation of the city under Ottoman rule, while the second coincides with its modernization with the Tanzimat reforms. The period from the end of the fifteenth century until the mid-eighteenth century can be defined as the 'Ottomanization' or 'Islamization' of the quarter. This process consisted of the establishment of several important public buildings and complexes at critical points in and around the quarter, which resulted in the formation of new quarters and a gradual concentration of the Muslim population around them. The construction of the Bedesten (covered market) facing the Genoese marketplace, establishment of the imperial shipyard (Tersane-i Amire) on the western side and the imperial armoury (Tophane-i Amire) on the eastern side of the Genoese walls can be considered among the earliest interventions. In this process, we should also recall the contribution of the famous sixteenth-century architect, Mimar Sinan, especially in the rearrangement of the Galata waterfront (Cuneo 1987) with several important buildings and complexes such as the Azapkapi (Sokollu) mosque on the east the Kılıç Ali Pasha complex near Tophane, and the Rustem Pasha Han, which was built upon the ruins of San Michele Church. In this period, some of the important churches were also converted into Islamic buildings, such as the church of San Domenico, which was transformed into a mosque for the Arab population expelled from Andalusia (İnalcık 1991; Kuban 1996).

The appearance of Ottoman Galata after the first urban interventions of the fifteenth and sixteenth centuries is best viewed in the plans of Matrakci Nasuh (1537) and Vavassore (1550). In Vavassore's plan, Galata is in the state of its largest expansion: we see an active port with several ships and a densely built urban fabric surrounded by city walls. Outside the city walls, there was a vast green area with a few houses and cemeteries. The miniature of Matrakci Nasuh, however, gives a certain emphasis to the historic peninsula, representing Galata mainly as a residential area, with the exception of a few mosques and churches. The waterfront is pictured as a narrow band in front of the city walls with a series of small-scale structures. In both views the edges of the settlement are marked by the Galata Tower at the highest point to the north, and by the complexes of the shipyard and armoury on either side of the waterfront.

From the seventeenth century on, parallel to the concentration of the Muslim population along the seashore, the non-Muslim population of Galata began to move north past the Galata Tower, to the area which is known as the Pera vineyard. This new quarter of northern Galata, known as Pera or Beyoglu, was developed in a very short time, especially after the establishment of foreign embassies (Akin 1998) and consequently of new public services (churches, schools, hospitals etc.) in this part of the city (Çelik 1986). New buildings constructed in various European styles enriched the multicultural and eclectic urban image of the district.

The second stage of transformation beginning from the mid eighteenth century, which can be called the epoch of 'modernization', comes after the period of Istanbul's great fires[3] which devastated the historic urban fabric, and coincides with the Tanzimat reforms. As most of the interventions of this second stage were aimed at the development of the street network and transportation facilities, it also had direct impact on the integration of Galata in the metropolitan area and the socio-economic life of Istanbul, which was on its way to hosting the new city centre by the twentieth century.

The Tanzimat reforms, aimed at the modernization of the administrative system, were launched by the Imperial Statute of 1839, which was followed by a number of laws and regulations about the social life and rearrangement of the urban areas based on the European models. In this period, a large number of timber structures were substituted by masonry buildings in accordance with the new building codes (Kuban 1996). The city was divided into fourteen districts, while Galata-Pera, as the sixth district, was allotted as the pilot area for experimentation of planned interventions such as the enlargement of streets and renewal of the infrastructure. In 1864–1865, as part of these urban interventions, the Genoese city walls were also demolished (except the Galata Tower and a few other towers and gates, and some wall portions situated in non-public lots) for the establishment of new arteries and buildings[4] (Çelik 1986; Akın 1998).

The construction of the bridges connecting the two sides of the Golden Horn was an important element in the nineteenth-century development of Istanbul. In fact, the idea of a bridge for Galata was already on the agenda in the sixteenth century when Leonardo da Vinci was invited to Istanbul to design a bridge, though for some unknown reason his project was not realized. The first pedestrian bridge in Galata arrived two centuries later, in 1836, connecting the western end of Galata to the historic peninsula. In a short time, it was followed by a timber bridge between Karaköy and Eminönü, the two important commercial areas of the city.

Another important turning point for urban transportation in Galata was the construction of the Tünel (tunnel), the underground railway system designed by French engineer Eugène Henri Gavand that connected the Karaköy port area to Beyoglu on the upper hillside of Pera (İnalcık 1991; Kuban 1996).

Between 1892 and 1910, the Galata waterfront was subjected to a series of interventions aimed at the aesthetic and hygienic improvement of the area. The works that were realized by an Ottoman official, Marius Michel, who obtained a seventy-five-year concession to rebuild the waterfront area in return for a certain percentage of the custom dues, consisted of a 758-metre-long quay and several new buildings for customs, warehouses and offices (Çelik 1986).

The new streets and development of transport facilities gave rise to construction activities. In the second half of the nineteenth century, numerous new buildings—bank buildings, commercial complexes (*han* and *pasaj*), bank offices, theatres, café houses, stores, hotels and restaurants—were constructed, according to the new demand created by the developing cultural, social and economic life of the area. Many of the buildings erected in this period represent the nineteenth-century Ottoman idea of modernization, which was strongly influenced by European styles from Neo-Baroque to Art Nouveau, and with the contribution of many European architects (such as Vallaury, Mongeri and Raimondo d'Aronco).

The Galata transformation process continued in the twentieth century after the foundation of the Turkish Republic. In the 1950s, a new circulation plan for Galata, with a number of new streets, was put into effect as part of the first development plan prepared by Henri Prost (Kuban 1996; Çelik 1986). The interventions made in this context resulted in the loss of a great number of historic buildings, among which numbered important monuments from the Genoese and Ottoman periods. In the 1960s, the eastern part of the Galata waterfront underwent a series of interventions with the aim of rearranging Tophane Square. The warehouses along the sea, one of which is today used as a museum of 'Modern Istanbul', were constructed in this period.

The last large-scale transformation, which was realized from 1984 to 1989 with the aim of creating a green band along the waterfront, consisted of the demolition of all the building blocks to the south of the previous Genoese walls, with the exception of a few listed buildings and some remnants of the city walls, seemingly 'preserved' in isolation from their historic context. For the last three decades, these open spaces have remained non-living, almost abandoned areas that serve solely to disconnect the historic fabric from its waterfront.

Today, Galata forms part of the city centre, with a concentration of economic and cultural functions playing an important role in the daily life of Istanbul. Though its urban image is the outcome of a continuous transformation process, the area still maintains its distinct character with the coexistence of buildings from all periods and various architectural styles, a considerable proportion of the population from different ethnic origins and religions, and a very active socio-economic and cultural life.

The Galataport Project: The International Gate of Istanbul

The historical multiple-dock system is still maintained in Istanbul, with eleven quays (in addition to other connection points exclusively used for public transportation) linked to each other within a functional and geographical network. Situated at the opening and the largest point of the Golden Horn, in a central location in front of the historic peninsula, Galata provides Istanbul's main international port in this network, and since 1986 has been exclusively dedicated to cruise ships.

The current arrangement of the port (consisting of two quays, named Karaköy and Salipazari) is the result of a series of urban interventions realized in the last century to improve the port establishments (administrative buildings, passenger terminals and warehouses) and transport facilities. The original shoreline today is situated 20 to 50 metres behind the row of buildings (administrative buildings, a terminal building and four warehouses) constructed on the infill area. There are several historic monuments in and around the port, such as the Kılıç Ali Paşa complex (sixteenth century), Nusretiye Mosque, clock tower and Summer Palace (nineteenth century), Tophane Fountain (eighteenth century) and many others, all bearing witness to different periods in the history of the place, though they stand in isolation, disconnected from their context, squeezed in among the tall buildings and the traffic jams. The urban space, which once used to be a meeting point for local people as well as incomers, is now invaded by parking lots. Furthermore, the cruise ships (up to eleven a day) berthing in the port create a visual barrier in front of the historic setting.

The Galataport project was planned in the same area, on a total surface of 112,147 square metres, extending 1,200 metres along the south-eastern bank of Galata from Karaköy to Tophane. The general framework of the project, together with the cruise port, comprises several tourist-related functions such as hotels, restaurants, commercial centres and other recreational facilities in order to create a tourist area that is planned and managed under the control of the National Privatization Administration. The first plan prepared by the authority was repealed for its incompatibility with the national law regarding waterfront areas. Nevertheless, the revised plan was approved with a minor change in the floor area ratio (1.50) and the maximum building height value (15.50–18.50 metres); while a 10-metre-wide waterfront infill (12,000 square meters) and a two-storey underground parking, were added. The plan includes the conservation of a few listed buildings but the replacement of all but two of the warehouses (constructed in the mid twentieth century), which are currently used as the Museum of Modern Art and the Mimar Sinan University, and gives a total construction area of up to 127,811 square metres.[5]

Istanbul is a city with a highly mobile population and strong dynamics of urban change widely influenced by global factors. The extreme rapidity of the physical and socio-economic transformation of the city has an overwhelming effect on the local identity of the place, while the cultural, social and economic benefits of 'development' are not evenly shared by the local population. Small businesses are being replaced with large-scale shopping malls, and traditional residential areas with luxurious residential towers—exclusively serving the elites—integrated with business centres. The development strategies seem to be determined at national level, based exclusively on the rules of international competitiveness[6] rather than local demands and social requisites. The result is a rapidly growing city with weakening ties with its history and local culture.

The waterfront of Galata has been functioning as Istanbul's cruise port for almost three decades. However, the consolidation of this function and all the prerequisites for the ambitious goal of being 'the best cruise port' and 'the main entrance gate of Istanbul' will evidently not favour the reconstruction of the historical, cultural and social integrity of Galata as a Historic Urban Landscape. Implementation of the project with the earlier proportions will certainly have a devastating effect on the historic heritage of a site which is already in a segmented state after the urban interventions of the last century. Even more unfortunately, the changing dynamics provoked by the project will create a multiplying effect on the cultural and socio-economic transformation of the context. Indeed, the project is already having a preliminary impact on land speculation. Newspapers report that real estate prices within the vicinity of the project area have doubled since the project launch in 2005, with an increasing request for nineteenth-century buildings to be restored and used as boutique hotels. Galata—which, contrary to the facing historic peninsula that has given itself wholly over to tourism, still preserves a distinct character as a lively quarter with its specialized streets and clusters of activities, small shops, cafes and restaurants mostly frequented by the young population of Istanbul—will be transformed by the realization of the project into a zone of VIP hotels, commercial centres and many other tourist-oriented functions.

Conclusion: Redesigning the Galata Waterfront

The Galata waterfront, which in its entirety as a port system was once composed of specialized zones, today represents an over-segmented urban space with a combination of port functions, historic buildings and open spaces which do not succeed in interacting with each other. Recalling the historic image of Galata, the port was the main generator of the social, economic and physical structure of the urban context, through a well-constructed system of relationships between sea, urban space, trade, monuments and social life. Therefore, the attempts to redesign the Galata waterfront should primarily be concerned with reconstructing these broken relationships, in the light of a holistic approach which does not exclude the contributions of any period, or the resultant shifts in the functional and symbolical meanings of the urban space.

The heterogeneous urban structure of Galata, with the coexistence of different periods, different styles and different functions that in many cases seem to be in conflict with each other, can be interpreted as historical discontinuity, or a lack of conservation. However, from another perspective, it also expresses the very continuity of the place, the adaptation of the urban space to introduce new elements and new uses, which, while becoming part of the urban context, also transform it into one which it has never been before. This dilemma of integration and transformation, in the case of dynamic urban contexts like Galata, forms part of the nature of the place, sometimes even shifting the focus of the conservation debate from what was there before to what was introduced later. For instance, one of the common discussions within the scope of the Galataport project regards a warehouse building constructed in Tophane in the 1960s (when Galata was Istanbul's main importing harbour), hiding the aspect of the nineteenth-century clock tower and detaching the Tophane Square visually and functionally from the waterfront. The building, which has recently been used as the Museum of Modern Art, has now become a subject for conservation, not for its architectural quality, or its representative value of the period, but in particular for the role it has assumed in the socio-cultural life of the city.

Certainly, in the case of complex heritage resources like historic cities that are created over a span of time, especially a metropolitan city like Istanbul, we cannot talk about the pure integrity of the historic urban context. Thus, it is necessary to embrace the time factor, the evolution process with all its cultural and socio-economical dynamics that created the cultural layers of the historic context and the values conveyed therein. For any kind of action regarding its future, it is the identity of the place that needs to be sought and taken as the main reference.

Notes

1 Recommendation on Historic Urban Landscapes. Art. 8.
2 In this article, reference is made to the Turkish translation of the book (Original source: *Die Häfen von Byzantion, Konstantinupolis, Istanbul*, Tübingen: Wasmuth 1994)

3   In the seventeenth and eighteenth centuries, daily life in Galata was marked by great fires. Inciciyan reports eight great fires from 1635 to 1771 that destroyed thousands of residential and monumental buildings (Inciciyan 1976).
4   With the demolition of the city walls, a total area of 9,000 m² was obtained for the establishment of new streets and constructions (Çelik 1986).
5   'Privatization of Istanbul Salıpazarı Cruise Port. A Brief Overview. National Privatization Administration ', February 2013.
6   Decision no. 2009/31 of the National Council of Planning officially declared the national strategy for Istanbul as the 'International Financial Centre' and defined a series of action plans for the development of infrastructure according to this vision.

Bibliography

Akın, N. 1998, *19. yüzyılın ikinci yarısında Galata ve Pera*. Literatür Yayıncılık, İstanbul.

Çelik, Z. 1986, *The Remaking of Istanbul: Portrait of an Ottoman City in the Nineteenth Century*. University of California Press, Berkeley.

Cuneo, P. 1987, 'Sinan's contribution to the design of Galata waterfront', *Environmental Design: Journal of the Islamic Environmental Design Research Centre*, 1–2, pp. 210–215.

Eyice, S. 1969, *Galata ve kulesi: Galata and Its Tower*. Türkiye Turing ve Otomobil Kurumu. Apa Ofset Basımevi, İstanbul.

Freely, J. 2000, *Galata*. Arkeoloji ve Sanat Yayınları, İstanbul.

Inalcık, H. 1991 'Ottoman Galata (1453–1553)', in *Varia Turcica, XIII: Premiere Rencontre Internationale sur l'Empire Ottoman et la Turquie Moderne*, Institut National des Sciences de L'Homme, 18–22 janvier 1985, Isis Press, Istanbul-Paris, pp.17–112.

Inciciyan, P.G. 1976, *18. Asırda Istanbul*, İstanbul Fetih Cemiyeti, Istanbul.

İstanbul Haritaları Ortaçağdan Günümüze: Maps of İstanbul from the Middle Ages to the Present Day, 1995, Türkiye Sınai Kalkınma Bankası. Mas Matbaacılık A.Ş. İstanbul.

Kuban, D. 1996, *İstanbul bir kent tarihi*, Türkiye Ekonomik ve Toplumsal Tarih Vakfı, İstanbul.

Müller-Wiener, W. 1998, *Bizans'tan Osmanlı'ya İstanbul limanı* (Original title: *Die Häfen von Byzantion, Konstantinupolis*; trans: Erol Ozbek) Tarih Vakfı Yurt Yayınları, Istanbul.

Özden, P. and Agar, D. (ed.) 2008, *Eğrisiyle Doğrusuyla Galataport*, TMMOB Sehir Plancıları Odası, Istanbul.

Privatization of Istanbul Salıpazarı Cruise Port: A Brief Overview, 2013, Prime Ministry Privatization Administration.

Recommendation on the historic urban landscape, 10 November 2011, UNESCO.

Yurdaydin, H.G. (ed.) 1976, *Nisahu's Silahi Beyan-i Menazil-i Sefer-i Irak*eyn. Turk Tarih Kurumu Basimevi, Ankara.

5 Alexandria's Waterfronts
Form, Identity and Architecture of a Port City

Cristina Pallini

Waterfront Scenes

The seduction of Alexandria is threefold. First, there is the legendary city celebrated in antiquity for its cultural institutions and architectural wonders; second, the port 'rediscovered' by Napoleon and revived throughout the nineteenth century by an enterprising international bourgeoisie; and finally, the twentieth-century literary myth (Festa-McCormick 1979; Re 2003; Starr 2005; Dodi 2010). While most narratives are characterized by a nostalgia for the lost cosmopolitan milieu and by a tendentious relationship with the materiality of the city, literature has indeed played a part in shaping an image of Alexandria in which the waterfront theme holds an important place. In Durrell's visionary Alexandria, the protagonists and the narrator are often to be seen on the 'magnificent long sea-parade' which frames the modern city, grouping the finest hotels and cafés with large galleries looking seaward; these resemble a row of aquariums, in which the inhabitants of the European city are suspended like 'glorious tropical fish'. (Durrell 1961: 221).

This coastal townscape where holiday resorts and residential areas flow into one another is also the scene of Naguib Mahfouz's Alexandrian novels, where the evocative potential of the Grand Corniche resounds in the emotions voiced by the protagonists. In *Miramar* the character of Hosni Allam, a young uneducated landowner, first appears leaning out over the rail of his balcony at the Cecil Hotel, his emotional frustration reflected by the great mass of sea that is 'locked-in' by the Corniche wall and arm of the jetty (Mahfouz 1967: 38). Later on, Hosni's spirits are raised as he drives faster and faster along the coastal road: 'Mazarita, Chatby, Ibrahimia and beyond' (42).

Drawing inspiration from his 1930s childhood recollections, Edouard Al Kharrat describes the easternmost stretch of Alexandria's waterfront: the colourful wooden cabins at Mandara, large tracts of untilled land, palm trees, street lamps along the coastal road—'glowing yellow spots against the blue canopy of the sky which still contained at its rim the last fires of the sunset' (Kharrat 1989: 40).

In *Girls of Alexandria* Edouard Al Kharrat depicts the Corniche during World War II as a daily scene of opposition between alien worlds: tanks, armoured cars and foreign troops, and the local observers, 'some barefoot in long tunics, others in short-sleeved shirts or complete summer suit' (Kharrat 1993: 48).

The Italian writer Enrico Pea, who worked as mechanic in a naval shipyard, has left some vivid scenes of daily activities in the western harbour, while also reflecting the socio-cultural complexity of Alexandria, 'the ideal location to speculate on the failure of western imperialism' (Pea 1949; cited in Palumbo 2003: 7).

However, suspended between illusion and reality, the literary images of Alexandria also include waterfront scenes that are now completely lost. On returning to Alexandria in 1930 the Italian poet Filippo Marinetti vividly describes the daily traffic of boats along the Mahmoudieh canal, mostly half-submerged under immense loads of cotton (Marinetti 1933: 77–78).

By contrast, for Giuseppe Ungaretti the Mahmoudieh canal is an enchanting childhood memory: its banks loaded with frogs, lined with luxuriant gardens and exotic and fragrant trees protecting the road with a refreshing shadow (Ungaretti 1931: 70).

The discovery, around 1910, of a submerged harbour dating back to an age earlier than the Ptolemaic greatly impressed Ungaretti. It was known that Alexander himself chose the site for the new city having observed the potential advantages of a small port sheltered by an island, halfway along a narrow stretch of coast separating the Mediterranean from an immense lagoon. The submerged harbour however, proved that Alexandria had been a port even before the emergence of Alexandria the city. Thus Ungaretti used *The Buried Harbour* as the title of his 1916 collection of poems and wrote a poem on that same theme. *The Buried Harbour* provided him with a metaphor expressing the very essence of poetic truth (Ungaretti 1916, trans. Bastianutti 1977: 47).

Staging the Past and the Future in Recent Waterfront Projects

When introducing the vanished world of cosmopolitanism in the Levant, the British historian Philip Mansel considers Alexandria as one of the few Eastern Mediterranean cities which did not experience a catastrophic twentieth century (Mansel 2010: 238). However, following the Free Officers' revolution of July 1952 and the Suez crisis of 1956, Alexandria faced a process of nationalisation, the exodus of its foreign population and the transfer to Cairo of its main institutional activities. Since the 1950s and 1960s, cosmopolitanism in Egypt has been equated with the colonial system that fostered it; thus Alexandria's public face was made more 'Egyptian', renaming streets and removing statues of former rulers. Fascinating even in its decline, and still characterized by buildings and districts that bore witness to its celebrated cosmopolitanism, Alexandria regained some popularity through a competition held in 1989 for the rebuilding of its legendary library, whose opening in 2002 has brought the city back into the stream of international tourism. Since the late 1980s, the waterfront theme has gained momentum, in Alexandria as well as in the international debate (Hoyle *et al.* 1988; Hall 1991; Breen and Rigby 1994, 1996; Bruttomesso 1999; Marshall 2001; Mah 2014). In Alexandria this debate addressed both the *Magnus Portus* of antiquity and the Corniche, as well as the western harbour, with its nineteenth-century port infrastructures.

The Library Project was conceived in the mid-1970s by leading members of Alexandria University and pursued as a matter of national interest; in 1985 it was presented to UNESCO, which later promoted a feasibility study. International experts prepared the competition brief and President Hosni Mubarak laid the first stone on 26 June 1988. The site, overlooking the sea—and most probably that on which the ancient library once stood—held a prominent position on the Grand Corniche, facing towards Fort Qaitbay, on Pharos island, on the site of the ancient lighthouse. By thus reviving the roots of Alexandria's historical traditions, to reassert their place in contemporary culture, the city was once again to relive its international vocation. As the Library of Alexandria was reaching completion, important archaeological discoveries aroused a revival of interest in Alexandria, ratified by the exhibition *La gloire d'Alexandrie*, held in 1998 at the Petit Palais in Paris and at the Musée de l'Ephèbe at Cap d'Agde (Empereur 1998).

Alexandria's facelift was prompted by a change in the leadership of the governorate: The Library of Alexandria was seen as a means to draw attention to the city's rich cosmopolitan heritage, which became the object of conservation and renovation projects (Girardelli 2001: 10–17; Awad 2005). The inauguration of the library in October 2002, and the predominant position it immediately acquired, opened a lively debate on changes to be made along the Corniche, which was at that time being widened to accommodate five lanes of traffic in each direction (1999–2005).

The first project, by Mohamed Awad (Alexandria and Mediterranean Research Centre) and by the architectural firm of Bertocchini & Ruggiero (Rome), was presented at the Ninth Venice Biennale in the Cities on Water session (September 2004). This thematic exhibition aimed at documenting ongoing and future changes in twenty 'waterfront cities' throughout the world, in order to recognize and comprehend present trends and the future prospects that might exist for waterfront projects.[1] It was eventually summarized in 'Ten Principles for a Sustainable Development of Waterfront Areas', which hovered somewhere between the promotion of historical urban identity and a more globalized design approach (Bruttomesso 2004, 125–163).

The eastern harbour of Alexandria symbolizes the different historical phases in the development of the city. Today it also represents the hub of the city centre and remains the most important physical feature identified with Alexandria's waterfront (Library of Alexandria 2005: 100). The project for the eastern waterfront of Alexandria proposed a number of buildings for cultural and recreational purposes, to promote tourism and to enhance the city's historical heritage. Great emphasis was placed on reshaping the promontory of Silsileh and Fort Qaitbay, the extreme points of the Grand Corniche, which were to be linked by a breakwater with a pedestrian promenade. A new aquarium and Institute of Marine Life was proposed for a site near Fort Qaitbay, while the promontory of Silsileh was envisaged as a sort of 'cultural and business district' grafted onto the new Library of Alexandria— to include a Museum of Underwater Archaeology, a convention centre and the Pharos Hotel—that would set a contemporary challenge to the wonders of antiquity.

Based on the Biennale project, in May 2006 the Library of Alexandria signed a memorandum of understanding with the developer Emaar Misr,[2] which financed further studies for waterfront redevelopment. These were entrusted to well-known architectural firms such as Mario Botta, Peter Chermayeff, Gensler, Pei Partnership Architects, Skidmore, Owings & Merrill and Jacques Rougerie. In September 2006 the library hosted an exhibition and a conference to present the resulting series of spectacular examples of *auteur* architecture. Two of these projects deserve closer attention. Skidmore, Owings and Merrill proposed a master plan for the whole bay, addressing problems of accessibility,[3] the 'cultural and business district' and the idea of a new breakwater around the harbour to protect the underwater archaeology and improve access to sites. A towering solar power generator was to glow by night close to the water's edge, evoking the ancient lighthouse while representing a sustainable future for the city.

In line with UNESCO's recommendations, the French architect Jacques Rougerie evolved the idea of an underwater museum to exhibit the ruins of the lighthouse and of the Ptolemaic palaces lying on the bottom of the eastern harbour.[4] An expert in water-based constructions, Rougerie explored the possibility of visiting these archaeological remains *in situ*: situated close to the new Library of Alexandria along the Corniche, his museum consists of an exhibition hall facing onto the bay and of a ring of underwater thematic halls surrounding the 'patio', illuminated by a column of clean water, with four sails emerging from the sea. Visitors would walk through fiberglass tunnels to reach the bottom of the bay and finally enjoy the sunken scenography, consisting of antiquities and occasional divers (see Bardon 2007: 12–13; Bossone 2008). Despite controversial reactions due to its technical challenges and high cost, Rougerie's project was seen by many as a further opportunity to strengthen Alexandria as a tourist destination able to attract a significant share of visitors to Egypt.

Away from the spotlight of international architecture, and while projects for the eastern harbour were still under discussion, the western harbour was transformed to accommodate super-sized cruise ships making the tour of the Mediterranean. Discussions around reshaping the old French-style arsenal and shipyards had started as early as 2000 among a group of professors from the Faculty of Engineering of Alexandria University and Costa Cruises, a British-American owned cruise line based in Genova, which in 2000 converted its entire fleet to full-time cruising and became one of the largest operators in Europe.[5] The Alexandria cruise terminal was inaugurated in 2007 as the first stage of a larger project: It can now accommodate 5,000 tourists at a time, with parking capacity for 350 cars and 80 buses. The building proper is a former maritime station, a large vaulted structure which was remodelled and extended to include a high-specification shopping mall and a pompous neo-Egyptian entrance hall (Aref 2009: 81–83 and 128–133).[6] When completed, the new port quarter will fulfil the requirements of a modern cruise terminal; however, super-sized cruise ships generally stop for one day only in Alexandria and many passengers spend no time there, leaving early in the morning and returning late at night after their excursions to the pyramids of Giza and to Cairo.

Multiple Waterfronts between Past and Future

The Magnus Portus of antiquity was immortalized by Strabo, who visited Alexandria around 30–25 BC and described the series of monuments and smaller harbours that could be seen around the rim of the bay: the Lochias promontory on which stood a palace, the small island of Antirrhodos, the Poseidonium pier with a temple to Neptune and Anthony's palace, the great temple dedicated to Caesar, the Emporion, the warehouses and the docks. Beyond this point began the Heptastadion, a seven-stadia dyke (c. 1,240 metres) extending from the mainland to the island of Pharos with its towering lighthouse. Built during the reign of Ptolemy II Philadelphus (309–246 BC), the Heptastadion also formed an aqueduct and preventative structure against currents and sandy sediments in the eastern harbour; it separated the eastern and western harbours, leaving two narrow passages for boats at the northern and southern extremities. Beyond the Heptastadion was the harbour of Eunostos and the Kibotos, an artificial basin cut at right angles into the mainland in order to facilitate access to the navigable canal towards Lake Mareotis on which there was an additional port (Strabo undated: paragraphs 8–10); el Fakharani 1991; Millet and Goiran 2007). Thus Alexandria bridged the gap between the maritime and river routes, her main street formed of a natural highway along a limestone ridge (Forster 1922: 5–12). Alexandria *ad Ægyptum*, as the Romans said, marks the north-west corner of the Nile delta, sufficiently near to Egypt to benefit from its riches, sufficiently distant to enjoy relative independence.

A number of late-seventeenth and early eighteenth century representations of Alexandria bear witness to a transitional phase between views and topographic maps, identifying the city with its waterfront and highlighting prominent landmarks that could guide sailors entering the eastern harbour, the only one accessible to non-Ottoman ships: these were Cleopatra's Needles, Pompey's Pillar, the base of the lighthouse and a few low hills. By this time almost nothing was left of the monumental waterfront described by Strabo; the elevation along the coastline clearly shows the defensive walls, beyond which tall minarets alternate with palm trees (Shaalan 2009).[7]

The *Mémoire* of Gratien Le Père and the engravings in the *Description de l'Égypte* offer a last detailed portrait of Alexandria prior to its rapid nineteenth-century development. The city had by then shrunk to a tongue of land extending seaward that had been formed over the years along the Heptastadion. While no trace remained of the lake-port of antiquity, the course of the canal, which had supplied Alexandria with fresh water and had formed the commercial highway to the interior of the country, was still visible (Le Pere 1818; Commission des Sciences et Arts d'Égypte 1822: plate 31). The western harbour used by the Ottomans was deep, wide and protected from northerly winds, and thus could easily be fitted up to become a modern port. Rocky and exposed, the eastern harbour was bordered by the Frankish Quarter and by a vast, sandy esplanade where European ships unloaded their goods.

Large-scale projects conceived in the first half of the nineteenth century—namely the Mahmoudieh Canal and the railway to Cairo and Suez—were intended to revive Alexandria as the bridgehead of the Isthmian route from the Mediterranean to the Red Sea. This implied laying the foundations of a new city onto the age-old urban layout, thus reshaping the port system and its multiple waterfronts: the two bays, the canal and the lake (Figure 5.1).

Correspondences between the actual city and the Alexandria of antiquity are often remarked upon by early nineteenth-century commentators. Le Père grasped the favourable natural features of the ports and observes the juxtaposition between the Turkish town on the isthmus[8] and the old town on the mainland; the first was made up of warehouses while the second was walled and abandoned, consisting of piles of ruins and debris.

As had taken place with the Turkish town, building the modern city led to a continuous pillage of antiquities. For the Turin writer Antonio Baratta this rendered the desolation of Alexandria even more affecting. At the time of the French expedition, there was still an abundance of remarkable remains and in 1826 many ancient buildings were still standing, but a few years later all were destroyed to make way for European-style houses (Baratta 1841: 322–323; 383–384). The British Egyptologist John Gardner Wilkinson suggested mapping wherever possible as, by 1841, the intersection of the two main streets could be ascertained only with difficulty: 'Little now remains of the splendid edifices of Alexandria; and the few columns, and traces of walls, which a few years ago rose above the mounds, are no longer seen' (Wilkinson 1843: 155).

Agreeing with Le Père's theory that the ancient city stretched well beyond the Arab walls, Wilkinson adds that the Saracen walls of Bab el Bahr (Sea Gate), near the great square of the Franks, which was then under construction, marked the profile of the ancient docks.

At the precise time that Wilkinson visited Alexandria for the second time in 1841, the ruler of Egypt, Mohamed Ali,[9] was forced by the Ottoman sultan and the European powers to give up his conquered territories and abolish the monopoly on agricultural products. As a result of this, Alexandria was to become a bridgehead of free trade. Its port-scape, however, had already changed profoundly.

The Mahmoudieh Canal and the Western Waterfront

The French architect Pascal Coste kept a log of his activity in Egypt, which began in March 1819, when Mohamed Ali appointed him to complete the canal that was to create a safe route to Alexandria for boats carrying products from upper, middle and lower Egypt. The route of the canal had been already cut following a plan by the Turkish engineer Chakir-Effendi but, due to design flaws, work had come to a halt (Coste 1878: 25–27). Coste succeeded in his task: The canal was opened in February 1821 and named Mahmoudieh in honour of Sultan Mahmoud II. The new canal was part of a scheme of hydraulic works to keep the Nile Delta permanently irrigated; it was to supply Alexandria with fresh water, thus giving new life to the port after centuries of decline, and restoring its relations with the interior of the country.[10]

The decision to link the final stretch of the canal to the western harbour marked for once and all the pre-eminence of the latter. Over the course of twenty years, a series of projects in rapid succession completely transformed the ancient harbour of Eunostos into a modern port. These projects included a transit dock for transferring goods from boats to warehouses and eventually to other modes of land and sea transport, a French-style arsenal built between 1829 and 1835 by the engineer Lefebvre de Cerisy at the northern end of the Heptastadion (where the necessary sea depth could be easily reached by removing sand and landfill),[11] and the Pasha's citadel on the promontory of Ras el-Tin, a panoramic setting reminiscent of the ancient palaces (1817).[12]

Paradoxically, the transit dock—reviving the role of the Kibotos—involved the destruction of many Roman, Greek and Egyptian antiquities.[13] However, looking at Coste's fine sketches (Poggioli-Barry 1998) and old photos, we realize that the mouth of the Mahmoudieh canal commanded a fine view of the port, crowded with merchant and military ships whose brightly coloured flags indicated the presence of diplomatic delegations. Cross-checking this kind of information with mid-nineteenth-century maps[14] and travel descriptions, we can deduce what could be seen on entering the western harbour and how the modern waterfront extended far inland along the Mahmoudieh canal.

Before the inauguration of the railway in 1856, anyone reaching Egypt and bound for Cairo would stop in Alexandria and then travel along the Mahmoudieh canal.[15] On leaving the city the sights would include the famous Pompey Pillar,[16] the warehouses where large quantities of grain and cotton were stored, the city walls at a distance and the green banks of the canal lined with fine mansions and gardens. A number of engineering works were also to be seen along the way, including the dam between lakes Maryut

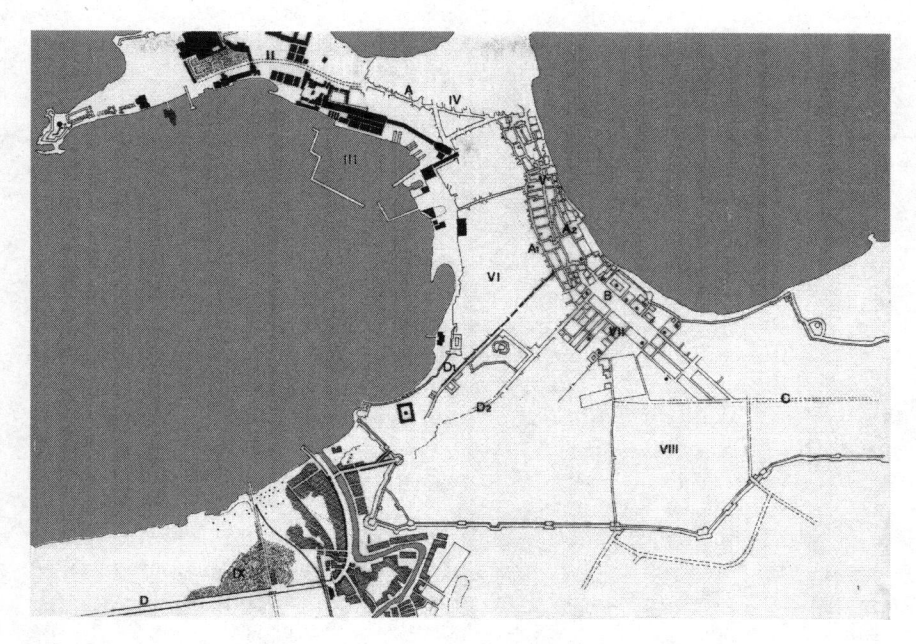

Figure 5.1 Map of Alexandria in 1855 (author's elaboration) showing port-related settlement and infrastructure along the western and eastern harbours. A. Ras el Tin Street; A1. Customs Street; A2. Frank Street; B. Place des Consuls; C. via Canopic Street; D1–D2. main connections to the canal; D. Lybian Route; I. dock for mooring boats at the mouth of the Mahmoudieh canal (1821); II. Ras el Tin Palace (1835); III. Arsenal (1835); IV Court area; V. Suq; VI. Turkish Town; VII. European Town; VIII. Arab Town; IX. unplanned settlements.

and Aboukir, the terminal lock on the Rosetta Nile and the telegraph towers designed by Coste, whose sight left visitors in no doubt as to Egypt's having entered the modern world. Most people presumably saw little else than a squat minaret; only an erudite few would have recognized even a vague reference to the legendary lighthouse. Among those few was certainly the British engineer Thomas Sopwith, whose exploratory journeys by train, on a track that ran parallel to the Mahmoudieh Canal, gave him access to a clear view of a waterfront scene crowded with people driving bargains over various kinds of merchandize that had been transported there by boats or by heavily loaded camels (Sopwith 1857: 77–78; 87).

The Eastern Harbour and the Corniche

The metamorphosis of the old Frankish quarter into the European town started on the Esplanade of the eastern harbour, where European ships unloaded their goods and Bedouins sold their cattle; here Pascal Coste designed the residence for Boghos Bey (1824) and the Italian engineer Francesco Mancini planned the great rectangular place generally known as the Place des Consuls (1834) (Awad 1996; Pallini 2009: 76–103, 60–70; Pallini 2014). Here Europe put its stamp on the arts and styles of building, on customs and habits; here the kinds of dress, local usage and the idioms of East and West met and mingled. (Regaldi 1884: 59–60).

It may be asked why Mancini so extensively adopted a neoclassical style in contrast to that of earlier Turkish towns and to the other styles then being introduced. This may have merely reflected his training in Italy during the Napoleonic period, but may also have been the means for establishing a lingua franca for modern Alexandria. While providing a European-style urban space where foreign traders and local merchants could exchange and stock their goods, the Place des Consuls turned its back to the sea. Thus the eastern waterfront was characterized by the rear facades of the *okelle*[17] bordering the old Frankish quarter street and the new square.

The first ideas for reshaping the eastern waterfront with a scenic coastal route were put forth by the Italian Pietro Avoscani in 1890,[18] who might have been inspired by the *Passeggiata dei Cavalleggeri* in his home town of Livorno.[19] In 1899 Avoscani's idea was finally implemented by the municipality. The scheme included a line of breakwaters across the mouth of the eastern harbour and a strong, high wall around the bay, accommodating at its foot the main sewer conduit and a broad boulevard at the city level. Forming a semi-circle of 3.947 kilometres, this structure, the Grand Corniche, was to 'restore to Alexandria the harbour that was hers in the past' (Wright and Cartwright 1909: 427).

The *grands travaux* were carried out between 1899 and 1907 and entrusted to the municipal engineers L. Dietrich, P. Arcoudaris and E. Quellenec, chief engineer of the Suez Canal Company (Malaval and Jondet 1912: 54–55; Hastaoglou-Martinidis 2010). Since 1901, works had been undertaken by the Italian Almagià contractors for completion in 1907 (Figure 5.2).

The Italian archaeologist Evaristo Breccia, Director of the Graeco-Roman Museum, considered the Corniche a colossal work which was to enrich the city with splendid promenades and, hopefully, with palaces and statues (Breccia, E. 1914: 15). E.M. Forster epitomized the new quay as one of the most remarkable sights in town:

> Seen from the south, when there is mist in the morning, its beauty is fairy-like; seen from the northern extremity it forms a complete ring around a circle of blue water. [. . .] To stretch right and left in an exquisite parabola and attain poetry through mathematics—that is its only aim, and an aim not unbecoming to the city of Eratosthenes and Euclid.
> (Forster 1917)

However, according to Alessandro Breccia (son of the aforementioned Evaristo) the Corniche was designed and implemented without a clear idea of

LE PORT-EST

Figure 5.2 Aerial view of the Corniche

how to use the port which, being open to the north, was often hit by violent waves (Breccia A. 1927: 21). What is certain is that part of the 100-metre-wide embankment—an area of 526 square kilometres—was to form a series of new building plots, providing a modern waterfront for both the Turkish and European towns, featuring a Central Business District and introducing a new hierarchy into the urban space (Ilbert 1996: 564–566). The evocative presence of the Magnus Portus certainly added value to these municipal ambitions. However, despite all efforts to move port activity to the west and gentrify the city centre, building activity along the Corniche made a very slow start and for many years the broad semi-circular road was separated from the city by stretches of desolate sands covered with enormous stone blocks.

The 1919 town planning scheme by the municipal engineer W.H. McLean proposed exploiting a number of these empty plots to create a Place des Obélisques and a Place des Mosquées (McLean 1921). But it was not until the late 1920s that a compact row of fine buildings about 25 metres high could be seen along the Corniche. These included a series of public and community buildings interrupting the row of apartment blocks, whose unified heights and architectural elements featured a compact 'urban façade'.[20] The Cecil Hotel, by the Italian architect Giacomo Alessandro Loria (1929), and the other Italian/Venetian-style buildings near Ramleh Station, echoed a debate then current among members of the municipality as to how Alexandria's independence could be expressed through the creation of its own architectural style (Figure 5.3).[21]

Figure 5.3 Italian/Venetian-style buildings along the Corniche near Ramleh Station

With a view to rationalizing Alexandria's somewhat random growth, which lacked any overall control, the 1919 town-planning scheme envisaged an extension of the Corniche over the entire length of the coast. Departing from Ras el-Tin Palace (transformed into a 'fairy-like residence' between 1920and 1925 by the Italian architect Ernesto Verrucci), and ending at the royal estate of Montazah, where Verrucci had also built a new *Haremlik* in the shape of a Tuscan-style castle, from 1923 to 1928 (Godoli 2008: 362–373), the new coastal road was to become a showcase for the Egyptian royal family. This role of the Corniche as concrete metaphor of the city's many identities became even clearer after the construction of three fine mosques designed by Mario Rossi: Abu 'l-'Abbas al Mursi in Place des Mosquées (1928–1944), Qa'id Ibrahim in Saad Zaagloul Square (1948–1951) and Muhammad Kurrayym near Ras el-Tin (1949–1953) (Turchiarulo 2012).

Construction work to extend the Corniche was completed in 1933 by the Italian contractors Dentamaro and Cartareggia. It involved the reclamation of land bordering the sea and the grouping of seaside-related features such as the well-known Stanley Beach, with its three levels of cabins in a fine theatrical setting. The beach proper started after Selselah, extending for nearly 14 kilometres; evocative names such as Chatby, Camp Caesar, Ibrahimieh, Sporting Club, Cleopatra, Sidi Gaber, Rouchdy, Bulkeley, Glymenopoulo and Sidi

Bishr followed one after another along the Corniche like beads on a gigantic rosary (Bernard 1936), greatly enhancing the reputation of Alexandria as a summer resort. The views to be seen from a drive along the Corniche in the early 1950s—at the time of the Officers' Revolution—could have reflected Alexandria's roles as port city, international resort and summer capital.

Conclusions

Many scholars argue that waterfronts express a 'plural identity' favouring the simultaneous presence of many activities; others instead define waterfronts as 'liquid borders', along which heritage structures may inspire us with ideas for the future. Some authors approach the waterfront theme from an economic standpoint, or else from the field of urban sociology, stating that waterfronts bear a tangible witness to a globalization process 'avant la lettre' *ante litteram* (Mah 2014). On the waterfront, writes Richard Marshall, we see glimpses of new city-making paradigms, partial visions for what our cities might be (Marshall 2001: 3–4). Conceived as such, the waterfront theme identifies an area of complex mediation between local and global space, where giant cruise ships and shopping malls are found next to spectacular aquariums, museums and high-end hotels.

Alexandria's waterfront projects conceived prior to the economic crisis of 2008, and before Egypt's January 2011 riots, bear witness to a changing physical and functional relationship between the city and its ports. While claiming the importance of a historical urban landscape, expressed by the slogan 'capitalizing on heritage', most of these waterfront projects pursue a set of self-referential architectural forms attuned with the international scene, as 'events' attracting broader urban tourism.

Why should one reference the port city's earlier developments when discussing these more recent projects?

According to Predrag Matvejevic (1999: 12), cities with ports differ from port cities, because the former build piers and warehouses out of necessity, while the latter grow in close relationship with their ports. The latter is the case with Alexandria, where historicizing the concept of waterfront development requires an understanding of the natural features of the site to perceive how the present urban/port structure is related to its pre-existing layers; the strategic position into which its roots have been planted.

The architectural wonders of antiquity clearly expressed the fact that Alexandria was intended as a 'haven' for trade and cultural exchange for many people from near and far (Saint-Marc Girardin 1840). While the lighthouse, the Heptastadion and the Kibotos were technical innovations showing that the port was the *raison d'être* for the city, the library and the museum turned the new level of economic exchange into cultural institutions.

Particularly when we consider the Italian contribution, the twentieth-century literary myth proves that Alexandria represented an original

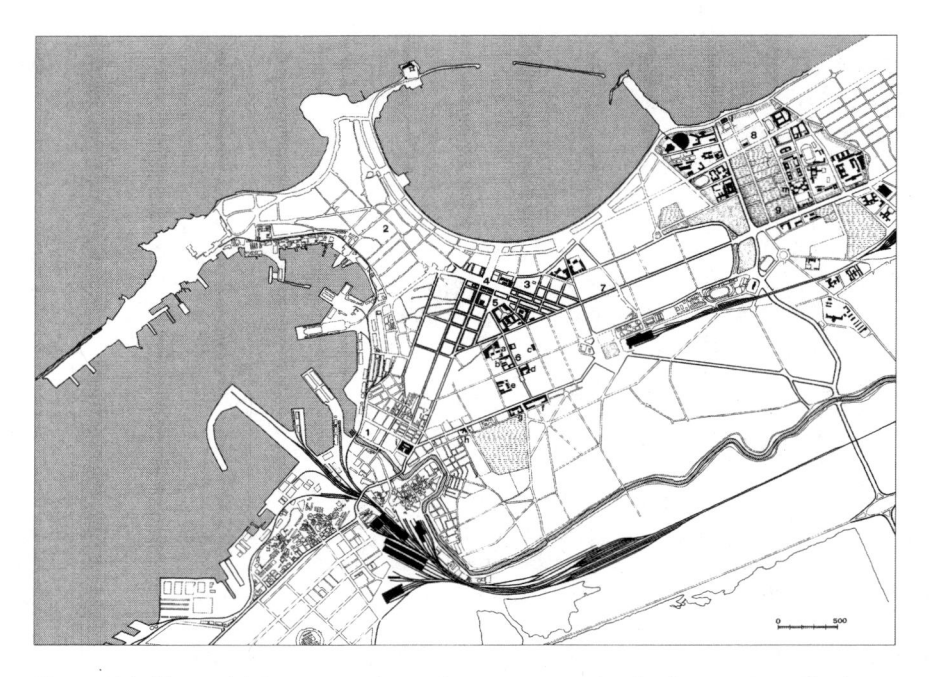

Figure 5.4 Alexandria's present-day urban structure (author's reconstruction), on which the nineteenth-century European city can still be identified. The western harbour is still occupied by port infrastructures, including the new cruise terminal, while the eastern harbour became the scene of waterfront redevelopment projects.

model of modern metropolitan civilization: composite, hybrid, yet oriented towards the future (Re 2003: 169).

A critical factor in the development of Alexandria's multiple waterfronts is the necessity for the project to concretely bridge the gap between the mythical past and a possible future. It may be added that the functional and symbolic performance of Alexandria's port-scapes bears witness to the plurality of contributions that have supported their physical construction (Figure 5.4). As in Tunis or Beirut, Alexandria's waterfronts reflect as in a mirror the diverse expressions of a given urban identity, as well as a cultural mosaic that took shape over many eons; in relation to this, the problem of a formal order has been one of volumetric and spatial relations or a 'three-dimensional plan'.

As in botany, where a rootstock plant is grafted to a scion to provide a source of growth, so a new waterfront must be rooted within an existing urban context. These 'roots' are the original features of a city, inscribed in its form and architecture and developed over a long period of time.

Notes

1 The exhibition included Mediterranean ports like Alexandria, Athens, Barcelona, Genova, Venice and Trieste; northern European ports like Delft, Rotterdam, Hamburg and Bilbao; inner ports like Berlin and Zaragoza; as well as Buenos Aires, Seoul and Incheon (South Korea), Shanghai and Qufu (China) and Yokohama (Japan).

2 A subsidiary of the Emaar Properties and Artoc Group for Investment and Development, a development company based in United Arab Emirates at the heart of the Dubai 'economic miracle'. I wish to thank Dr. Y. Aref (AlexMed) for this information.

3 Centralized parking to reduce traffic congestion, a new tram route, boardwalk, floating piers and water taxis.

4 The first indications of the existence of important underwater cultural heritage in the eastern bays of Alexandria were found at the very beginning of the twentieth century. Scientific archaeological research started in the late 1960s with the support of UNESCO, which sent a survey mission to Alexandria composed of the pioneering archaeological diver Honor Frost and the geologist Vladimir Nesteroff; they compiled a detailed report and laid the groundwork for further excavations. From 1994 to 1998, a Franco-Egyptian team inspected the submerged ruins of the Pharos lighthouse and other remains in the Eastern Harbour, an underwater archaeological site covering an area of 2.5 hectares and comprising approximately 2,500 pieces of stonework of archaeological interest. In 1998, a second mission of international experts sponsored by the Egyptian authorities and UNESCO focused on conservation and development options for the underwater archaeological sites of Alexandria.

5 Meeting with Dr. S. Baiumi and Dr. A. El Sherif at the Faculty of Engineering, Alexandria University, June 2000; meeting with Dr. A. El Sherif, August 2007.

6 See also *Alexandria Port*, Microsoft PowerPoint file by the Alexandria Port Authority, 2007.

7 Plans in Jondet (1921): pl. IX Christian Melchien (1699) *Plan du Port d'Alexandrie observé par toutes les observations comme aussi par la latitude*; pl. XI (1713) *Plan et élévation de la rade d'Alexandrie en Égypte par Marquese de la Garde*; pl. XII (1738) *Carte et Plan du Port Neuf d'Alexandrie*. See also Shaalan (2009: 8–19; 7–23).

8 The so-called Turkish town had developed since the late sixteenth century on the landfill of the Heptastadion; see Annaloro and Lange (2011).

9 Mohamed Ali (Kavala, Macedonia 1769–Cairo 1849) is considered the founder of modern Egypt, where he arrived in 1799, a general in the Ottoman army commanding Albanian troops sent to halt Napoleon's advance. Taking advantage of conflicts between Turkish officials and Mameluke dignitaries, in 1806 he persuaded the Ottoman government to appoint him governor of Egypt. Apart from his military exploits, the mark he left on Egyptian history was linked to his radical administrative, economic and cultural reforms.

10 There was a canal between the Nile and Alexandria in antiquity which had been restored at different times. See Hairy and Sennoune (2006) and Hairy (ed.) (2009).

11 Lefebvre de Cérisy directed the initial activity of the arsenal with artisans from Toulon, Malta and Livorno. After he left in 1839, the French engineer D.E. Mougel designed the adjoining shipyards. See Clot Bey (1840: 221–237).

12 Similar to the Topkapi Palace at Sarayburnu, Istanbul, Mohamed Ali's palace was built *à la constantinopolitaine*, including a harem, a divan and a pavilion for sea bathing; right outside the palace were the barracks and a military hospital.

13 Carefully surveyed by Coste in his drawings; see Armogathe and Leprun (eds) (1990); and Poggioli-Barry (1998).

14 Among the best known is Charles Muller 'Plan d'Alexandrie comprenant toutes ses fortifications et edifices principaux', of 1855.
15 Construction of the railway from Alexandria to Cairo started in 1852 under the direction of Robert Stephenson and was completed in 1854; the line was inaugurated in 1856 and extended to Suez in 1958. It runs parallel to the Mahmoudieh Canal along the shores of Lake Maryut.
16 A monolithic column over 20 metres high made of red granite from Aswan, marking the site of the Temple of Serapis.
17 The *okelle* is built around a large courtyard with shops facing onto it, but it is also a hotel, a bazaar, a warehouse, a workshop and even a stock exchange. It may be summed up as a large public building where the industrious activity of a people is carried out; see Edmond (1867: 215).
18 Avoscani had worked in Alexandria since 1837 as an architect, diplomat and commercial agent; see Balboni (1906: 394–408).
19 Conceived to include an existing road in a public coastal promenade, construction of the Passeggiata dei Cavalleggeri began in 1835, providing a structure for further urban expansion.
20 The French, Italian and Swedish consulates, as well as the Egyptian Maternity Hospital, the Bureau Sanitaire et Quarantenaire and the local Court House.
21 This group of buildings, currently called 'Little Venice', has been acquired by Sigma Properties, a property management company that specializes in developing and reutilizing heritage buildings (see sigmaproperties.net).

Bibliography

Annaloro, M. and Lange, G. (2011) *Alexandrie, une architecture ottomane*, Marseille: Parenthéses.
Aref, Y. (2009) 'Plan and Projects for Alexandria: 1952 to Present', in L. Ferro and C. Pallini (eds.), *Alessandria d'Egitto oltre il mito [Alexandria Beyond the Myth]*, Boves (Cuneo): ArabaFenice, 128–133.
Armogathe, D. and Leprun, S. (eds.) (1990) *Pascal Coste ou l'architecture cosmopolite*, Paris: L'Harmattan.
Awad, M. (1996) 'The Metamorphoses of Mansheyah', *Méditerranéennes*, (special issue on *Alexandrie en Égypte*), 8–9: 42–58.
Awad, M. (2005) 'The Conservation and Rehabilitation of Alexandria's City Center', in M. Awad (ed.), *Patrimoines partagés en Méditerranée: Elément clés de la rehabilitation (Euromed Heritage II)*, Alexandria: Alexandria Preservation Trust, 41–53.
Balboni, L.A. (1906) *Gl'italiani nella Civiltà Egiziana del Secolo XIX*, vol. I, Alexandria: Stabilimento Tipo-litografico V. Penasson.
Baratta, A. (1841) 'Alessandria d'Egitto', in *Museo scientifico, letterario e artistico*, 3rd Year, Turin: Fontano, 322.
Bardon, A. (2007) 'Un musée qui donne l'ivresse des profondeurs', *Le Courrier de l'UNESCO*, 3: 12–13.
Bernard, J. (1936) 'Les plages alexandrines', in *Alexandrie portique de l'Orient*, Alexandria: Imprimerie A. Procaccia, 73–79.
Bossone, A. (2008) 'Underwater Museum Planned for Egypt's Alexandria', *National Geographic News*, 16 September 2008.
Breccia, A. (1927) *Il Porto di Alessandria d'Egitto. Studio di geografia commerciale*, Cairo: Institut Français d'Archéologie Orientale pour la Société Royale de Géographie d'Égypte.

Breccia, E. (1914) *Alexandrea ad Ægyptum: Guide de la ville ancienne et moderne et du Musée gréco-romain*, Bergamo: Istituto Italiano di Arti Grafiche.

Breen, A. and Rigby, D. (1994) *Waterfront Cities Reclaim Their Edge*, New York: McGraw-Hill.

Breen, A. and Rigby, D. (1996) *The New Waterfronts: A Worldwide Urban Success Story*, New York: McGraw-Hill.

Bruttomesso, R. (1999) *Water and industrial heritage: the reuse of industrial and port structures in cities on water*, Venice: Marsilio.

Bruttomesso, R. (ed.) (2004) 'Metamorfosi delle città d'acqua', in *Metamorph: 9 Mostra Internazionale di Architettura*, Venice: Vettori, Fondazione La Biennale di Venezia, 125–163.

Clot Bey, A.B. (1840) *Aperçu général sur l'Egypte*, Brussels: Meline, Cans et Cie.

Commission des Sciences et Arts d'Égypte (1822) 'Carte Generale des cotes, rades, ports, ville et environs d' Alexandrie, Plate 31', in *Description de L'Égypte Book 15, Vol. 5 Antiquités*, Paris: Imprimerie Impériale.

Coste, P.-X. (1878) *Mémoires d'un artiste: Notes et souvenirs de voyages (1817–1877)*, Marseille: Cayer et C.ie.

Dietrich Bey, L. (1909) *Rapport sur L'assainissement de la ville d'Alexandrie*, Alexandrie: Société de Publications Égyptiennes.

Dodi, C.A. (2010) *Villes invisibles de la Méditerranée, Naples, Alexandrie, et Tanger*, Paris: L'Harmattan.

Durrell, L. (1961) *Balthazar*, New York: Dutton.

Edmond, C. (1867) *L'Égypte a l'Exposition Universelle de 1867*, Paris: Dentu.

El Fakharani, F. (1991) 'The Kibotos of Alexandria', *Giornate di Studio in onore di Achille Adriani, Studi Miscellanei*, 28: 21–28.

Empereur, J.-Y. (1998) *Alexandrie redécouverte*, Paris: Fayard-Stock; Empereur, J.-Y. *Alexandria Rediscovered*, London: British Museum Press.

Festa-McCormick, D. (1979) *The City as a Catalyst: A Study of Ten Novels*, London: Associated Universities Press.

Forster, E.M. (1917) 'XXth-Century Alexandria: The New Quay', *Egyptian Mail*, 2 December 1917.

Forster E.M. (1922) *Alexandria: A History and a Guide*, Reprint Gloucester, MA: Peter Smith, 1968.

Girardelli, P. (2001) 'Città irreale', *Controspazio* 5: 10–17.

Godoli, E. (2008) 'Ernesto Verrucci's Architectural Works for Alexandria', in M. Cozzi (ed.), *The Presence of Italian Architects in the Mediterranean Countries*, Florence: Maschietto, 362–373.

Haag, M. (2004) *Alexandria. City of Memory*, New Haven, CT: Yale University Press.

Hairy, I. (ed.) (2009) *Du Nil à Alexandrie. Histoire d'Eaux*, Alexandria: Centre d'Études Alexandrines-CNRS, Harpocrates.

Hairy, I. and Sennoune, O. (2006) 'Géographie historique du canal d'Alexandrie', *Annales Islamologiques*, 40: 247–287.

Hall, P. (1991) *Waterfronts: The New Urban Frontier*, Berkeley, CA: University of California.

Hastaoglou-Martinidis, V. (2010) 'The Cartography of Harbor Construction in Eastern Mediterranean Cities: Technical and Urban Modernization in the Late Nineteenth Century', in B. Kolluoğlu and M. Toksöz (eds.), *Cities of the Mediterranean*, London: I.B. Tauris, 78–99.

Hoyle, B.S., Pinder, D.A. and Sohail Husain, M. (1988) *Revitalizing the Waterfront: International Dimension of Dockland Redevelopment*, London and New York: Belhaven Press.

Ilbert, R. (1996) *Alexandrie 1830–1930*, Cairo: IFAO.

Jondet, G. (1921) *Atlas historique de la ville et des ports d'Alexandrie*, Cairo: Institute Français d'Archéologie Orientale.

Kharrat, E. Al (1989) *City of Saffron*, London: Quartet Books.

Kharrat, E. Al (1993) *Girls of Alexandria*, trans. F. Liardet, London: Quartet Books.

Le Père, G. (1818) *Mémoire sur la ville d'Alexandrie,* Paris: Imprimerie Impériale.

Library of Alexandria (2005) *MedCities. The Mediterranean City: Dialogue Among Cultures,* Alexandria: Bibliotheca Alexandrina.

Mah, A. (2014) *Port Cities and Global Legacies: Urban Identity, Waterfront Work and Radicalism,* UK: Palgrave Macmillan.

Mahfouz, N. (1967, 2nd US edn 1990), *Miramar*, Washington, DC: Three Continents Press.

Malaval, B. and Jondet, G. (1912) *Le Port d'Alexandrie,* Cairo: Imprimerie Nationale.

Mansel, P. (2010) *Levant: Splendour and Catastrophe on the Mediterranean*, London: John Murray.

Marinetti, F.T. (1933) *Il Fascino dell'Egitto* (1981), Milan: Mondadori.

Marshall, R. (ed.) (2001) *Waterfronts in Post-Industrial Cities*, London: Taylor and Francis.

Matvejević, P. (1999) *Mediterranean: A Cultural Landscape*, Berkeley, CA: University of California Press.

McLean, W.H. (1921) *City of Alexandria Town Planning Scheme*, Cairo: Imprimerie Nationale.

Millet, B. and Goiran, J.-P. (2007) 'Impacts of Alexandria's Heptastadion on Coastal Hydro-Sedimentary Dynamics During the Hellenistic Period: A Numerical Modelling Approach', *The International Journal of Nautical Archaeology*, 36(1): 167–176.

Pallini, C. (2009) 'La costruzione di Alessandria Moderna', in L. Ferro and C. Pallini (eds.), *Alessandria d'Egitto oltre il mito [Alexandria Beyond the Myth],* Boves (Cuneo): ArabaFenice, 76–103.

Pallini, C. (2014) 'Il ruolo della Commissione d'Ornato nella ricostruzione di Alessandria d'Egitto', in S. Adorno, G. Cristina and A. Rotondo (eds.), *Visibile Invisibile: percepire la città tra descrizioni e omissioni,* Catania: Scrimm, 375–388.

Palumbo, P. (ed.) (2003) *A Place in the Sun: Africa in Italian Colonial Culture from Post-Unification to the Present*, Berkeley, CA: University of California Press.

Pea, E. (1949) *Vita in Egitto,* Milan: Mondadori.

Poggioli-Barry, A. (1998) *Pascal Coste. Toutes les Égypte,* Marseille: Parenthèses-Bibliothèque Municipale de Marseille.

Re, L. (2003) 'Colonialism and the Egyptian Works of Enrico Pea and Giuseppe Ungaretti', in P. Palumbo (ed.), *A Place in the Sun: Africa in Italian Colonial Culture from Post-Unification to the Present*, Berkeley, CA: University of California Press, 163–196.

Regaldi, G. (1884) *L'Egitto antico e moderno,* Florence: Successori Le Monnier.

Saint-Marc Girardin (1840), 'De la destinée des villes. Constantinople, Alexandrie, Venise, Corinthe', *Revue des deux mondes,* IV: 574–581.

Shaalan, C. (2009) 'Mapping Alexandria: A Long History of Change', in L. Ferro and C. Pallini (eds.), *Alessandria d'Egitto oltre il mito [Alexandria Beyond the Myth]*, Boves (Cuneo): ArabaFenice, 8–19.

Sopwith, T. (1857) *Notes on a Visit to Egypt by Paris, Lyons, Nimes, Marseille and Toulon*, London: C. Roworth and Sons.

Starr, D.A. (2005) 'Recuperating Cosmopolitan Alexandria: Circulation of Narratives and Narratives of Circulation', *Cities*, 22(3): 217–228.

Strabo (undated) 'Chapter 1 in Geography, Book XVII'. Available at: www.alexandrianlibrary.org/?page_id=252.

Turchiarulo, M. (2012) *Building 'in a style': Italian Architecture in Alexandria, Egypt: The Work of Mario Rossi*, Rome: Gangemi.

Ungaretti, G. (1916) *A Major Selection of the Poetry of Giuseppe Ungaretti*, trans. Bastianutti, D. (1977), Toronto: Exile Editions.

Ungaretti, G. (1931) 'Chiaro di luna (Quaderno egiziano) [Moonlight—Egyptian Notebook]', in P. Montefoschi (ed.), (2000) *Vita di un uomo, Viaggi e Lezioni [A Man's Life, Travels and Lessons]*, Milan: Mondadori, 70.

Wilkinson, J.G. (1843) *Hand-Book for Travellers in Egypt*, London: John Murray.

Wright, A. and Cartwright, H. (1909) *Twentieth Century Impressions of Egypt: Its History, People, Commerce, Industries and Resources*, London: Lloyd's Greater Britain Publishing Company.

Part III

Waterfronts Revisited: Regeneration, Redevelopments and the Historic Urban Landscape

Section 1

Local Stories and the Impact of a Global Model

6 Internationalizing Port Regeneration
Models and Emulators

Stephen V. Ward

Introduction

It is widely recognized that the redevelopment of harbour waterfronts in port cities across the world (Breen and Rigby 1996) has created many rather similar environments. Yet there has been little detailed discussion of the flows of investment, knowledge and expertise which generated these similarities. As will be shown, a few projects came to be widely imagined as 'models', where physical transformations created immensely positive impacts for city economies and external images. Civic leaders elsewhere sought to emulate or, to varying extents, actively copy these models. More specific agents, particularly developers, politicians, planners and architects, also promoted these positive imaginings, often trading on their associations with early model schemes. There were also other motives, including bilateral technical assistance and desires to establish international networks for mutual knowledge exchange. Gradually, as will be shown, weaknesses in the original models were recognized, producing a more genuine learning process, from which negative as well as positive lessons were drawn.

Throughout the world, common factors had caused ports to change their ways of working. From around 1960, technological and other changes in shipping operations made older ports increasingly redundant. The changes included the growing scale and specialization in bulk cargoes such as oil or minerals; the decline of scheduled passenger lines and rise of cruise passenger traffic; the adoption of 'roll-on, roll-off' ferries; and, most importantly, containerization.

Together these changes meant that ships had to get bigger, but that loading and unloading times could be reduced to hours instead of days. It was virtually impossible to adapt the oldest ports to these new demands. Traditional layouts with enclosed docks reached through narrow channels and lock gates, or slender finger piers projecting into sheltered natural water, were fundamentally unsuited to new forms of maritime trade. Docksides were typically cramped and cluttered with obsolete cranes, railway tracks and warehouses. Beyond the dock perimeters lay the central and inner cores of major cities, once housing the large workforces formerly needed to operate ports. Finally, the need for labour has been reduced so that ports no longer have to be located in highly populated areas. More spacious locations also more readily allow quicker access to national road systems than was possible within older urban locations. In consequence, port functions have tended to shift to more spacious settings in less central locations.

Yet the underused or abandoned older docks which remained had immense development potential. Heritage value was inherent in many port buildings and structures beneath the grime. Suitably enhanced by appropriate investment and re-imaging, these older ports could diversify the economies of their host cities. However, the shift from working port to post-industrial space, newly based on retail, finance and tourism, was often socially painful and politically contentious.

The Baltimore Model

No city was more influential in seaport regeneration than Baltimore (Ward 2011). During the 1980s, it promised a way of moving from grimy dereliction to a future based on tourism, leisure, retailing and office-based services. The basic story is well known: The Inner Harbor effectively closed in the 1950s and some city investment maintained it sufficiently to allow future reuse (Lyall 1982). At that time, however, efforts focused on renewing the Charles Center, adjoining the Inner Harbor, which were an essential prelude to tackling the harbour itself. An important plan for this appeared in 1964 (Wallace 2004) though little happened until a historic warship was introduced to attract tourism in 1972, along with public access and free, city-funded entertainments.

All this encouraged more ambitious investments. From the mid-1970s, several major public projects opened (Wrenn with Casazza and Smart 1983). The Maryland Science Center (1976), the World Trade Center office tower (1977) and the Marina (1978) were all envisaged in the 1964 plan. Several additional developments then followed: the Convention Center in 1979, the privately funded Harborplace festival marketplace (a tourist-oriented shopping mall seeking to reproduce the atmosphere of a traditional urban market) in 1980, and a new Hyatt hotel and the National Aquarium in 1981. The eastern Inner Harbor saw further developments from the mid-1980s, with a concert hall, museums and other cultural facilities.

By then Baltimore's reputation as a model of regeneration was well established. In 1983 an estimated 4,000 visiting representatives from eighty-seven cities around the world arrived, eager to learn (Olsen 2003). Those involved in its development and design also began to market their expertise. They were undoubtedly crucial in making Baltimore *the* first international model for the post-industrial waterfront. A key figure was James Rouse, who had developed the Inner Harbor's main private development and premier visitor destination, Harborplace. A charismatic and widely known figure, he actively took the Baltimore model to other cities (Bloom 2004). He had already used his earlier Boston experiences in his home city. In 1972, he had joined with Boston architect Ben Thompson to realize the latter's dream of reviving the historic Quincy Market and Faneuil Hall to create Rouse's first festival marketplace. The other key figure was Martin Millspaugh, a former journalist who led the Inner Harbour redevelopment agency. He invited Rouse to repeat his Boston experience in Baltimore at what became Harborplace (Olsen 2003). Initially controversial for removing a popular waterfront open space, Harborplace proceeded only after a narrow victory in a citizen poll (Rusk 1996). In its first full year of operation it drew 18 million visitors.

At this point, Rouse retired from the development company he had founded, though its involvement in US waterfront regeneration projects continued. During the 1980s it developed festival marketplaces at South Street Seaport in New York; Bayside, Miami; Riverwalk, New Orleans and elsewhere (Metzger 2001). Yet Rouse had not retired, and he took the model much further afield. In 1981, with Millspaugh, he founded the Enterprise Development Company (EDC) (Olsen 2003). It soon became a powerful global promoter of the Baltimore approach (Global Harbors Documentary Inc. 2008a).

Within a few years, EDC promoted festival marketplaces, some in waterfront locations in several smaller US cities. Except for the first, Waterside in Norfolk (which opened in 1983), these all failed because they lacked the critical mass of attractions found in Baltimore and Boston (Olsen 2003). They also suffered from economic changes and governmental spending cuts during the Reagan era. Increasing difficulties with these smaller US projects encouraged EDC to look further afield. Rouse had not initially wanted to be a globetrotting evangelist for Baltimore. Before EDC's first and most important international project, in Sydney, came up in 1983, he had refused 120 invitations to visit non-US cities to give development advice (Perkins 2001).

An Australian developer, Thomas Hayson, persuaded Rouse to break this habit. Hayson was impressed by the Inner Harbor's similarity to the disused Darling Harbour in Sydney (Perkins 2001; Millspaugh 2008). The New South Wales government sought its renewal and Hayson had agreed to participate (Young 1988). Having read about Baltimore, Hayson visited the city, contacting Millspaugh and a reluctant Rouse. Both immediately saw Darling Harbour's potential. They were soon advising him and the new Darling Harbour Authority. EDC also invested in Hayson's Harbourside festival marketplace, which was very similar to Rouse's Baltimore development.

EDC was also active at Port Vell in Barcelona (Meyer 1999). In 1985 it undertook master planning for Barcelona's port authority on the area's regeneration, later joining in the development of the quayside Maremagnum leisure and retailing complex. Another important EDC venture was the Kop Van Zuid in Rotterdam (Figure 6.1) (Millspaugh 2007). Here the company joined a consortium with the Rotterdam municipality, Dutch investment and construction companies to produce a strategic vision in 1988. EDC proposed the public-private partnership delivery structure, following the

Figure 6.1 The Entrepot Haven, Kop van Zuid, Rotterdam, now luxury apartments, restaurants, shops and marina, 2007

Baltimore template (Hajer 1993). The actual development included some Baltimore features, notably a festival marketplace in the old Custom House, though with important differences.

An important Japanese example opened in 1991 at the Tempozan Harbor Village (Olsen 2003;Global Harbors Documentary Inc. 2008b). Developed by a consortium led by the Osaka Port Authority, with EDC as consulting developer, it more closely followed the Baltimore model, with a festival marketplace, an aquarium, a cruise ship terminal and several other attractions. Also in 1991, the Laganside Development Corporation, responsible for the Belfast waterfront, chose a development consortium comprising EDC and two Northern Irish developers.

Yet Rouse's EDC was not the only agent of Baltimore's dissemination. Some of Rouse and Millspaugh's professional associates independently helped spread elements of the model. Most important was the practice led by Benjamin Thompson. Thompson himself had invented the festival marketplace as a design concept and his firm designed Rouse's most successful marketplaces. Independently of Rouse, they worked in Guatemala City and Buenos Aires during the 1990s (BTA Architects Inc. 2007). At the wider planning level, they planned the reuse of the Custom House Dock in Dublin in 1987. Waterfront areas in several other cities including Auckland and Cardiff were also master-planned by them.

Another important diffuser of the Baltimore (and Boston) approach was Cambridge Seven Associates (CSA undated). This practice designed both Boston's pioneering aquarium and Baltimore's later, more ambitious effort. CSA's other work included Osaka's Tempozan aquarium and marketplace (where EDC was also involved), along with later similar projects in Lisbon and Kuwait. Other longstanding professional collaborators of Rouse were RTKL Architecture and Urban Design (RTKL undated). After working with him in Baltimore, their global practice has master-planned several waterfront developments, notably in Shanghai and at Leith and Salford in the UK. Many Baltimore actors therefore helped spread the lessons. But, even without them, there was much learning and borrowing of ideas from Baltimore by other cities. Knowledge of the city (also of Boston) framed the thinking of several British urban development corporations in the 1980s and 1990s. This was particularly so for London and other cities undertaking dock regeneration schemes (Imrie and Thomas 1999).

During the 1980s, therefore, Baltimore's Inner Harbor captured the imaginations of international city leaders, planners and developers considering waterfront regeneration. The very improbability of declining Baltimore becoming a successful 'comeback' city created a compelling, if partly illusory, narrative. By the 1990s, Baltimore's decline, apparently halted in the 1980s, had resumed. Moreover, the imagined showpiece for public-private partnership actually contained surprisingly little that was private investment, beyond Rouse's Harborplace. Public sector agencies had developed most of what visitors saw. Nor were Baltimore's individual attractions even genuinely innovative. Boston had been more significant, but its stronger economy and established touristic status made it a less compelling role model of a city arising from the dead.

The London Docklands: A Contested Model

If Baltimore wove the first truly global narrative of port reuse, the vast London Docklands regeneration can also not be ignored (Figure 6.2). Covering 2,150 hectares, the territory of the London Docklands Development Corporation (LDDC) dwarfed the Inner Harbor. In contrast to Baltimore, however, the attention earned by the intervention was certainly not all admiring and the narrative of the Docklands was fiercely contested (Brownill 1993). Regeneration had begun long before the appearance of the LDDC in 1981. Renewal at St Katharine Docks, near Tower Bridge, began in the late 1960s, with a mix of public and private developments, in new and reused heritage buildings. By the early 1980s, tangible results were modest but had won some favourable international comment (Anon 1982). Soon, however, the new LDDC transformed the prevailing ideology, mode of operation, pace and scale of change, prompting mixed international perceptions.

Figure 6.2 West Silvertown Urban Village, Royal Victoria Dock, London Docklands, 2009, showing the Millennium Dome and the extended Canary
Wharf in background

Culture, tourism and leisure activities dominated Baltimore, but the
LDDC went much further. It pioneered private sector housing and major
office, largely finance-related, developments in waterfront settings. Far more
than Baltimore, the London Docklands became the demonstration project for the capitalist-led form of Anglo-American political economy that
dominated in the 1980s and 1990s. It was the most complete expression of
the Thatcherist vision of a Britain transformed. Here capitalist enterprise
would be (and largely was) freed from state regulation and the 'dead hand
of socialism' (Heseltine 1987). Traditional working-class dock communities
were marginalized, supplanted by a new, more affluent population with a
'yuppie' lifestyle. Here too, at the Docklands' showpiece, Canary Wharf,
could be glimpsed the emergent world of globalized finance.

This development drew on transatlantic precedents quite different to
those of Baltimore. The idea for a major new financial district was launched
in 1985 by G. Ware Travelstead, a Texan entrepreneur, and backed by US
banks (Brownill 1993). In 1987 the Canadian developers Olympia and
York, led by the Reichmann Brothers, took control. Since 1980, they had
been developing Battery Park City as a financial district on former port

land in New York (Gordon 1997). The Reichmann Brothers followed many aspects of this development at Canary Wharf. Its master plan, prepared by Skidmore, Owings and Merrill, partly resembled that of Battery Park City. Visual similarities were reinforced by hiring the architect of Battery Park's towers, César Pelli, to design the main tower at Canary Wharf.

A key difference was, however, its remoteness from London's established financial district, in contrast to Battery Park's proximity to Wall Street. Rather like Baltimore, therefore, the very improbability of Canary Wharf created its own narrative of boldness and success. Important also were LDDC's place marketing efforts, directed at international business, developers and potential new residents rather than city leaders or planners. Combined with wider 1980s reforms to the UK business climate, the Docklands was physical testimony that a relatively unregulated London was open for business. In these circumstances, city leaders and planners elsewhere were naturally curious. As in Baltimore, many began to visit and learn about the massive transformation.

But the London Docklands soon earned strong negative as well as positive perceptions. Almost immediately, many British planners, architects, commentators and politicians were critical (Thornley 1991). To them, the Docklands was ideologically driven, undemocratic, socially insensitive and aesthetically crude, more about developer profits than wider planning or design considerations. Specific aspects of the Inner Harbor (particularly Rouse's Harborplace) had also, initially, been viewed negatively in Baltimore. Yet in that city positive impressions soon dominated and were actively promoted externally by EDC and others.

By contrast, criticisms of the Docklands reflected wider international suspicions of Anglo-American political economy in the Thatcher-Reagan era. Some of Britain's European neighbours equated the Docklands with Thatcher's rejection of the stronger state intervention and market regulation favoured elsewhere in Europe. In France, for example, much professional comment about the Docklands was very negative, seeing it as a model built on illusion (Hollamby and Da Luz 1988; Villeneuve 1988; Ducher 1989). Nobody wanted to see the London Docklands transposed to a French setting. More mixed lessons were drawn in other European countries. In Amsterdam, for example, the LDDC's success in creating housing in waterfront settings was emulated in the Dutch city's Eastern Docks. In Sweden, early regeneration in Gothenburg's port closely followed London (Hall 1991).[1] Yet by 2001 planners of the Norra Älvstranden district in the port wanted a 'vibrant quarter that would not be similar to the London Docklands' (cited Cadell *et al.* 2008: 32).

A more positive Docklands narrative followed former LDDC employees or consultants, or Docklands developers who took its experience to new settings. A key internationalizing figure was Reg Ward, the LDDC's first chief executive. He led it when it was most dynamically pro-development and least planning- or community-friendly (Brownill 1993). In late 1987 he left the LDDC, soon becoming advisory consultant to several cities in Australia and New Zealand. He subsequently worked in St Petersburg, St Kitts and Barcelona (*LDDC 2011*).[2]

Australia was generally receptive to UK ideas and practice. Already, independently of Ward's role, the organizational model of the urban development corporation, based directly on LDDC, had been adopted in Australian waterfront settings, notably for Sydney's Darling Harbour Authority, created in 1984 (Searle 2005). Yet it was in Sydney's great rival, Melbourne, that links with the London Docklands were closest. In 1988, a business organization, the Committee for Melbourne (CFM) asked Ward for ideas about the moribund port area (Pappas 2005; Warrender 2007). CFM had been formed in 1985 to re-energize Melbourne's economy (Figure 6.3). Like London, therefore, the perceived imperative, at least for business, was to boost the city to potential investors. A dynamic initiative to regenerate the docks would signal a wider desire to change the city (Wood 2009).[3] Ward reported in 1989 and CFM published two further reports on the docks in 1990. These prompted the forming of the Melbourne Docklands Authority (MDA) in 1992, aimed at regenerating the area.

Though Ward's specific proposals were not adopted, he was a catalyst and an inspirational figure. Melbourne is generally seen as the Australian

Figure 6.3 Melbourne Docklands, 2011. View towards city centre showing offices and Docklands Stadium.

city where port renewal most closely followed London's approach. Tellingly, only a very few port regenerations outside London adopted the actual name 'Docklands' in their titles. However, CFM and Melbourne planners also examined other cities undergoing regeneration, including Baltimore, Boston, Glasgow and Liverpool. There were also later denials of parallels with the London Docklands (e.g. Procter 1997).

A rather different example was Angus Gavin, former Principal Urban Designer and Development Manager for the Royal Docks area of the eastern docklands (Gavin 1996). By 1992 he was master planning central Beirut's reconstruction after the Lebanese Civil War. Guided by him, the Solidere public-private company overseeing reconstruction used international experience extensively. The London Docklands was a leading referent, but there were others, including Baltimore, Sydney and Barcelona.

Other Models and Networks of Knowledge Circulation

As this suggests, widening experiences of port regeneration gave more possible referents, some becoming new models. Sometimes, as for Baltimore, developers actively promoted these new models elsewhere. EDC's main rival in this was the international development consultancy arm of the Victoria and Alfred Waterfront Company in Cape Town (Van Zyl 2005). This waterfront regeneration began in 1988, drawing on Baltimore and Boston (Figure 6.4). Soon South Africa's biggest tourist attraction, it prompted international demands for the expertise that created it. During the 1990s commissions started to arrive. These included Libreville (Gabon), St Louis

Figure 6.4 Victoria and Alfred Waterfront, Cape Town, 2012. Real and 'new' historic townscape combine with working port activities in this iconic South African port regeneration.

(Mauritius), Lagos (Nigeria), Gelendzhik (Russia) as well as Gunwharf Quays in Portsmouth, UK (Portsmouth Society 1998; Cook 2004) and further work on the Maremagnum at Port Vell in Barcelona.

Especially after the 1992 Olympics, Barcelona also attracted interest from world city leaders, planners, architects and developers (Monclús 2003). Like Baltimore and Cape Town, its image was assiduously fostered. In Barcelona, however, the promoters were often city politicians or officials. Since the mid-1990s, the city has actively marketed itself as a model, especially in Latin America. Its own waterfront planning was distinctive, especially the new beaches formed in the 1990s. Yet it was the most Baltimore-like part of Barcelona, Port Vell, which became a partial model for the Puerto Madero in Buenos Aires (Keeling 2005). Under a formal co-operation agreement between the two cities, Barcelona architects undertook early planning of this area in the late 1980s.

Network organizations promoting port regeneration also appeared during the 1980s. Amongst the first was the US-based Waterfront Center, founded in 1981 (Waterfront Centre undated). The Association Internationale Villes et Ports (AIVP) appeared in 1988, originally involving countries speaking French or Latin languages (AIVP undated). Within Europe, the EU has funded projects linking several ports in mutual learning programmes. The Waterfront Communities Project (2004–2007) involved Hamburg, Gothenburg, Schiedam, Aalborg, Odense, Oslo, Edinburgh, Gateshead and Hull (Interreg 3B 2009). The current URBACT II programme's CTUR project focuses on cruise liner traffic, urban regeneration and heritage (URBACT undated). Led by Naples, the other partners are Alicante, Helsinki, Leixoes (Portugal), Dublin, Valencia, Rhodes and Rostock.

Conclusions

The global flows of knowledge about port regeneration resemble the circulation of other innovations. An initial example (Baltimore) was recognized as the main innovator, winning disproportionate attention even though other examples were more truly inventive (notably Boston). Yet Baltimore was imagined as *the* model for others because it synthesized earlier initiatives, produced impressive results earlier than anywhere else and was extensively marketed by its promoters. Despite clear disparities between perceptions and realities in the Inner Harbor, it had a disproportionate impact on early thinking. Other 'models' appeared, particularly the London Docklands, but were more controversial and less systematically promoted than Baltimore

As more port regeneration occurred, other projects were admired for various real and imagined reasons. Some also became new exemplars, especially if they too had active promoters. Often, though, design and organizational know-how was now being sought, not the specific template that early emulators took from Baltimore. Further actual refinements of the original model were now relatively minor. Increasingly there has been a shift towards mutual learning networks. These promote multidirectional knowledge flows with more emphasis on actual learning rather than simply imagining. Yet, even in such networks, some partners, often larger cities, will tend to dominate. In general, though, when city leaders, planners and developers have many possible referents, they are more discerning.

All this partly insures against the rather uncritical acceptance of a few external models, particularly that of Baltimore, which characterized early port regeneration. Over time there has been a reaction against the 'fun city' and 'financial yuppie city' models that Baltimore and London pioneered. In recent years port cities have also been less ready to surrender the maritime functions of their historic docks. It is now increasingly common to see more nuanced port regenerations, combining working port functions with other activities.

Notes

1   S. Brownill interview with C. McCauley, 28 May 2009.
2   Author's interviews with P. M. Warrender (and personal communications), 5th, 10th, 12th August 2009.
3   Personal communication with Wood, 15 June 2009.

Bibliography

AIVP (undated) *Home Page*. Available at: www.aivp.org/spip.php?sommaire&lang=en (accessed on 26 November 2013).
Anon (1982) 'Londres: Contrastes et Mutations', *Urbanisme*, 190/191: 74–75.
Bloom, N.D. (2004) *Merchant of Illusion: James Rouse, America's Salesman of the Businessman's Utopia*, Columbus: Ohio State University Press.
Breen, A. and Rigby, D. (1996) *The New Waterfront: A Worldwide Urban Success Story*, London: Thames and Hudson.
Brownill, S. (1993) *Developing London's Docklands: Another Great Planning Disaster?* London: Paul Chapman.
BTA Architects Inc. (2007) 'Urban Mixed-Use'. Available at: www.bta-architects. com/c/portfolio_umarketplaces.html (accessed on 26 November 2013).
Cadell, C., Falk, N. and King, F. (2008) *Regeneration in European Cities: Making Connections*, York: Joseph Rowntree Foundation.
Cook, I. (2004) *Waterfront Regeneration, Gentrification and the Entrepreneurial State: The Redevelopment of Gunwharf Quays, Portsmouth*, Spatial Policy Analysis Working Paper No 51, Manchester: School of Geography, University of Manchester.
CSA (undated) 'Cambridge Seven Associates Inc.: Impactful Architecture'. Available at: www.c7a.com (accessed on 26 November 2013).
Ducher, D. (1989) 'Docks de Londres: Un modèle en trompe-l'œil', *Urbanisme*, 229, 22–25.
Global Harbors Documentary Inc. (2008a) 'Global Harbors: A Waterfront Renaissance'. Available at: www.globalharbors.org/index.html (accessed 26 November 2013).

Global Harbors Documentary Inc. (2008b) 'Model for the World: Examples of Port Cities Influenced by Baltimore's Waterfront Development'. Available at: www.globalharbors.org/model_for_the_world.html (accessed on 26 November 2013).

Hajer, M.A. (1993) 'Rotterdam: Re-Designing the Public Domain', in F. Bianchini and M. Parkinson (eds.), *Cultural Policy and Urban Regeneration: The West European Experience*, Manchester: Manchester University Press, 48–72.

Heseltine, M. (1987) *Where There's a Will*, London: Hutchinson.

Gavin, A. (1996) *Beirut Reborn: The Restoration and Development of the Central District*, London: Academy Editions.

Gordon, D.L.A. (1997) *Battery Park City: Politics and Planning on the New York Waterfront*, Amsterdam: Gordon and Breach.

Hall, T. (1991) 'Urban Planning in Sweden', in T. Hall (ed.), *Planning and Urban Growth in the Nordic Countries*, London: Spon, 167–246.

Hollamby, T. and de Luz, P. (1988) 'Londres ouvre ses docklands à l'investissement privé', *Urbanisme*, 225: 12–17.

Imrie, R. and Thomas, H. (eds.) (1999) *British Urban Policy: An Evaluation of the Urban Development Corporations*, 2nd edn, London: Sage.

Interreg 3B (2009) 'Waterfront Communities Project'. Available at: www.north-searegion.eu/iiib/projectpresentation/details/&tid=19&theme=6 (accessed on 26 November 2013).

Keeling, D.J. (2005) 'Waterfront Redevelopment and the Puerto Madero Project in Buenos Aires, Argentina', in V.O. Chabrera, R.B. Kent and J.S. Martí (eds.), *Cities and Urban Geography in Latin America*. Castellon de la Plana: Publicaciones Universitat Jaume I, Serie Colección Américas: 113–136.

LDDC (2011) 'LDDC People: Death of Reg Ward'. Available at: www.lddc-history.org.uk/veterans/index.html (accessed on 26 November 2013).

Lyall, K.C. (1982) 'A Bicycle Built-for-Two: Public-Private Partnership in Baltimore', in R.S. Fosler and R.A. Berger (eds.), *Public-Private Partnership in American Cities: Seven Case Studies*, Lexington MA: Lexington Books, 17–57.

Metzger, J.T. (2001) 'The Failed Promise of a Festival Marketplace: South Street Seaport in Lower Manhattan', *Planning Perspectives*, 16(1): 25–46.

Meyer, H. (1999) *City and Port: Transformation of Port Cities London, Barcelona, New York, Rotterdam*, Utrecht: International Books.

Millspaugh, M. (2007) 'Rotterdam: The Kop Van Zuid'. Available at: www.globalharbors.org/rotterdam_kop_van_zuid.html (accessed 26 November 2013).

Millspaugh, M. (2008) 'The Sydney Story: Darling Harbor'. Available at: www.globalharbors.org/sydney_darling_harbor.html (accessed on 26 November 2013).

Monclús, F.J. (2003) 'The Barcelona Model: An Original Formula? From "reconstruction" to Strategic Urban Projects (1979–2004)', *Planning Perspectives*, 18: 399–421.

Olsen, J. (2003) *Better Places, Better Lives: A Biography of James Rouse*, Washington, DC: The Urban Land Institute.

Pappas, G. (2005) 'How Melbourne Became a City to Be Copied', *The Age*, 6 October 2005. Available at: www.theage.com.au/news/business/how-melbourne-became-a-city-to-be-copied/2005/10/05/1128191785284.html (accessed on 17 November 2013).

Perkins, K. (2001) *Dare to Dream: The Life and Times of a Proud Australian*, Sydney: Golden Wattle.

Portsmouth Society, The (1998) 'Cape Town Lessons for Gunwharf', *Portsmouth Society News*, January 1998.

Procter, C. (1997) 'Ashton Raggatt McDougall's Masterplan for Melbourne's Largest Project—Rejuvenation of the Docklands—Is Out in Public', *Architecture Australia*. Available at: www.archmedia.com.au/aa/aaprintissue.php?issueid=199703&article=1 (accessed on 26 November 2013).

RTKL (undated) 'Featured Projects'. Available at: www.rtkl.com/Projects (accessed on 26 November 2013).

Rusk, D. (1996) *Baltimore Unbound: A Strategy for Regional Renewal*, Baltimore: Abell Foundation.

Searle, G. (2005) 'The Redfern-Waterloo Authority: Sydney's Continuing Use of Development Corporations as a Primary Mode of Urban Governance', paper in 2nd 'State of Australian Cities Conference', Griffith University, Brisbane, November–December.

Thornley, A. (1991) *Urban Planning Under Thatcherism: The Challenge of the Market*, London: Routledge.

URBACT (undated) 'CTUR Results'. Available at: http://urbact.eu/en/results/results/?resultid=32 (accessed on 26 November 2013).

van Zyl, P.S. (2005) 'V&A Waterfront Development: An African Success Story in the Integration of Water, Working Harbour, Heritage, Urban Revitalization and Tourism Development'. Available at: http://capeinfo.com/component/content/article/115 (accessed 26 November 2013).

Villeneuve, S. (1988) 'L'envers de la flambée du foncier', *Urbanisme*, 225: 18–21.

Wallace, D. (2004) *Urban Planning/My Way*, Washington, DC: American Association of Planners.

Ward, S.V. (2011) 'Port Cities and the Global Exchange of Planning Ideas', in C. Hein (ed.), *Port Cities: Dynamic Networks and Global Networks*, London: Routledge, 70–85.

Warrender, P.M. (2007) *Pamela: In Her Own Right*, Prahran, Victoria: Hardie Grant.

Waterfront Centre (undated) 'The Waterfront Center'. Available at: www.waterfrontcenter.org/index.html (accessed on 26 November 2013).

Wood, S. (2009) 'Desiring Docklands: Deleuze and Urban Planning Discourse', *Planning Theory*, 8: 191–215.

Wrenn, D.M. with Casazza, J.A. and Smart, J.E. (1983) *Urban Waterfront Development*, Washington, DC: The Urban Land Institute.

Young, B. (1988) 'Darling Harbour: A New City Precinct', in G.P.Webber (ed.), *The Design of Sydney: Three Decades of Change in the City Centre*, Sydney: Law Book Co., 190–213.

7 The Historic Urban Landscape of the Liverpool Waterfront

The Three Graces in a New Perspective

John Pendlebury

Introduction

Deindustrialization in the 1970s created huge swathes of vacant waterfront land in many countries. With the decline of industry and introduction of remedial measures to raise water quality, an opportunity was created for very different uses, albeit necessitating large costs for infrastructure. In the UK in the 1980s waterfronts were a major focus of public regeneration policy: many of the government-created development corporations, aimed at stimulating market investment, were centred on waterfront areas. The first two of these were London and Merseyside, the latter including the Liverpool waterfront. In the long property boom of the late 1990s and early 2000s market investment continued apace, as waterfronts were seen as vital sites of economic growth in the post-industrial period.

In the process, waterfront spaces have often been considered as in some ways separate from the surrounding city (see, for example, Marshall 2001; Desfor *et al.* 2010), although this is perhaps only continuing a tradition. Industrial docklands were, historically, often a place apart. At the heart of the economy of the port city, from the nineteenth century they were often phenomenal engineering constructions, physically separate from the surrounding city, sealed off by high walls, designed to help regulate customs and excise, and to prevent the theft of valuable cargo. Thus, when we are talking about the potential for the reuse of dock spaces following deindustrialization, we might not be talking about re-integration with the city, but integration of a space that has long been liminal—the threshold to the city, yet apart, not 'of' the city. The role of docklands heritage has also been ambiguous; it is important as a frame for new development but sometimes seen as a restraint on development, or as a history that is in need of sanitisation (see, for example, Atkinson *et al.* 2002).

This chapter will focus upon a case study of Liverpool. At the heart of the Liverpool waterfront are the so-called Three Graces; a relatively recent labelling of the trio made up by the Royal Liver Building, the Cunard Building and the Port of Liverpool Building. These buildings are the face of Liverpool, monumental early twentieth century buildings at Pier Head and a confident late-imperial assertion of Liverpool's greatness facing out across the water. Views of these buildings from and across the River Mersey are considered a central element of the river landscape of Liverpool (see, for example, Rodwell 2008). However, they are also atypical of the waterfront historically in being so 'public', in connecting with the city and in making this external show. In practice, most of Liverpool's docks, like those in many industrial cities, have long been a place apart, shut off behind high walls and further separated by infrastructure such as the now-removed aerial train and a dual carriageway. In Liverpool, where these walls survive, they are often now protected as listed buildings.

After briefly describing the history of the docks in Liverpool and the early regeneration efforts of the Merseyside Development Corporation, focused upon the Albert Dock area, the chapter will concentrate upon the most recent decade. This period has seen the valorization of the historical and material significance of the Liverpool waterfront through its inscription as a World Heritage Site (WHS)—Liverpool Maritime Mercantile City—in 2004. However, it has also seen immediate pressure on this status caused by the need and desire for economic growth. At the time of writing, this has reached a culmination with the 'Liverpool Waters' scheme, which has led to the WHS being added to the list of sites that are recognized as in danger. The final discussion in the chapter briefly considers this scheme through the lens of the Historic Urban Landscape.

Liverpool Docks: Rise, Fall and Rise

In the eighteenth and nineteenth centuries, Liverpool was central to the expansion of the British Empire. Its location on the east bank of the mouth of the River Mersey was integral to this as the city developed into a great port and maritime centre. The eighteenth century saw the city established as the principal European hub for the triangular transatlantic slave trade. The wealth generated saw great physical expansion and development, and technological innovation; for example, in 1715 the first commercial wet dock in the world was built in the city (Giles and Hawkins 2004). In the nineteenth century, after the ending of Britain's involvement in the slave trade, the city continued to develop and flourish. By the middle of the century, 45% of UK exports by value went through the port (Giles and Hawkins 2004). The middle of the century also saw further technological innovation and the beginning of the construction of the city's heroically scaled warehouses, many of which still form an important element of the city's dockland heritage. The name most associated with their creation is Jesse Hartley, dock engineer from 1824 to 1860 and responsible for construction at the Albert, Stanley and Wapping docks (all in Liverpool), amongst others. The most gargantuan of all the warehouses, the Tobacco Warehouse at Stanley Dock, was built at the very end of the nineteenth century (Figure 7.1). The development of the port city was not confined to docks and warehouses; it included the Three Graces, and also, for example, the monumental civic buildings around St George's plateau, including St George's Hall itself, opened in 1854.

Figure 7.1 Stanley Dock tobacco warehouse

The history of the Liverpool waterfront became one of continuous change and growth; throughout its long history as working, productive docklands, change was constant. As ships grew in size and further development was required, activity moved further north towards the mouth of the river, away from the city centre, with the modern container port at Seaforth constructed in 1972 and the historic South Docks closed in the same year. In total the docklands waterfront spanned some 11 kilometres by this stage (Giles and Hawkins 2004), but there was also significant decline and dereliction evident. So, for example, the Albert Dock, already recognized as being of significant historical importance, was in decay, with wartime bomb damage unrepaired and the dock itself largely silted up. Development plans for this era indicate much of the central docks area (indeed, much of the city centre) as 'areas of secondary or inessential land uses' or 'areas of obsolescence' (City Centre Planning Group 1965: 166). By 1973 the Albert Dock at least was identified as an area with 'potential for comprehensive rehabilitation'. However, as Francis Amos (1973), who was the city planning officer, narrated, the Albert Dock area had been subject to large speculative development plans by the well-known British developer of the period, Harry Hyams. Prefiguring the story of Liverpool Waters, the City Council was prepared to set aside the heritage of the area and its own development plan. However, in contrast with Liverpool Waters, central government 'called in' the application for its own determination. In the meantime market conditions changed and Hyams lost interest. The Albert Dock had in fact been listed as early as 1952, very early in the British post-war listing system, and by the time of Hyams' proposal had been upgraded to the highest category (Grade I). A broader appreciation of the aesthetic qualities of the dockland areas (and of the city more generally) can be found in the townscape study, *Seaport* (Hughes 1964), following a pattern of appreciation of industrial functionalism that had been set in the *Architectural Review* over the previous twenty-five years or so (Figure 7.2).

Figure 7.2 Industrial aesthetics in Liverpool Docks

Figure 7.3 Albert Dock restored

In the 1980s, waterfronts became perhaps the major focus of public regeneration policy in the UK and were the focus of many of the government-created development corporations, aimed at stimulating market investment. These were handsomely resourced organizations, autonomous from local government and free of democratic accountability, other than to the central government minister. They had a very clear brief to achieve physical regeneration and development. The exemplar of this process, on a phenomenal scale, was the London Docklands Development Corporation (LDDC), discussed elsewhere in this volume, but this waterfront focus was also evident in many other cities. The Merseyside Development Corporation (MDC), together with the LDDC, were the first corporations to be created in 1981. The MDC's development strategy sought to achieve tourism and leisure uses for the waterfront. Albert Dock was restored and reused, with a combination of uses including a maritime museum, an art gallery, a television studio, offices and apartments (Stratton 2000) (Figure 7.3). While this was a relatively quick success for the MDC, the scale of dockland regeneration required was daunting. The MDC's area of operation was trebled in 1988. Progress was slow, albeit with some tangible successes (Couch 2003).

Since the 1980s, across the UK waterfronts have continued to be seen as vital sites of economic growth in the post-industrial period. After the property slump of the early 1990s, when many of the newly built buildings on waterfronts remained unlet, market investment continued apace in the long property boom of the late 1990s and early 2000s. It is to the last decade, and Liverpool's inscription as a WHS, that I now turn.

Liverpool Maritime Mercantile City World Heritage Site

The Liverpool Maritime Mercantile City WHS was inscribed in 2004 in recognition of Liverpool's historic significance as an outstanding example of a world mercantile port city (on the basis of criteria ii, iii and iv[1]). Embedded within this rationale are its contribution to technological innovation and its pivotal role in the transatlantic slave trade. The boundary of the site connects a series of discrete areas, including sections of the waterfront and the main commercial core of the city. A defined buffer zone incorporates much of the rest of the city centre. WHS status was effectively part of a process of cultural reinvention for the city, subsequently culminating in the award of European Capital of Culture for 2008, although as part of this process the city had been criticized for being oblique about its role in the history of slavery (McLernon and Griffiths 2002). Indeed, UNESCO encouraged this to be more directly addressed in the WHS nomination (Pendlebury 2009).

It was apparent at the time of the nomination that extensive development was both anticipated and seen as desirable by the various UK authorities within the site, its buffer zone and its wider setting, explicitly identifying the boost that WHS status was hoped to bring (Department for Culture, Media and Sport 2003). In turn this was situated within a wider discourse linking conservation and regeneration (Farr and Giles 2008:7; Biddulph 2010). Whilst the Albert Dock and some neighbouring sites had been regenerated, much of the waterfront remained a wasteland and significant problems of poor historic building condition were evident throughout the proposed site and its buffer zone. Concerned about the impact of this development, UNESCO were 'unusually insistent that a policy framework should reflect the needs of the site' and imposed 'unprecedented conditions' (Denyer 2005). These conditions related to the height of new constructions prompted by the tall building proposals then coming forward, which were considered of critical significance in Liverpool, given the importance of its morphology and waterfront. The City Council wrote a draft tall buildings policy which was published for consultation in December 2004 (Liverpool City Council 2004), which suggested three clusters of tall buildings, all within either the site itself or the buffer zone. This policy, applied without any degree of consistency (Short 2007), was much criticized (for example, Rodwell 2008) and was quickly shelved. UNESCO's concerns also related to development proposals at the symbolic heart of the site at Pier Head and proposals for a large new building, styled the 'Fourth Grace'.

The inscription of the WHS attracted the general support of the many agencies and government bodies involved in regenerating Liverpool, yet there was concern from the beginning within the business community that the tightly drawn boundaries might stifle investment. Indeed, stakeholders seemed to coalesce around having the WHS status revoked or at least revised to rid the city of the buffer zone (Short 2007). Conversely, some conservation bodies have been intensely critical with what they perceive as a poor track record on maintaining historic buildings and a laissez-faire approach to development within the city (for example, see Hradsky 2009; Merseyside Civic Society 2009)—a critique that has been mirrored in the local and national press (for example, see Hunt 2008).

It is in this context that, following the World Heritage Committee's main annual meeting in 2006, a reactive monitoring mission visited the city in the October of that year. The proposal for a Fourth Grace had been dropped by this time. However, Pier Head remained a significant concern, both in terms of the lower-key development that had replaced the Fourth Grace scheme but also, more significantly, due to plans for a new building for the Museum of Liverpool (now built and operational) which stands forward and to the side of the Three Graces, close to the waterfront (Figure 7.4).

Reporting to the World Heritage Committee in mid-2007, the mission team indicated that they did not consider the integrity of the site to be under imminent danger but foresaw potential threats to its future functionality and integrity (UNESCO-ICOMOS 2007). They expressed concern over developments on the waterfront and were also concerned that the 'world heritage perspective' had not been effectively communicated and 'sold' to local stakeholders. However, perhaps their most powerful conclusion was that the planning framework was inadequate for appraising development

Figure 7.4 The Three Graces with the addition of the new Museum of Liverpool

proposals. This led in due course to a new Supplementary Planning Document (SPD) for the WHS, a substantial 150-page document, which was adopted in October 2009 (Liverpool City Council 2009: 152).

The subsequent World Heritage Centre/ICOMOS Reactive Monitoring Mission (UNESCO-ICOMOS 2011: 23) in November 2011 was upbeat in many respects, reflecting upon the improved condition of parts of the WHS and that many of the fears expressed in 2006 had been unfounded. So, for example, the Museum of Liverpool and other developments in the Three Graces area were considered to be reasonably successful and certainly not a threat to the Outstanding Universal Value of the WHS (although they remain strongly criticized by others, see Rodwell 2012). The mission acknowledged the development of the SPD and commended the open process of its formulation. It did, however, partially disagree with the content of the SPD. Specifically, it challenged the suggestion put forward in the SPD relating to 'opportunities for two secondary clusters of high-rise buildings' in the buffer zone, away from the primary cluster of the Central Business District. More fundamentally it indicated the threat to the WHS and its status posed by the emerging Liverpool Waters proposals.

Liverpool Waters

From its inscription in 2004, the WHS had something of a difficult history in Liverpool, with constant negotiation between the state and extra-state authorities about the nature of its integrity and how this might be managed. However, in many respects these negotiations can be seen as just a prelude for the Liverpool Waters proposal. This is a huge waterfront redevelopment scheme, paralleled by a similar scheme on the other side of the Mersey: Wirral Waters. In the words of its proposers, Peel Holdings,

> The Liverpool Waters vision involves regenerating a 60 hectare historic dockland site to create a world-class, high-quality, mixed use waterfront quarter in central Liverpool. The scheme will create a unique sense of place, taking advantage of the sites' cultural heritage and integrating it with exciting and sustainable new development. . . .

> Liverpool Waters will draw on the unique identity of the site and the city to define character areas, delivering a high density and accessible quarter, which is both economically and environmentally sustainable, and which will significantly reinforce Liverpool's strong identity. Based on strong contextual and place-making principles, the area will be characterized by activity and diversity, providing public spaces that encourage formal and informal use. It will establish a stimulating and dynamic environment that re-vitalizes the whole area, and responds to the needs of different communities. . . .

> As an integral part of Liverpool's iconic skyline, and continuing its tradition of innovation, Liverpool Waters will symbolize the city's 21st century renaissance alongside its 19th and 20th century heritage on the world stage.
>
> (Liverpool Waters undated)

This is a massive project, divided into a series of sectors, which the developers have discussed in terms of a 50-year implementation period with both substantial mid-rise development and two groups of tall buildings (Figure 7.5). Parts of the scheme fall both into the WHS and the buffer zone. The sheer scale and proposed implementation over many decades have prompted some scepticism over the likelihood of implementation (see, for example, Rodwell 2012).

Whilst in the planning process, a series of different evaluations of the proposals were undertaken. The assessment commissioned by the developers as part of the extensive planning application documentation was undertaken by Peter de Figueiredo (2011), an architect and historic environment consultant, who had previously worked for English Heritage and been involved in the inscription and management of the WHS. Perhaps unsurprisingly, Figueiredo's conclusions on the proposal were largely positive. Ostensibly using ICOMOS methodology and English Heritage guidance, he considered the direct impact on heritage assets as to be largely positive or neutral, whilst acknowledging some detrimental impact on views, albeit viewing this as inevitable to a degree with any development of the site. He also stressed 'gains', such as the access and regeneration benefits the scheme would arguably bring, and invoked Liverpool's 'spirit of optimism and innovation'. He considered the proposals to be largely compliant with the SPD for the site.

The impact study commissioned by English Heritage was undertaken by a team led by Stephen Bond of the Heritage Places consultancy (2011). It reached very different conclusions to the first study, judging the scheme to

Figure 7.5 Artist's illustration of Liverpool Waters

have potential for substantial harm to the Outstanding Universal Value of the WHS. At the heart of the negative consequences of the proposals were judged to be issues of scale and density and impacts on key views. There was also felt to be a lack of understanding of the historical morphology and organization of the docks. So, for example, in the buffer zone, 'low, horizontal and transverse historic emphases will be replaced by height, verticality and the longitudinal' (Bond 2011: 363). The proposals were felt to display little innovation and, in the main, to fail to conform with the WHS SPD. The evaluation did acknowledge heritage benefits of the long-term safeguarding of the Central Docks area plus some benefits from one of the tall building clusters, as well as non-heritage benefits related to regeneration and public access.

The Reactive Monitoring Mission in November 2011 had access to these impact assessments (as well as a third, positive, evaluation undertaken by Liverpool City Council). Its conclusions, however, closely followed those made by the English Heritage study. For example,

> the development would result in the definitive modification of the functional hierarchy and morphology expressed by the port circulation system (river—sluices—docks—water basin), as well as by the historical typologies of the port industrial structures and services, thus seriously affecting the authenticity of the World Heritage property.
>
> (UNESCO-ICOMOS 2011: 13)

Furthermore, the Mission made specific reference to the 2011 UNESCO *Recommendation on the Historic Urban Landscape* and its invocation for proposals to be informed by the 'the complex layering of urban settlements, in order to identify values, understand their meaning for the communities and present them . . . in a comprehensive manner' (UNESCO 2011, article 26). Liverpool Waters, in their view, failed to respond to this challenge.

Plans for the scheme were first unveiled in March 2007, planning applications made in October 2010 and outline planning consent granted by Liverpool City Council in March 2012. The central government announced it was waiving its right to call a public inquiry over the scheme and to exercize its right to determine the planning applications in March 2013—a perhaps surprising decision that provoked concern from the heritage sector (ICOMOS-UK 2013). UNESCO placed the Liverpool WHS on its danger list in June 2012. This was reaffirmed in 2013 with the following observations:

> . . . there have been no actions to remove the potential danger . . . [and] that if the proposed Liverpool Waters development is implemented as currently planned, it would irreversibly damage the attributes of Outstanding Universal Value and the conditions of integrity that warranted inscription, and could lead to the potential deletion of the property from the World Heritage List.
>
> (UNESCO WHC 2013: 4)

Discussion: Liverpool Historic Urban Landscape

A focus on the public-supported, market-dictated regeneration of ports and waterfronts has been a central characteristic of UK urban policy for thirty years. In the process, waterfront spaces have often been considered as in some ways separate from the surrounding city; indeed, this has been part of the appeal to developers wanting to secure their investment in a controlled and closely managed space. But, as discussed, this is only continuing a tradition; the industrial dockland has long been a place apart.

Within dockland regeneration, the role of heritage has also been ambiguous. It has been important as a frame for the new development, but sometimes seen as a restraint on development or as a history that is in need of sanitization. The visual indicators of former maritime uses are often highly prized as aestheticized signifiers of former uses. So railings, bridges, cranes and so on become an important part of the ambience of the new place. More problematic is the recycling of large industrial structures. Sometimes, such as with Albert Dock, they become a focal point for regeneration efforts—but their scale, their typological characteristics (method of construction, floor to ceiling heights, depth of floor plan) can make them difficult and expensive structures to reuse. Nevertheless, for the most part they are protected by listing and there is an acceptance that, in general, they should be retained. The form of new development is often contentious, especially with the new fashion for building tall over the last decade or so. Issues of style are also vexed, with a particularly divisive emphasis in the Vienna Memorandum (UNESCO 2005) given to interventions being 'contemporary' in nature (Rodwell 2012).

Liverpool has perhaps been a very typical British example in all these respects. However, the Liverpool Waters proposals also raise a series of wider issues. The translation of notions of authenticity and integrity, derived from an object-based logic and applied to the complexities of the management of dynamic places, is a difficult and problematic process, with the idea of 'Outstanding Universal Value' difficult to define at urban scale (Pendlebury *et al.* 2009). Arguably there are fundamental tensions between the desire to preserve a sense of the past and the recognition that heritage cities are the product of many layers of development and habitation, as part of an ongoing process of evolution and change. For Dennis Rodwell (2012), the British planning system is rather better at dealing with the micro-conservation issues of protected buildings and areas than with the macro issues of city character, as evidenced by the number of UNESCO WHS monitoring missions to the UK in recent years, which were largely concerned with the impact of wider urban change. Equally, however, he acknowledges the ongoing tension in ICOMOS between the preservationist camp upholding the 'classic values of conservation' and the 'managing change' camp.

The sheer over-bearing scale of the Liverpool Waters plans is an extreme case study of the tensions inherent in the evolution of historic cities and docklands specifically, and how change might impact on notions of authenticity, integrity and Outstanding Universal Value. But how do we understand these concepts in the context of a city such as Liverpool and mobilize them in the context of a proposal such as Liverpool Waters? Whilst we can be suspicious of the different provenances of the impact appraisals undertaken on the scheme, it is still striking how such different conclusions can be reached by apparently well-qualified consultants in terms of their evaluation of the scheme's impact on heritage assets, the city and WHS more generally and indeed with how the proposals comply or otherwise with the WHS SPD. It is understandable that city authorities wishing to achieve the regeneration of extensive areas of derelict dockland (however fantastic the claimed benefits may seem and however diversionary such investment would be from the rest of the city) will prefer to accept an evaluation with a more positive, less critical conclusion on the impact the proposals will have on the heritage of the city.

In a conference held in Liverpool, English Heritage Chief Executive Simon Thurley (2008) listed four reasons for the conservation of port heritage: the physical evidence of the shipping industry; an understanding of the history of place; the aesthetics of dockland structures and their 'raw, sublime beauty' (Thurley 2008: 3); and the meaning that former maritime activity and its physical remains may have to the people of that place. While there might be concerns about each of these in the case of Liverpool Waters, a more fundamental objection seems to be something else: that is, the morphology of the proposals and their three-dimensional manifestation—their verticality—and perhaps the sheer scale and bulk of what is proposed for the townscape. It is the likely visual impact of the scheme on the wider historic landscape, and specifically, with Liverpool, the importance of views of the city from over the water, that raises most concern.

The development of the concept of Historic Urban Landscapes (HUL) was a specific response to this sort of problem (Bandarin and van Oers 2012). The UNESCO recommendation on HUL defines the concept very broadly, including a wide range of physical characteristics of place but also, for example, 'perceptions and visual relationships. . . . social and cultural practices and values, economic processes and the intangible dimensions of heritage as related to diversity and identity' (UNESCO 2011: para. 9).

HUL provides 'the basis for a comprehensive and integrated approach for the identification, assessment, conservation and management of historic urban landscapes within an overall sustainable development framework' (para 10), through mechanisms such as civic engagement, research, regulation and fiscal incentives. It is essentially a comprehensive three-dimensional planning approach for historic cities.

The broad approach suggested by the HUL recommendation does not present a direct and obvious evaluation methodology for a proposal such as Liverpool Waters. The HUL approach places emphasis upon process, one element of which is a development framework, such as the SPD that has been developed. However, as we have seen, the proposers of Liverpool Waters consider their proposals to be compliant with the SPD, a view supported by the local authority and, implicitly, by the state party through its decision not to intervene. Conversely, English Heritage, UNESCO-ICOMOS and other conservation groups have taken the opposite view. Both sides ultimately analyze the Liverpool Waters proposals through a reductive, component-based logic judiciously selected, rather than the more synthetic aspirations of HUL.

Liverpool is inscribed as a WHS that is an outstanding example of a world mercantile port city, a function it no longer holds. The evidence for this past role survives in part because its loss has not been adequately replaced by a new, successful economic function, such that the city has often served as a synonym for dereliction and decay. The objectives for the site(s) occupied by the Liverpool Waters proposals are therefore necessarily as much about place making as place protection. There is an opportunity in Liverpool to change the docks, so long a place apart, into a more integrated element of the future city. The proposers of Liverpool Waters proclaim these objectives as part of their vision. There is justifiable scepticism over these claims. The proposals probably do lack adequate response to context and place specificity, and it is likely that the developers see a sanitized place of possibility, separated physically and in terms of identity from the surrounding city. However, if we accept the principle of the desirability of major development, whilst HUL adds a conceptual approach to the debate, we still seem to lack tools that are sufficiently persuasive to create any sort of consensus over the form such development should take. In this context, it is perhaps unsurprising that decision-makers accept what seems to be on offer.

Note

1 Criterion (ii): Liverpool was a major centre generating innovative technologies and methods in dock construction and port management in the eighteenth, nineteenth and early twentieth centuries. It thus contributed to the building up of international mercantile systems throughout the British Commonwealth.

   Criterion (iii): The city and the port of Liverpool are an exceptional testimony to the development of maritime mercantile culture in the eighteenth, nineteenth and early twentieth centuries, contributing to the building up of the British Empire. It was a centre for the slave trade, until its abolition in 1807, and for emigration from northern Europe to America.

   Criterion (iv): Liverpool is an outstanding example of a world mercantile port city, which represents the early development of global trading and cultural connections throughout the British Empire. (UNESCO 1992–2013).

Bibliography

Amos, J.C. (1973) 'Liverpool', in J. Holliday (ed.), *City Centre Redevelopment: A Study of British City Centre Planning and Case Studies of Five English City Centres*, London: Charles Knight & Co Ltd, 175–206.

Atkinson, D., Cooke, S. and Spooner, D. (2002) 'Tales from the Riverbank: Place-Marketing and Maritime Heritages', *International Journal of Heritage Studies*, 8(1): 25–40.

Bandarin, F. and Van-Oers, R. (2012) *The Historic Urban Landscape: Managing Heritage in an Urban Century*, Chichester: Wiley-Blackwell.

Biddulph, M. (2010) 'Liverpool 2008: Liverpool's Vision and the Decade of Cranes', in J. Punter. (ed.), *Urban Design and the British Urban Renaissance*, Abingdon: Routledge, 100–114.

Bond, S. (2011) *Assessment of the Potential Impact of the Proposed Liverpool Waters Master Plan on OUV at Liverpool Maritime Mercantile WHS for English Heritage*, Dulverton, Somerset: Heritage Places.

City Centre Planning Group (1965) *Liverpool City Centre Plan*, Liverpool: City and County Borough of Liverpool.

Couch, C. (2003) *City of Change and Challenge: Urban Planning and Regeneration in Liverpool*, Aldershot: Ashgate.

Denyer, S. (2005) ICOMOS, interview with Michael Short, 29 April.

Department for Culture Media and Sport (2003) 'Pier Head Set to Join Pyramids as World Heritage Site', 30 January 2003. Available at: www.culture.gov.uk/global/press_notices/archive_2003 (accessed on 24 July 2013).

Desfor, G., Laidley, J., Stevens, Q. and Schubert, D. (eds.) (2010) *Transforming Urban Waterfronts: Fixity and Flow*, London: Routledge.

Farr, S.-J. and Giles, C. (2008) 'Understanding the Historic Environment of Port Cities: The Case of Liverpool', in *On the Waterfront: Culture, Heritage and Regeneration of Port Cities*, Liverpool: English Heritage. Available at: https://www.historicengland.org.uk/images-books/publications/on-the-waterfront/ (accessed on 28 April 2016).

Figueiredo, P. de (2011) *Liverpool Waters Heritage Impact Assessment: Non-Technical Summary*, Liverpool: Liverpool Waters.

Giles, C. and Hawkins, B. (2004) *Storehouses of Empire: Liverpool's Historic Warehouses*, London: English Heritage.

Hradsky, R. (2009) *Triumph, Disaster and Decay: The SAVE Survey of Liverpool's Heritage*, London: SAVE Britain's Heritage.

Hughes, Q. (1964) *Seaport: Architecture & Townscape in Liverpool*, London: Lund Humphries.

Hunt, T. (2008) 'Liverpool, Capital of Vandalism', *The Times*, 8 March 2008.

ICOMOS-UK (2013) *ICOMOS-UK Statement on Liverpool Maritime Mercantile City World Heritage Site*, London: ICOMOS.

Liverpool City Council (2004) *Tall Buildings: Consultation Draft Supplementary Planning Document*, Liverpool: LCC.

Liverpool City Council (2009) *Liverpool Maritime Mercantile City World Heritage Site: Supplementary Planning Document*, Liverpool: City Council.

Liverpool Waters (undated). 'Home Page'. Available at: www.liverpoolwaters.co.uk/content/home.php (accessed on 4 September 2013).

Marshall, R. (ed.) (2001) *Waterfronts in Post-Industrial Cities*, London: Spon.

McLernon, P. and Griffiths, S. (2002) 'Liverpool and the Heritage of the Slave Trade', in A. Phelps, G.J. Ashworth and O.H. Johannson (eds.), *The Construction of the Built Heritage: A North European Perspective on Policies, Practices and Outcomes*, Aldershot: Ashgate, 191–206.

Merseyside Civic Society (2009) Available at: www.liv.ac.uk/mcs/mcsnews.html (accessed on 13 August 2009).

Pendlebury, J. (2009) *Conservation in the Age of Consensus*. London: Routledge.

Pendlebury, J., Short, M. and While, A. (2009) 'Urban World Heritage Sites and the Problem of Authenticity', *Cities* 26(6): 349–358.

Rodwell, D. (2008) 'Urban Regeneration and the Management of Change: Liverpool and the Historic Urban Landscape', *Journal of Architectural Conservation*, 14(2): 83–106.

Rodwell, D. (2012) 'Rethinking Heritage', *Context*, 127: 29–31.

Short, M. (2007) 'Assessing the Impact of Proposals for Tall Buildings on the Built Heritage: England's Regional Cities in the 21st Century', *Progress in Planning*, 68: 97–199.

Stratton, M. (2000) *Industrial Buildings: Conservation and Regeneration*, London: E & FN Spon.

Thurley, S. (2008) 'Heritage in Regeneration: Inspiration or Irrelevance?', in *On the Waterfront: Culture, Heritage and Regeneration of Port Cities*, Liverpool: English Heritage. Available at: https://www.historicengland.org.uk/images-books/publica tions/on-the-waterfront/ (accessed on 28 April 2016).

UNESCO (1992–2013) 'Liverpool—Maritime Mercantile City, UNESCO'. Available at: whc.unesco.org/en/list/1150 (accessed 9 September, 2013).

UNESCO (2005) *Vienna Memorandum on 'World Heritage and Contemporary Architecture—Managing the Historic Urban Landscape'*, Paris: World Heritage Centre.

UNESCO (2011) *Recommendation on the Historic Urban Landscape*, Paris: UNESCO.

UNESCO World Heritage Committee (2013) 'Liverpool SOC 2013 Report', in *37th Session of the World Heritage Committee*, Paris: World Heritage Centre. Available at: http://whc.unesco.org/archive/2013/whc13-37com-7A-en.pdf (accessed on 28 April 2016).

UNESCO-ICOMOS (2007) *Report of the Joint UNESCO-ICOMOS Reactive Monitoring Mission to Liverpool-Maritime Mercantile City, United Kingdom*, Christchurch, New Zealand: World Heritage Committee.

UNESCO-ICOMOS (2011) *Report of the Joint World Heritage Centre/ICOMOS Reactive Monitoring Mission to the World Heritage property Liverpool—Maritime Mercantile City, United Kingdom*, Christchurch, New Zealand: World Heritage Committee.

8 Genova, a Success Story![1]

Francesco Gastaldi

The regeneration process that took place in the area around the Porto Antico (old harbour)—which was converted to new, mainly leisure-related, urban functions—has fostered Genova's tourist appeal and leisure sector. The completion of the conversion process of this part of the waterfront, from a port-related commercial area to a functional urban space, has put an end to the trend of port areas developing in a definite separation from the close urban context. This is now considered the most enhancing intervention for the city, given that it also represents an important basis for a renewed image of the city. The regeneration process undertaken to transform the old port area to urban functions has a very long history: the first intervention hypotheses for the area were elaborated in the mid 1960s. The 1980 Genova municipality master plan at first envisaged urban functions in municipally owned areas located within state property that were part of the Porto Antico: the Darsena and the Porto Franco (now the Expo area). According to the plan's design, these areas were reserved at services for the neighbouring historical centre, representing important resources for improving public services (such as technological areas, parking spaces, and sports and school support infrastructures).

In 1984 the local executive committee entrusted the Genoese architect Renzo Piano with the first assignment of rethinking the means and the location for the 1992 Columbus Exposition within the context of the celebrations for the fifth centenary of the discovery of the Americas. It became clear how the historic centre and the harbour area represented the ideal location for the event, and that the works built for the event could become the hub for the new development of the city. During the same year, a group of Genoese entrepreneurs put forward a proposal—developed by the architect Piero Gambacciani—to create a small marina with hotels and a shopping centre. The project was completed in January 1986. This transformative vision was substantially welcomed by both public authorities and private investors, and it was supported by analyses and research on the tourist and commercial traffic that could originate from such an operation.

In May 1985 an important shift became official: the Liguria regional government, the municipality of Genova and the port authority signed a non-binding agreement which set forth the closure of the old industrial docks for their rehabilitation for tourist and leisure purposes. In the same year, the municipality established a special office for the Columbus celebratory events and the parliament approved law no. 418—relating to the celebration of the fifth centenary of the discovery of the Americas—which earmarked the first 40 billion liras for the exposition and the historical and artistic refurbishment interventions at the locations linked to Columbus. The year after, another 75 billion liras were allocated for three years and the government appointed the general commissioner for the exhibition.

On 5 June 1986 the assembly of the Bureau International des Espositions resolved to locate another specialized exposition for 1992 in the city of Genova.

In 1987, in accordance with the Liguria regional government and the municipality of Genova, an amendment was approved to the 1964 master plan for the harbour. It allowed the dismantling of customs barriers and the modification of commercial land use to transform the docks into an urban area with functions related to services, tourism (also nautical), culture and leisure. Moreover, the establishment of the use of ship containers for freight transport physically prevented any further use of the Porto Antico docks for such purposes (Figure 8.1).

The indications contained in the amendment were aimed at kick-starting the refurbishment of the historic centre; creating areas for leisure activities; improving accessibility through metropolitan public transport; and improving mobility, parking, and the pedestrian use of spaces, with special regard to the areas facing the sea. For the part of the historic harbour between the Embriaco and the Morosini bridges, the master plan amendment foresaw the creation of a hub for nautical activities—a stretch of water of about 65,000 square metres that would welcome 800 boats.

In August 1988, the municipality of Genova commented positively on the amendments to the plan for the harbour and stressed how land uses—to be agreed between the municipality, the port authority and other competent bodies—needed to host other functions that were not competitive but instead in harmony with those already present in the neighbouring historic centre. Moreover, extreme permeability between the harbour and the city needed to be pursued through the removal of all fences and limitations on the space, which instead was to be open to public use.

At that time, a diffused and transversal consensus on the operation initiated by the local administration on the city's waterfront area started to develop among a wide stratum of the population and among the city's most prominent opinion leaders.

In May 1988, during a convention at the Istituto Gramsci Ligure, the idea came about to locate a big aquarium in one of the historic docks—following the example of what happened in the American city of Baltimore. With law no. 373 of 23 August 1988, which had the international exposition as its objective, definition of the project began once and for all.

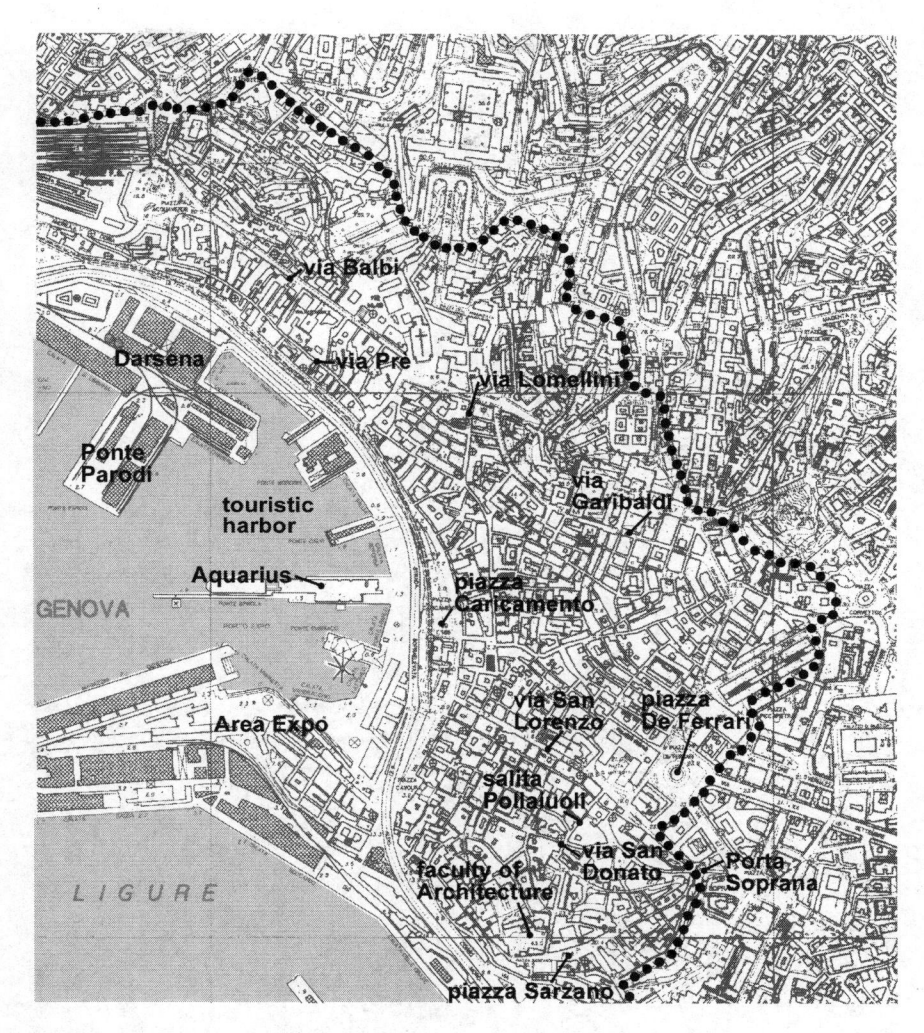

Figure 8.1 Plan of the old port and of the historic centre of Genova

There was the feeling that we were witnessing a concrete possibility of inverting the declining trend of the city, which throughout the 1980s had manifested a profound identity crisis because of the industrial depression (largely related to state heavy industry). A new awareness of the fact that the waterfront—refurbished and functionally reconnected to the city—could represent an opportunity to relaunch the city, also in terms of its image, started to spread widely. The idea that economic development in the fields of tourism and leisure could be achieved through appropriate promotion aimed at tapping into new opportunities thus became a widespread opinion.

The first results started to appear in 1992, with the 'Christopher Columbus: the Ship and the Sea' international exhibition, part of the programme of celebrations for the 500th anniversary of the discovery of the Americas by the Genoese sailor Christopher Columbus. The project involved the most diverse purposes for this area, with regard to both the exteriors (an area with streets, spaces and squares, all by the sea) and internal aspects of, among others, the Magazzini del Cotone (cotton warehouses), a building about 400 metres long.

The project consisted of permanent structures and works which, once the exposition activities were over, would provide the set of urban functions. Starting from the wharves facing Palazzo San Giorgio, the exposition area stretched for about 5 hectares, from the Molo Vecchio to the Spinola Bridge, and it bordered the Deposito Franco building and the area in front of the Porta Siberia gate (Figure 8.2). It comprised 416,000 square metres, including the spaces for the exhibition (Magazzini del Cotone), parking lots, commercial areas, a convention centre, the aquarium and the Piazza delle Feste (Figure 8.3), overlooked by the Grande Bigo,[2] a symbol of the event.

The process of urban transformation, requalification and maintenance involving the historic centre of Genova and the Porto Antico waterfront began in 1992, and was later confirmed and evolved with the G8 Summit held in July 2001 and Genova's election as the European Capital of

Figure 8.2 Old port and aquarium

Culture in 2004. These events contributed positively to triggering processes to reverse the trend of physical, economic and social decline that were present in many parts of the central area of the city. They also contributed to the creation of a new open waterfront space in the city forming a connection between the historic port basin and the ancient nucleus of the city (characterized by an urban system with a medieval matrix, which in later ages developed through the spread of building renovations and construction of super-elevations, with some large structural interventions, such as the opening of some streets with sixteenth- to eighteenth-century buildings).

At the same time, other public works were included in this renovation strategy, some of which took place in the historic centre, such as the restoration of the Sant'Agostino museum complex and the opening of the Tosse Theatre, and others in nearby areas, including the Palazzo Ducale cultural centre and the Carlo Felice Theatre (Seassaro 2001; Gastaldi 2004b; Gastaldi 2010).

The waterfront-historic centre binomial also featured in more substantial urban policy decisions during the 1990s and the first few years of the 2000s, similarly catalyzing greater interest and more funding. Consequently, the interest in this area has progressively grown to be representative of the whole city (Gastaldi 2005; Guala 2005).

Figure 8.3 A view of the central area of the port of Genova

Interventions related to big events (urban renovation and maintenance, such as renewal of public spaces, and restoration of the building facades and of the main places of architectural value) have been carried out in context of changes to the road network, the consolidation of a pedestrianized city, the regularization of traffic flows with the goal of emphasizing the sense of identity of the population (Piazza de Ferrari, Via Garibaldi with its museum centre) and in the context of new axes or urban hubs (Via San Lorenzo, the Expo area and the façades of Sottoripa, Via Cairoli and Via Balbi).

In conjunction with the public interventions related to these great events, the public administration encouraged the transformation process by attracting other forms of capital that were external to the ordinary budget, to use them for the central area of the city: EU integrated or complex funding programmes for urban redevelopment (Urban Programme II), national and regional Italian programmes, and public-private partnerships have all acted on the commercial fabric of the city. These programmes created a synergy between the physical enhancements of buildings and public spaces (quite significant ones, like Piazza Sarzano, Piazza delle Erbe, and Salita del Prione) and socio-economic revitalization programmes.

After the 1992 celebrations, the Società Porto Antico S.p.a. was established. The municipality of Genova had a 80% holding and the Chamber of

Figure 8.4 Old port and view of Genova

Commerce—which was and still is the licensee (until 2050) for 71,000 square metres of covered surface and 59,000 square metres of open space—had a 20% holding. The company's objective, according to its articles of association, was to manage the waterfront real estate in such a way as to support the creation of new functions that could change the area into a centre attracting national and international tourism (Figure 8.4). The Genova Aquarium opened in 1992 for the Expo, and in twenty years it has become the main driving force in redefining the waterfront in terms of tourism and leisure (with more than 1.2 million visitors per year).

Furthermore, as for the Darsena, the relocation of the Faculty of Economics and Commerce to the Cembalo neighbourhood has created new residential and commercial functions, and the Nautical High School has also been relocated here too. In addition, the Famagosta neighbourhood was demolished. This was followed by the partial reconstruction of the Bacinetto Building. Also, the Museum of the Sea and Navigation at Galata was set up as part of the 2004 event, and the neighbourhoods of Caffa and Metellino restored.

In the case of the Darsena, the works were also part of a strategy to recover declining areas that were no longer utilized as part of the port and could therefore be returned to the city. This operation was solidly based on the introduction of functions that integrated tourism with cultural attractions, safeguarding the memory of the port environment.

During the 1980s the historic centre of Genova (113 hectares, 20,000 inhabitants) was struck by a serious phase of decay affecting its built heritage as well as the quality of its public areas. Furthermore, the city's commercial network had been seriously weakened by the closure of many port-related economic activities, which resulted in the gathering of high rates of marginalized people in this area. The recent influx of non-EU immigrants further and often dramatically complicated the situation, creating social alarm to the extent that the area became progressively ostracized by the people of Genova, who considered it an area to avoid. In common opinion, the historic centre was considered a dangerous place, a progressively marginalized area and a symbol of the city's crisis, where negative elements could settle and be amplified.

At the beginning of the 1990s, some new events—resulting from a clear strategy agreed to by public policymakers—offered a first sign of a reversal in the trends. An important role in the complex process of urban regeneration and active valorization of the waterfront-historic centre nucleus was played by the University of Genova, which put down roots within the heart of the city, transferring some faculties there at the beginning of the 1990s such as the Faculty of Economics and the Faculty of Architecture, and strengthening other existing structures. As part of a programme to increase its teaching space, the Faculty of Literature and Philosophy has purchased a new building and has been redesigning its entrances towards the area of Via di Prè, one of the most derelict parts of the district.

All these activities, especially the works on the road system and on the historical buildings (Palazzi dei Rolli), have led UNESCO to recognize the historic centre of Genova as a World Heritage Site.

A total of 650 million euros were spent between 1993 and 2005, the larger part of which was made available by public organizations other than the municipality of Genova (approximately 75%).[3]

All these public policy decisions and actions have triggered enduring processes of improvement and regeneration of the urban quality, favouring subsequent projects including the involvement of private operators. In turn, this has nourished an increase in the value of some areas, changed the image of the city, led the people of Genova to rediscover their own city, revitalized the property market and gradually increased tourism.

The first signs of development in the wake of gentrification were seen in the first half of the 1990s. It is important to note how this process in Genova has not occurred because of all-inclusive targeted planning, nor as a result of a strategy put into practice by large property operations: it is in fact the consequence of a series of individual actions (not initially predictable) that have spontaneously triggered greater transformations through a micro-adaptation of the residential housing stock, the social fabric and the economic situation from the bottom up. Meanwhile, during recent years Genova has progressively chosen to limit other forms of expansion on the hillside areas that surround the city, and has, most importantly, directed attention and invested resources in the oldest part of the city.

In the Porto Antico area tourists make up a new temporary population, whose visits are increasing throughout the city thanks to the effect of the aquarium and to the renewed cultural attractions which place Genova inside the circuit of the Italian cities of art.

The Piazza Caricamento area has been increasingly set up as a 'main entrance' for the arrival of tourist groups (coaches and organized trips) and also in part for tourists arriving by car, as well as for those coming to the city via the Piazza Principe railway station. The most popular tourist tours of the city move along Via San Lorenzo, a favoured route towards the most famous attractions of the city (the cathedral, Palazzo Ducale and Porta Soprana).

On one hand, there remains widespread prejudice against walking on foot, especially with regard to the less-frequented alleys which are still considered to be dangerous. On the other hand, the maintenance of port activities (ferries, cruise liners) inside the Porto Antico basin is recognized as a positive strategic factor that safeguards the 'urban image' and identity of the neighbourhood.

The layout of Genova's historic centre follows the pattern of a medieval settlement which has highly stratified along the centuries (buildings have been joined together and built up, inner alleys closed and blocked), with numerous aristocratic palazzi of high architectural value. In this context, restoration actions are extremely complex. They often require burdensome procedures in terms of analysis, time and money.

The actions under way are part of a municipal administration strategy which considers the phase of the city's expansion on the hills definitively over and instead focuses on the restoration of the historic built heritage and pays greater attention to urban quality (regeneration of historic centres, industrial suburbs, districts of council housing). The municipality's main objective consists of a progressive regeneration of the central historic area (closely related to the waterfront regeneration process) and for this reason the different programmes follow the same goals: to promote and fund specific interventions on the built heritage in order to trigger widespread and spontaneous restoration processes. According to the public administration's strategy, once triggered, such regeneration actions should become self-perpetuating, and therefore should not give rise to further requests or dependence on public funds. The local administration has decided to focus its numerous efforts on the weakest areas (Via dei Giustiniani, Piazza delle Vigne, the Maddalena District) where spontaneous regeneration actions do not tend to occur, in an attempt to support and trigger wider mechanisms of diffused and spontaneous urban regeneration. In many cases they are targeted projects where the public body plays a coordinating role among different (also private) agents involved at different levels. The main actions are promoted jointly by the municipality, ARRED (Agenzia Regionale per il Recupero Edilizio—Regional Agency for the Building Heritage Restoration), ARTE (former IACP, Institute for Public Housing), the university, the port authority and private contractors (single or in partnership).

The projects that started in the mid 1990s involved a multidimensional and integrated approach to deal with problems such as the decay of the economic, employment and social structure, decline in the state of repair of the built heritage and in the quality of public spaces. As a result, the municipal administration is undertaking some major changes in its decision-making procedures and in its operating mode, promoting a relationship between private and public agents capable of creating effective transformation processes in one of the most complex and decayed areas of the city. Moreover, the municipality has shown a great ability to draft projects aimed at acquiring regional, national and EU resources and, accordingly, at implementing an administrative practice marked by a feeling of competitiveness among public bodies.

Today these actions are also fostering many interventions by private contractors, and we can observe direct benefits on the social and economic structure (increase in tourism, opening of new economic activities, built heritage restoration processes). Moreover, it is important to observe how the interventions accomplished have affected symbolic and particularly representative sites and buildings in the urban fabric—places that convey the image of the city, places that the citizens can identify as part of their daily life. These interventions gave a vital contribution to casting light on and unveiling the city's hidden resources (historical-cultural heritage, sea environment) and to making the inhabitants aware that such resources can promote new chances of economic development.

Conclusions

There are many elements that, starting from the case of Genova, could be key features for improving the institutional capacity of other cities. The organization and management of projects linked to great events (Columbus Expo 1992, G8 Summit, Genova Capital of Culture 2004) have been experiences of particular interest because of the ability of the public authorities, within a limited time frame, to manage programmes and negotiations between the public and private sectors. Moreover, the experience has created knowledge, intangible resources (activated during the processes), networks of relations, capacities and competences of remarkable importance. Genova's public administration has even been able to rediscover and reactivate competences and capacities that it was not conscious of having. Moreover, these big events have acted as a stimulus towards a rediscovery and active valorization of elements of identity, triggering new directions of development.

The relocation of the Faculty of Architecture has played a leading role, but all the other transformations that have followed through the course of time have supported the phenomena. Processes of urban regeneration have caused a progressive development of a new consciousness throughout the city with regard to the cultural value of the historic centre. The large rise in property values confirms the results achieved. The trend in property values therefore represents a significant measurement of the effects induced by urban transformations and is a useful indicator of the effectiveness of the work undertaken.

The restoration of the waterfront and the maintenance operations in the historic centre have led residents to change their perception of their own city. The renewed ownership of the waterfront and the notable quantity of historical places recuperated, and the conversion of large disused industrial sites through the introduction of new uses, have translated into a growing sense of belonging, and have reinforced elements of identity through the rediscovered use of collective and representative functions at a metropolitan level. In addition, the overall image of the city is seen from the outside not only as more linked to the harbour and industry (which had often been seen in a static or decadent way), but also as a new element linked to art, culture, architectural beauty and new forms of acceptance in a dynamic and more progressive vision.

Notes

1   A previous version of this paper was presented at the national convention of the Italian Association of Landscape Architecture, which was titled 'Landscape and Archeology' and was held in Naples on 7 June 2013.
2   The Bigo is inspired by the crane historically used in Genova's harbour to load and offload goods, and contains a panoramic lift.
3   Interventions for the organization of the Expo in 1992 are not included (Source: Comune di Genova).

Bibliography

Atkinson, R. and Bridge, G. (eds.) (2005), *Gentrification in a Global Contest: The New Urban Colonialism*, Routledge, London

Gabrielli, B. (2005), 'Politiche per la città di Genova', *Urbanistica Informazioni* vol. 202, pp. 19–20

Gabrielli, B. (2006), 'Genova: Una grande manutenzione', *Economia della Cultura* vol. 4, pp. 565–572

Gastaldi, F. (2004a), 'Rigenerazione e promozione urbana a Genova: Dal piano della città a Genova città europea della cultura 2004', in Fedeli, V. and Gastaldi, F. (eds.), *Pratiche strategiche di pianificazione. Riflessioni a partire da nuovi spazi urbani in costruzione*, FrancoAngeli, Milano, pp. 64–79

Gastaldi, F. (2004b), 'Genova: La difficile transizione verso un'economia "a più vocazioni"', *Equilibri* vol. 1, pp. 29–38

Gastaldi, F. (2005), 'E dopo il 2004? Necessità di sguardi e di azioni su un'altra Genova', *Gomorra* vol. 8, pp. 92–97

Gastaldi, F. (2009), 'Rigenerazione urbana e processi di Gentrification nel Centro Storico di Genova', in Diappi, L. (ed.), *Rigenerazione Urbana e ricambio sociale. Gentrification in atto nei quartieri storici italiani*, FrancoAngeli, Milano, pp. 89–116

Gastaldi, F. (2010), 'Genova. La riconversione del waterfront portuale. Un percorso con esiti rilevanti. Storia, accadimenti, dibattito', in Savino, M. (ed.), *Waterfront d'Italia. Piani politiche progetti*, FrancoAngeli, Milano, pp. 88–104

Guala, C. (2005), 'The Carnival is over: Genova 2004 e dintorni', *Urbanistica Informazioni* vol. 204, pp. 63–65

Guala, C. (2007), *Mega Eventi: Modelli e storie di rigenerazione urbana*, Carocci Editore, Roma

Petrillo, A. (2004), 'Dopo la grande tristezza. Ripensando vent'anni di periferie genovesi', *Urbanistica Informazioni* vol. 193, pp. 41–42

Pichierri, A. (1989), *Strategie contro il declino di aree di antica industrializzazione*, Rosenberg & Sellier, Torino

Rugafiori, P. (ed.) (2004), *Genova del Saper Fare: Lavoro, imprese, tecnologie*, Skirà Editore, Milano

Seassaro, L. (2001), 'Tra porto e città: Logiche aziendali, neoutilitarismo e contrattualismo', *Urbanistica Informazioni*, vol. 178, pp. 45–46

Smith, N. (2001), 'Rescaling politics geography, globalism and new urbanism', in Minca, C. (ed.), *Postmodern Geography: Theory and Praxis*, Blackwell, Oxford, pp. 147–168

Zukin S. (1982) *Loft Living: Culture and Capital in Urban Change*, John Hopkins UP, Baltimora

Zukin S. (1995), *The Cultures of the Cities*, Blackwell, Oxford

The Difficulties Faced by
Waterfront Renewal Projects
in Italy

Rosario Pavia

Unlike other parts of the world, in Italy waterfront renewal programmes have almost never managed to make it off the drawing board. With the exception of Genoa, designed by Renzo Piano, our country boasts no important waterfront experiences. I will try to explain why.

Waterfront renewal has a relatively short history and is closely linked to the reorganization of port systems. Underlying this process is the 'containerization' of maritime transport. The container has revolutionized the dimensions and technologies of ports and ships. It was responsible for introducing globalization processes into the maritime and port economy. It began in the United States and in the ports of northern Europe, and it soon produced the decentring of harbour activities to more suitable areas, far from the city. In the end, it was precisely this decentring that freed up many harbours that had been absorbed by the growth of the city. They soon became the basic ingredient for waterfront renewal programmes. Beginning in the 1970s in North America, from New York to San Francisco to Baltimore, the process soon extended to London, Amsterdam, Hamburg and later to Barcelona. London and Barcelona would become paradigmatic examples; their waterfronts became strategic areas for the renovation of the entire city. The process is now in full swing in other European cities, as well as in Shanghai, Shenzhen, Hong Kong, Dubai and Buenos Aires, entrusted to the vast club of the architectural and engineering star system.

Why has this process never gone beyond competitions and proposals in Italy?

The first answer to this question lies in the fact that, unlike in other countries, Italian ports were never the object of important processes of delocalization (only Genoa and Trieste were witness to a partial decentralization of their harbour activities). Actively functioning in the heart of the city, in material terms Italy's ports are separate bodies with respect to their urban surroundings. Many years ago Italian cities lost their ties with the sea and their harbour spaces. This fracture was sanctioned at the institutional and administrative level. On one hand, we find municipal governments with their urban master plans; on the other, the port authorities (for minor ports, the Port Captaincies Corps maritime authority) with their port master plans.

These two master plans pursue different objectives and different logics, despite the introduction of law no. 84/94 (the Italian Port Reform Law) imposing coordination and agreement between these institutions. Yet this is not enough: the time required for the approval of a port plan is extremely lengthy and poses a serious obstacle to waterfront renewal programmes; for their part, urban master plans are often too indefinite and lacking the proper normative references governing areas of overlap between port and city.

Given the lack of a process of delocalization, and hindered by the intense urbanization of coastal areas, waterfront projects in Italy are forced to fully accept a complex reality that imposes a forced coexistence between city and port.

Structurally, waterfront areas are areas of conflict. This conflict pitches various interests and powers against one another: the municipal government, the port authority, heritage committees and port operators. The latter, concessionaires of state-owned lands, benefit from consolidated advantageous positions. Their presence as members of decision-making boards of port authorities (the Harbour Committee) often becomes an obstacle to any programme of waterfront renewal able to question the current state of affairs. These are the real reasons why it is so difficult to implement urban projects in waterfront areas.

From this point of view, the waterfronts in Naples and Taranto are exemplary. The following sections offer a closer look.

Naples

In 2004 the Naples Port Authority announced an international competition for the renewal of the monumental waterfront of the Port of Naples: an extremely complex area in front of the Maschio Angioino medieval castle, situated between the quay of San Vincenzo, the Beverello quay and the complex of the Immacolatella. The centre of this area is occupied by the beautiful Maritime Station designed by Cesare Bazzani and countless large cruise ships. Automotive congestion, disorganization and the advanced state of decay of the quays have impeded, and continue to impede, the city's ability to make use of this extraordinary waterfront.

The competition, carefully prepared by Nausicaa (comprising the Port Authority and the municipal, provincial and regional governments), focused its requests to participants on the necessary coexistence between the working port and the city. This was the central node of the competition and the project.

In 2005, after two phases, the jury, under the direction of Professor Bernardo Secchi, awarded the competition to the entry entitled *Euvè*. This project gave the theme of the waterfront an urban dimension, proposing a grand public space open to the water and strongly interconnected with the city. The project was clearly attentive to the operational problems of the port, though decisive about its intentions to restore the historic relationship between the city and its harbour.

The project concentrated on the margin between port and city, between Via Nuova Marina and the Del Piliero quay (the point of departure for the large ferries serving Sicily), and between Via Ammiraglio Acton and the Beverello quay (the mooring point for ferries to the islands and the rest of the Gulf of Naples). This port context, with its ships and its flows, served as the backdrop to the project, the spectacle to be restored to the city. Its position along the city boundary was a way of allowing the port to continue operating. The project transformed this line separating city and port into a 'filtering line', offering the city the possibility of looking out over its port without interfering with its activities. The requirement to improve visibility of the port was resolved by shaping the ground plane and lowering the level of the 'filtering line'. This element was imagined as a commercial street set into the ground. Atop this element, almost as a continuation of Via Nuova Marina, there was to be a long walkway open towards the port and interconnected with the galleria (designed by Alvaro Siza), connecting the Maritime Station with the Piazza del Municipio metro station. The walkway was to continue along the Beverello quay, exploiting the roof of a new passenger terminal. The 'filtering line' was used to structure the relocated volumes of buildings that the competition brief called for to be demolished.

From 2005 to 2008 a series of appeals impeded the awarding of the design. In 2008 the winning group began developing the project, submitting the designs on schedule in 2009. Upon submission, the director of the local monuments Heritage Committee, the architect Stefano Gizzi, prohibited the destruction of the building known as the Magazzini Generali (wholesale warehouses), which had been designed by Marcello Canino (though only half built) and situated on the Del Piliero quay—and this despite the fact that the competition brief clearly called for its demolition. After a phase of negotiations, the Naples Port Authority decided to accept the Heritage Committee's suggestions, promoting a protocol of understanding between the Port Authority, Nausicaa, the City of Naples, the Heritage Committee and the constitution of a technical work group to orient and evaluate the design activities in accordance with specific suggestions.

After the winning group developed the guidelines expressed by the work group, the project was redefined in 2010. The Magazzini Generali building was placed at the centre of the waterfront reorganization. The building was divided into two fronts, the first almost flush with the water and consisting of the Magazzini Generali restored to their original dimensions; the second defined by the filtering line system, rendered lighter and more coherent with the needs of the city and local operators.

The new arrangement (Figures 9.1 and 9.2) had already received initial evaluation and signs of acceptance, not the least of which being the approval in 2011 of the technical and functional modernization of the Beverello quay by the High Council for Public Works, meaning that this part of the project could begin construction immediately. The approvals process could later be concluded through a formal local authorities planning conference, which

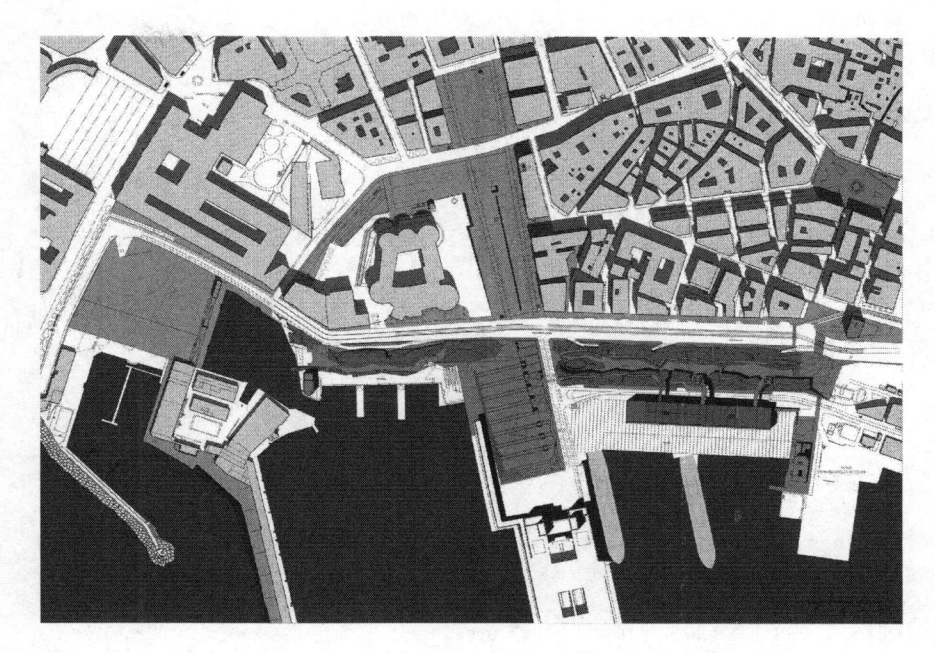

Figure 9.1 Between the harbour and the city. Redevelopment project for the monumental waterfront of Napoli (IT). Master plan.

Figure 9.2 Redevelopment project of the monumental waterfront of Napoli (IT). Rendering of the ferry-boat terminal at the Molo Beverello.

would render the project truly buildable. Instead, the imminent possibility that the project would actually be realized gave rise to strong opposition from the Harbour Committee itself, in particular a group of operators who wished to maintain the status quo. Nausicaa was disbanded, the port plan has yet to be approved and the new municipal government has yet to examine the fate of such a strategic area for the city. After seven years, the polemics have abated into silence, with the serious risk of making so much work worthless.

Taranto

The recovery of the S. Cataldo quay as a waterfront pursues the objective of reintegrating the city of Taranto and its port (Figure 9.3). This is to be achieved through a system of pedestrian interconnections from the S. Eligio quay and Piazza Fontana, extending to the extremity of the S. Cataldo quay, with its statue of the saint.

This operation, made possible by the relocation of the eastern port entrance, is founded atop the realization of a lengthy landscaped walkway that runs from the old city, along the Porta Napoli bridge, continuing as a long promenade that wraps around the eastern side of S. Cataldo quay at 3 metres above sea level.

The promenade becomes the backbone of the new waterfront. Its development will make possible the reorganization of pedestrian and bicycle paths, improve service vehicle traffic and allow access to loading/unloading areas in the harbour. Raising this surface above grade separates pedestrian, urban and port traffic. The continuity of the promenade creates a vast public space linking the historic city with the end of the port, served by new facilities for sport, leisure and recreational activities.

The end of the promenade is marked by a new mixed-use building that becomes a focal point overlooking the sea and the city. The process of introducing a new waterfront culture to the City of Taranto begins with this complex system that links the port, the city and the environment with a single new element.

The architectural concept driving the design of the mixed-use building improves the conditions of the site. With respect to the road level and the ground level of the Port Authority building, the enlargement of the eastern docks of the S. Cataldo quay, part of the port programme, produces a level change of 1.5 metres. The area of intervention, situated between the eastern docks and the operative quay to the west, thus assumes the form of a basin.

This basin becomes the matrix of the architectural design. Exploiting this change in level allows for an optimization of the available space and ensures the integration of the design of the mixed-use building with the rigid morphology of the quay. It recreates the close relationship with the loading/unloading dock and the nearby statue of S. Cataldo.

The immensity of the basin further divides the mixed-use building into two volumes and an open space. This latter opens onto a sunken Mediterranean garden, a *hortus conclusus*, protected by the height of the quay.

Inside the basin, the volumes slip past one another, extending toward the quays and the end of the dock, integrating vehicular and pedestrian flows.

The design of the mixed-use building follows the shape of the harbour basin, exploiting the level change between the docks and the level of the road. The 1.5-metre raised level is home to cultural functions (exhibition spaces, media library, virtual maritime museum) and a vast covered parking structure. On the upper level the complex is divided into two volumes separated by an open space that serves to ensure the continuity of the system of public spaces and landscaped areas of the urban itinerary along the S. Cataldo quay. On one side the building opens up to overlook the Mediterranean garden, created inside the empty space of the harbour, while on the other side it looks toward the docks. The volume adjacent to the eastern docks is linked to the loading/unloading areas, offering a multipurpose space for use by the Maritime Station (Figure 9.4). Here the design includes areas for ticketing, check-in, customs controls, seating, tourist information, spaces for local operators and dining facilities. The upper level serves as a belvedere for cruise ship passenger traffic.

The space between the two buildings functions as a plaza offering access to the Maritime Station and operators' offices, as well as to the spaces of the second volume. At the level of the internal plaza, this building contains a 250-seat auditorium, a multipurpose space for commercial activities and small offices. The upper level features a large restaurant-bar and a panoramic terrace. The roof of the building, accessible from a system of terraces, functions as a belvedere-solarium.

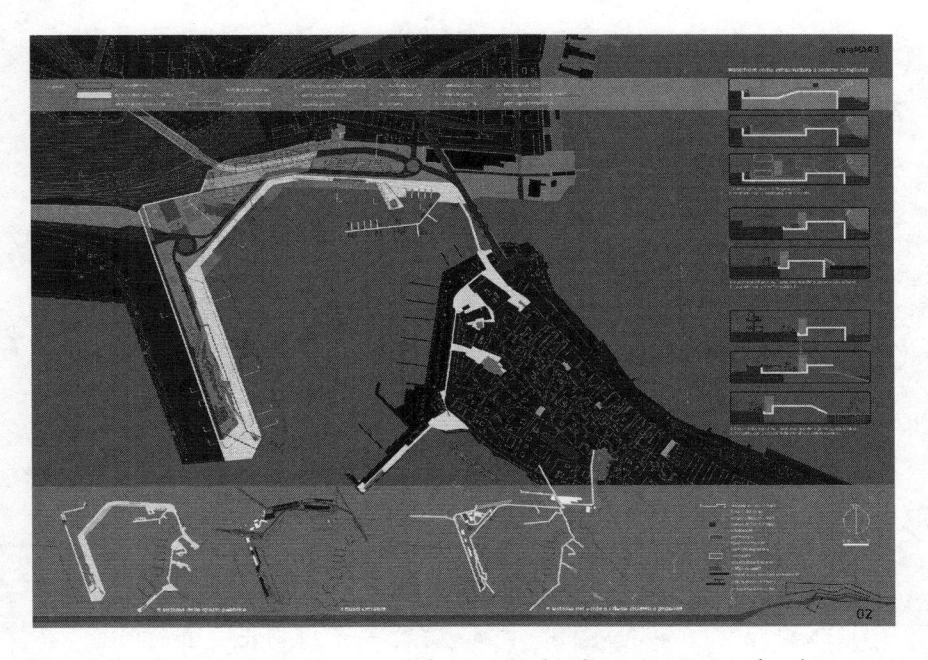

Figure 9.3 Between the harbour and the city. Redevelopment project for the waterfront of Taranto (IT). Master plan

Figure 9.4 Redevelopment project for the waterfront of Taranto (IT). Rendering of the Maritime Station.

The sinuous and organic forms of the two volumes extend towards the Mediterranean garden. The composition assumes the fluid form of a group of volumes and paths that extend towards the sea and the new point at the end of the quay and the statue of S. Cataldo. The new complex is poised to become a new centre of attraction that brings the city to sea. The mixed-use building is integrated with the very structure of the quay. The complex is born of the sea and the relationship between the city and its harbour.

The final design of the mixed-use building is currently in the approvals phase; however, the realization of the project is not without its obstacles. The levels of environmental pollution of the ground beneath the quays must be controlled. This will no doubt require remediation work and authorizations that will significantly delay completion of the project.

Prospects

The examples of Naples and Taranto demonstrate how difficult it is to implement waterfront renewal programmes in Italy. All the same, an important aspect regarding the project in Taranto must be pointed out, as it indicates an operative prospect for future development.

Unlike Naples, the master plan for the Port of Taranto is approved, and it excludes the project site from the area of its influence. This simplifies approval procedures because they belong to processes of urban planning and joint decisions taken by the city government and the port authority instead of being separate decisions. This important step requires further refinement as part of a more general revision of the current methods of preparing port and urban master plans. The Guidelines for the Preparation of Port Plans, defined by the Italian Ministry of Infrastructure and Transport twelve years ago (circular dated 15 October 2004, protocol no. 1777MM) need to be reviewed and simplified. It is necessary to use greater care when identifying areas in which it is possible to promote waterfront renewal programmes. When areas of overlap between the city and the port are situated outside the spaces of a port's daily operations, they can be defined and removed from the port plan. A similar modification should be defined as part of the joint agreements between municipal governments and port authorities established by law no. 84/94. Though complex, and accompanied by the difficulty in identifying an equilibrium between diverse interests (municipal government, port, private operators), the agreement is central to new strategies for the regeneration of port cities. In similar terms, there is a need for a specific national programme promoted by the Ministry of Territorial Cohesion and the Ministry of Infrastructure, created to manage a consistent quota of European Structural Funding (2014–20). A further step should also be taken into consideration: the definition of a single structural plan for cities and ports. This is the correct phase for identifying areas of overlap between cities and ports, the ideal sites for waterfront renewal programmes.

Bibliography

Pavia, R. (2010) *La riqualificazione del waterfront monumentale del porto di Napoli*, in *Portus*, 20: 25–29.

Pavia, R. (2010) Waterfront. L'interfaccia del conflitto, in Savino, M. (ed.) *Waterfront d'Italia. Piani, politiche, progetti*, Milano: Franco Angeli, 13–17.

Pavia, R. (2011) 'Waterfront Story', *Urbanistica*, 146: 82–87.

Pavia, R. and Di Venosa, M. (2012) *Waterfront. Dal Conflitto all'integrazione*, Trento: List.

10 Messina's Waterfront Regeneration

What a Chance to Reinvent the City!

Michelangelo Savino

Geographic, Historic and Economic Issues of a City and Its Port

While taking a look at the conformation and history of Messina, we can observe that its development along the centuries is the consequence of very peculiar factors and conditions.

First, its location in the middle of the Mediterranean Sea helped the city to become one of the most important emporium cities in history; second, its location in the Strait of Messina made the city a safe and sure haven in the dangerous crossing of that sea passage; third, its location in Sicily, on an extreme offshoot stretching towards the continent, made it a strategic military point and essential link from the island to the other part of the country; and fourth, the morphology of the site, characterized by rugged but weak mountains that have pushed the city towards the sea, around the deep basin of the historic port, encloses the mythical *Falce* (sickle) which protects it from a violent and aggressive sirocco. From the port, the city stretches along the Tyrrhenian Sea and Ionian Sea shores for almost 40 kilometres. History tells us of a rich and powerful city, not only a trade centre but an excellent place of production and cultural crossroads. Proud and rebellious, Messina made the Spanish viceroy in Sicily live here at least six months every year (spending the rest of the year in Palermo, the formal capital of the kingdom), and many times disputed the crown of Spain and kings of Naples' abuse of power, while suffering its immediate effects (such as economic penalties, political repressions and destruction: e.g. in 1678 when the city was intensely bombed by the Spanish army from its own citadel, or in 1848 with the siege of Bourbon kings of the Two Sicilies, and the alternate vicissitudes of the Second World War when the port and city were victims of attacks by both contenders).

History also tells us of a city that many times had to face devastating natural disasters and unbelievably—mainly after the destruction caused by the 1908 earthquake/seaquake—has been capable of rebuilding itself again every time, by making far-reaching changes to its urban structure, so much so that it is impossible to recognize the past in the current city framework: only the profile of the port is still recognizable, the thread of its history having been broken too many times.

Indeed, it is around the port that the city always found the reason and sense of its life, until not long ago: initially the port represented the main communication system with the continent, and also with other parts of the island, because the connections with nearby surroundings were very difficult and slow; then the outlet of a productive system that was very lively until 1908 (Messina was one of the first industrial sites in southern Italy); and after that the 'door to Sicily' and the main logistical core for flows of merchandise and people to and from Sicily, providing frequent connections throughout the Strait and to the island through the railway network.

During the 1950s and 1860s, Messina experienced a dynamic phase of post-war development that led to its transformation into an industrial and logistical city (one of the few in southern Italy at that time). The port and its trade were also triggers for industrial and technological innovation: the first hydrofoil was devised and built in Messina in 1956 (Musolino and Perna 2007).

All these elements persisted until the economic and social crisis came about that is still ongoing today. Despite the lack of wars and earthquakes, since the 1970s the city has recorded a decline: the cause is a deep-rooted social and economic decadence that has weakened the most dynamic forces in the city. Many industrial activities, such as commercial activities, are in trouble; meanwhile the weight of public administration has grown (supported by the state and regional welfare policies) to such an extent that it has become all encompassing. This declining situation has been taken over by real estate speculation, which after the 1908 earthquake substituted industry and trade as the main economic activities. Indeed, due to the effects of the quake on the fixed, financial and human capital, the rebuilding of the city became a tool and an aim of the urban economy,[1] owing to its unregulated expansion on the coastal plain, the river beds and the steep slopes of the mountains (La Spada 1996). The port activities were mostly reduced to ferries and cruises, and the port remained as a mere 'mirror' reflecting the more dense, compact, congested and disfigured city.

The events of these last three decades sum up a decline considered unstoppable by a lot of people. They are the results of a progressive exhaustion of resources, abilities and a worsening of the quality of life, in which only the option of a large-scale project seems to provide a solution capable of redeeming the city (Farinella 2008).

A New Vision of the City

The debates about the future of the city, which began at the end of the 1970s and have gone on until today, started from the common assumption that the first step should be its radical redevelopment. However, the main question has also concerned the role that the city must be able to build for itself.

The city has to be relaunched at a regional level: Messina is still the third largest city in Sicily, in terms of the number of inhabitants, but it is no longer a significant centre even within its own area, where other smaller but alternative towns are growing into hubs of financial, economic, cultural etc. import. Messina also has to be boosted at a supra-regional level, for instance, by strengthening relationships and supporting integration with the City of Reggio Calabria, to become an attractive 'metropolitan area of the Strait' for new investments and new business initiatives. Finally, it has to be relaunched at national and international levels by proposing a new image of itself, as a city of art and culture, a new tourist destination in the Mediterranean Sea. The ambitions are not lacking; what seems to be missing are strategies (and related policies), capable and determined stakeholders, and economic resources.

During the 1990s some conditions were going in its favour: large regional funding programmes to rehabilitate some highly decayed urban residential areas. At the same time, ministerial funding and EU funding supported other projects which joined new ideas for urban regeneration and economic revitalization. The proposal of a new city plan and a strategic plan stimulated a discussion about the city of the future. While the hypothesis of a 'metropolitan city of the Strait' (including the urban areas of Messina and Reggio Calabria on the opposite shore of the strait) has been set aside (for political reasons and because of 'practical' administrative issues, which have made difficult the relationships between the two cities belonging to different regions and with different statutes), the idea of a city that should invest in innovation (knowledge and technologies) or in more dynamic fields (such as tourism) has been going forward. The Messina 2020 Strategic Plan (Comune di Messina 2010),[2] first presented in July 2009, represents the synthesis of this vision and the first framework of public policies targeting the city's renewal.

With regard to the objective of changing Messina into a centre for innovation and knowledge-based economy, the city can rely on an ancient university and some international and prestigious research centres, but it seems to be lacking ideas and the social agents that could grant its implementation. For the second, easier to achieve objective, the city could take advantage of many resources: it could be the strategic hub for all the flows to eastern Sicily, the Aeolian Islands, southern Calabria, and even a focus for the main tourist routes, owing to its location in the Mediterranean Sea. In this way the port still represents a factor for real strategic development.

The Strategic Plan defines and integrates some project ideas (already introduced but not sufficiently outlined) included in the plan for the development of the port that was presented in 2004 (Autorità Portuale di Messina 2004).

Law no. 94/1984 set up the elimination of the old Enti Portuali and the institution of new bodies—the so-called Port Authority—with different competencies, assignments and special competencies on docklands and port areas, involving a whole rethinking of development strategies for the port

infrastructure and its modernization (Pavia and di Venosa 2006). Consequently, in 2005, the newly instituted Messina Port Authority drew up an
interesting enhancement plan. The Messina Port Development Plan proposed a different vision for the organization of the city, finding the local
government very unprepared.[3] It suggested transferring all the port facilities
for ferry services to the southern part of the city close to the edge of the
built-up area (Tremestieri); only the passenger connections with Calabria
were kept in the historic port, and all the industrial trade was relocated to
the port of Milazzo or the Giammoro terminal (to be built), 30 kilometres
westwards from the city. What is more, the historic port was designated for
tourist and cruise traffic functions only. This kind of choice involved maintaining some shipbuilding activities and renewing the port facilities but also
creating new accommodation, housing and leisure activities in the Falce,
involving the recovery of the archaeological ruins of the sixth-century military citadel, the institution of a modern art museum and a park. The site
next to the Palazzata (the built-up waterfront in the historic port, redesigned
after the 1908 earthquake) was proposed as the location for a new cruise
ship station (recovering the old customs house); on the area still occupied by
the disused Messina Exhibition buildings, and in place of the still-operating
private ferry terminal, the plan suggested public gardens, leisure activities
and a cultural centre. This area was redefined as a 'promenade', and new
and small leisure ports along the coast were to stimulate economic revitalization (Autorità Portuale di Messina 2006).

The Port Authority proposed an image of the city strongly devoted to
tourism where the port facilities, together with new accommodation and
new commercial activities, were intended to kick-start a whole regeneration
of the central areas of the city in order to become more welcoming for all
who would be stopping in the city during their Mediterranean cruise. More
interventions (mainly infrastructure on airports and roads) set out in the
plan were to make Messina not only a cruise stop, but also a boarding and
landing point for passengers.

The port would return to its role—in this vision—as the pulsing heart of
a new urban economy, but now voted to tourism.

From Port to Waterfront

The regeneration project for the port of Messina has more than these aspects
that could transform the urban organization, such as the cruise terminal
that supports a strong turn of local economy towards tourism and transforming Messina into a hub for passengers headed to theAeolian Islands,
to Reggio Calabria or Taormina; the empowerment of its cultural resources
supporting the building of new attractions; the enhancement of the quality
of life with the regeneration of declining urban areas; and the provision of
new facilities. At the same time, the resizing of the commercial activities and
development of a new cruise terminal would impose a large-scale redesign

of the port access through a city affected by highly congested urban traffic. Furthermore a reorganization of the railway network should be planned as well as improvement of the road infrastructures.

On many occasions it has been proposed to redraw the railway line, as in Messina—running along the coastline—it creates a break between the city and sea. Some years ago a rerouting of the railway line (at least an underground line despite some geological hindrances) was proposed, claiming government funds for the bridge on the Strait[4] to free access to the sea, plus relocation of the main station (and recovery of the old station for other, perhaps commercial purposes) and redevelopment of the partially vacant railway areas. Having to connect the new ferry terminal, located in the southernmost area of the city, to the historical port and having to find a solution for such a congested road network, the municipality (supported by the Port Authority) proposed a new motorway (along the coastline, the Via del Mare) to improve the north-south displacements in the city. All these infrastructural plans depend on the local government's resolution that all the coastal industrial areas—developed along the old railway line, according to the nineteenth-century zoning philosophy—can be considered suitable for new uses.

The whole area targeted by the redevelopment plan is a coastal strip of about 7.5 kilometres in length going from the Falce to the new ferry terminal in Tremestieri, with a width of 450–600 metres. Overall, it is an area of about 359 hectares, 10% of which are currently occupied by railway infrastructure; its regeneration could involve not only the waterfront but also all the city behind, the built-up plain and the narrow valleys densely occupied by public housing in a state of great decay.

The waterfront design is a great urban regeneration opportunity that is more than coastal area redevelopment, more than the realization of new public spaces and new commercial and tourist facilities, more than the building of large urban facilities and new residential zones (Bruttomesso 2006): it is the concept of a new urban organization which can involve a variety of parts of the city. It is the construction of a different economic and social structure, which can lead to a different scenario for the future of the city (Savino 2010a).

The Redesigned Waterfront

In the first documents (according to the concept already presented in the Strategic Plan) for the waterfront plan—PIAU, or Innovative Urban Programme, according to the ministry prescriptions—it was evident that there had been a profound change in the meaning of the waterfront renewal, as well as in the political rhetoric, as it now integrated some indications from the Port Plan concerning new uses for the historical port and the new ferry terminal, with a clear formulation of the new urban functions that would be developed along the coast (Comune di Messina 2009).

Despite the fact that the historic port is to keep its traditional functions, though renewed by a new cruise passenger terminal, all of the southern coast band would be affected by a far-reaching urban transformation. The first step of this regeneration process is the renewal of the Falce, with the replacement of the old industrial plants, part of the shipyard and the navy areas, with new housing, commercial activities, accommodations, a marina, a park, the citadel museum and an archaeological area. Then, while preserving the historic listed railway station building, all the railway area is to be transformed into a new urban area, where prestigious public buildings (for services and equipment), private uses (mainly hotels and other accommodation facilities, such as a congress centre and leisure activities) have to be promoted and green areas should change the face of the present city. The new city, from the Falce to the future railway station, would replace existing industrial areas, stimulating the 'spontaneous' regeneration of twentieth-century built-up areas (so it is supposed!). Southward from the future railway station (forecasted for an area of 40 hectares), the plan hypothesizes a large commercial area (approximately 13 hectares, next to the area where unplanned and congesting malls, shops and commercial activities need to be reorganized) close to the research and technological innovation centre,[5] a planned freight terminal platform near the Tremestieri terminal[6] and a junction with the proposed Via del Mare and the existing highway.

This not-well-defined plan proposes a radical urban regeneration that should outline a brand-new urban fabric, the removal of all infrastructural barriers, the realization of large new public facilities, the recovery of the beach, and the creation of beach resort facilities for inhabitants and tourists, accommodations, etc.

The municipality decided to hold an international competition for the design of the new area: in its guidelines for the competitors, the municipality provided a synthesis of all the studies about site conditions that could be useful for the designers. It also asked MBM (a firm from Barcelona), Oriol Bohigas and his staff,[7] for a sketch, a sort of preliminary master plan.

The proposal was interesting as well as disruptive. The MBM group proposed a complete redrawing of the coast with an artificial island and a strong skyline in contrast to the traditional shape of the city; in addition, a large urban park (35 hectares) was proposed to connect the Falce, downtown and the new waterfront areas, providing the location for significant attractive metropolitan-scale facilities for art, culture, tourism and leisure. This would be a powerful urban driving force for the relaunch of the city.

An innovative element was represented by digging a new sea arm for leisure port activities (in the place of the railway area) which separated the city from the new artificial island, about 12 hectares in size (the 'Marina'), where tourist and recreational amenities should be concentrated; high skyscrapers would tower up on the island and would design a new city profile. This represents a truly unusual proposal for Messina (maybe just in a challenging way) and a strong break with the past. Indeed, building development in Messina has never gone against a more or less low-building tradition, inherited from post-earthquake rebuilding and due to the national anti-seismic regulations. The MBM project tried to lay down a scenario that completely changes the conservative images of the city.

The daring preliminary indications in the MBM design were modified by the administration's guidelines for the contest held in November 2010: the artificial island disappeared, but not the suggestion of high-density buildings (which would be proposed in many designs), the sea arm was erased but the leisure port—[8]though moved elsewhere—remained in all the presented projects.

A Disputed Contest

The first phase of the competition ended on July 2011. Five design groups were selected to take part in the second phase of the competition, with a more detailed master plan than the concept proposed in the first phase.[9] The participants were also requested to create a preliminary design for a multifunctional service centre to be located in the vacant railway area. The second phase, with delivery of the projects extended to February 2011, was in actual fact concluded in July 2012. The group Favero & Milan[10] was announced as winner of the contest.

The winning design focuses the regeneration on a new Piazza Europa (located in the vacant railway area), which is dominated by a tall multifunctional service centre towering over the area, highlighting the city profile. A hotel and private service buildings (about 13,000 square metres) and new residential block (112,000 square metre surface area, of which 101,000 residential, 8,000 tourist accommodation and 3,250 for commercial activities) overlook the seafront, where the lodging area is south-facing to enjoy an incomparable view over the Strait. A large park completes the regeneration of the central area facing the leisure port, partially dug into the existing coastline, which is protected by breakwaters. At the north and south edge of this new 'urban heart', two more low-density roof-terraced residential blocks are proposed (13,000 square metres in the northern side of the citadel district, 24,000 square metres in the southern part of the regenerated area). The road connecting the historical port and the southern area of the city crosses the residential district located in a green area.

The final ranking was contested by the other competitors and final judgement was suspended on appeal to the TAR (Regional Administrative Court) presented by the runners up in the competition. As is usually the case in (local, national or international) competitions held in Messina, everything was stopped and the waterfront regeneration process came to a halt. Is this just for the moment?

The court case has put to an end the enthusiasm and interest in the competition; the contest results were not published nor the designs widely discussed.

There have been no public debates about the outcomes of the competition and about any feasible urban frame for the future of the city.

The End of the Story?

The epilogue to the waterfront competition has opened many questions about the future of the city. First of all, the debate about what the city can achieve appears to have been interrupted, or at least postponed; the unfair end to the competition, instead of stimulating a broad public discussion about the new urban organization and the waterfront redevelopment—mainly about the urban regeneration resulting from such a large-scale design—completely put a stop to any debate about the city's future. Whether the suggested architectural solution by the competition winner can be appreciated or not, it should be supposed that the projects or the original urban solutions could be good suggestions[11] for urban renewal. The natural outcome of the competition should be an intense community debate about a new city layout. In this perspective the first aim of the competition very much failed.

The opportunity for a new city design to push towards the formulation of an awe-inspiring scenario for the future of the city at this moment in time seems to be lost. In the same way, to a certain extent the chance to mobilize the community and the social and economic stakeholders seems to have vanished, it could be said.

Likewise, the conclusion of the competition did not accelerate the debate for a new city master plan, a framework that could not be lacking in a design of such importance because it represents the political framework for all regeneration processes. Only the city master plan can assure a coherent integration of regeneration projects (which usually only interest finite parts of the city) in the general development of the city and attempt to create the political and cultural conditions for one to be started.

About the waterfront that should be rocking the boat, nothing seems to be shaking!

The economic crisis, however, is having a dramatic impact: by cutting (financial, technical, human) resources for public institutions that would be the promoters or at least triggers of the regeneration process and weakening the restricted panel of private stakeholders, who in southern Italy are few and not willing to act unless conditions are very much in their favour).

The latest political change in the *local government* of Messina has created more doubts about the future of the waterfront regeneration process. The new mayor—very appreciated by the population and also renowned in the international press for his unconventional profile—[12]and the city council are facing a dramatic political and economic situation. The agenda has been seriously changed by different political issues and the rigorous abandonment of large projects.

The dreaded financial default of the municipality, the collapses of the public transport company and waste collection department, the lack of resources for welfare politics in a city that is finding itself poorer and needier, where the already scarce quantity of public facilities are now becoming profoundly insufficient in terms of quality too, has led to an expected suspension of urban regeneration. These circumstances are also causing a sort of distrust towards great urban projects suspected of draining resources intended for more useful public interventions.

Waterfront regeneration (as many public interventions in Italy, but mostly in Sicily show, where it is possible to visit a virtual museum of unfinished public works)[13] does not seem to assure real urban regeneration nor an improvement in the quality of life, but only provides a magnificent stage set against a background of urban miseries!

Undoubtedly, in Italy at least, the first phase of waterfront regeneration has not been at all convincing (Savino 2010b): it has not proven to be a decisive turn in the way of designing the city nor provided impressive arguments for the port or waterfront to be the starting point for a new strategy to conceive innovative regeneration policies and tools.

Could it be possible, with the crisis behind us, to construct the conditions for a second and really innovative chapter in waterfront regeneration that would become a new opportunity for an urban renaissance?

Notes

1 According to many studies, the construction industry became the dominant economic activity in the city, replacing manufacturing and trade, anticipating the forms of contemporary capitalism. The rebuilding of the destroyed city, the provision of private and public dwellings, as well as the development of public building and facilities (using national funds and government support) was the tool of entrepreneurs for enrichment; real estate speculation was the aim of all economic activities and urban policies, including planning (Saitta 2013).

2 See www.comune.messina.it/messina2020/, last access October 11 2015.

3 Indeed, the municipality's first reaction was staunch opposition to the plan. It was later approved only in 2007, after the local administration's resignation and substitution by a special commissioner.

4 The project of a 'permanent connection' over the Strait of Messina is a dramatic issue that is still in progress. Since the 1970s it has influenced many city development plans, however, a real solution for the connection has never been implemented. During the past decade the bridge project was subject to incredible acceleration, mainly during the right-wing governments which pushed not only for a technical design for the bridge structure, but also land reorganization and a new infrastructure system related to bridge access. Major changes were planned for the whole structure of the city (deviation or closure of a railway track, building of a new railway station, new highway access to the city and consequently the reorganization of the main regional road system). Everything would have to be funded with resources provided for construction of the bridge, as 'compensatory works for the city'. The continuous (mostly political) uncertainties about the future of the project have made many of these projects totally unlikely (Bettini *et al.* 2002; Pieroni 2000). The current economic crisis probably means that the bridge project has been given up once and for all, despite the significant funding spent to complete feasibility studies and surveys, obtain soil core samples and

acquire the first expropriations of the areas for building the bridge structures and the 1 kilometre of railway track in Villa San Giovanni.

5 The technological and education centre for innovative renewable energy technologies was to consist of a science centre, advanced services for enterprises and a higher education centre.

6 The 55-hectare freight terminal platform would have met Ministry of Transport requirements for European Corridor 1.

7 The Municipality of Messina has had a strong relationship with these designers for years, since they have drawn up some urban regeneration plans as well as the Tono-Mortelle coastal area executive plan presented in 2007.

8 Upon its first presentation, the artificial island design aroused many objections, mainly concerning the special nature of the site. Excluding the distinctive nature of the historic port, the other part of the Messina coast presents great difficulties for any kind of port equipment (the remarkable depth a few metres from the coastline; the strong currents; the strong, mainly sirocco winds), as demonstrated by the frequent silting or the effects of storms that often make the new Tremestieri terminal unusable, which also require sizeable funds for emergency rehabilitation works on the port.

9 The first rankings showed the group led by Bruno Gabrielli with the top score; then the Ramboll Group (a team including several engineering companies); the Favero & Milan engineering firm came third; the fourth position went to the VIA Engineering group with Guendalina Salimei and Giovanni Fiamingo; and last the proposal—inappropriately presented—by the MBM group from Barcelona.

10 The initial ranking was unexpectedly changed: the Favero & Milan team was declared first in the list; second, the design team coordinated by Bruno Gabrielli; then the Ramboll Group and the VIA Engineering group; MBM remained in last position.

11 From a few of the published project details, it is possible to say that all the participants followed the call requirements correctly. Only the Guendalina Salimei and Giovanni Fiamingo waterfront project seems to break away from the competition guidelines by proposing original and innovative waterfront solutions, albeit with some feasibility issues.

12 See von Elhers (2013) and Savinao (2014).

13 To understand the quantity and the consequences of many unfinished public works in Italy and the problems affecting many Italian cities or the low provision of facilities in a large number of urban areas (mostly in the South of Italy), it could be interesting to look at the contents of the 'Osservatorio partecipato sul fenomeno delle opere incompiute in italia' (Shared Observatory on Unfinished Works in Italy"), see: www.incompiutosiciliano.org.

Bibliography

Autorità Portuale di Messina (2004) *Piano Regolatore del Porto*, Messina: www. porto.messina.it/dettaglio.asp?id=181&porto=1, last access October 11 2015.

Autorità Portuale di Messina (2006) 'Messina', in R. Bruttomesso (ed.), *Città-Porto. City-Port. Catalogo della X Mostra Internazionale di Architettura «Città-Porto»*, Venezia: Marsilio, pp. 208–11.

Bettini, V., Guerzoni, M. and Ziparo, A. (2002) *Il ponte insostenibile. L'impatto ambientale del manufatto di attraversamento stabile dello Stretto di Messina*, Firenze: Alinea.

Bruttomesso, R. (ed.) (2006) *Città-Porto/City-Port. Catalogo della X Mostra Internazionale di Architettura di Venezia*, Venezia: Marsilio.

Comune di Messina (2009) *Programma innovativo in ambito urbano. Porti & Stazioni. Documento preliminare alla progettazione*, Messina: www.piaumessina.it/, last access February 25 2014.

Comune di Messina (2010), Il Documento definitivo del Piano strategico, Messina: www.comune.messina.it/messina2020/, last access May 3 2016.

von Ehlers F. (2013), Bürgermeister aus Versehen, Der Spiegel, n. 40: www.spiegel.de/spiegel/print/d-114948815.html, last access May 3 2016.

Farinella, R. (2008) 'Coste e Waterfront. Riflessioni su un tema maturo', in M. Balzani and E. Montalti (eds.), *I progetti nelle città della costa. Dal ridisegno del waterfront al piano spiaggia*, Sant'Arcangelo di Romagna, RN: Maggioli Editore, pp. 37–61.

La Spada, E. (1996) 'Città e periferia a Messina', *DRP. Rassegna di studi e ricerche*, 1: 81–126.

Musolino, M. and Perna, T. (2007) 'La metamorfosi socio-economica nel XXI secolo', in F. Mazza (ed.), *Le città della Sicilia. Messina: storia cultura economia*, Soveria Mannelli: Rubettino, pp. 297–338.

Pavia, R. and di Venosa, M. (2006) 'I porti delle città: piani e progetti', *Urbanistica*, 131: 7–34.

Pieroni, O. (2000) *Tra Scilla e Cariddi. Il ponte sullo Stretto di Messina*, Soveria Mannelli: Rubettino.

Saitta, P. (2013) *Quota zero. Messina dopo il terremoto: la ricostruzione infinita*, Roma: Donzelli.

Saviano C. (2014), "Pisapia e Accorinti i più amati tra i sindaci del cambiamento", La Repubblica, February 19: www.repubblica.it/politica/2014/02/19/news/ricerca_piepoli_sindaci-79037585/, last access May 3 2016.Savino, M. (2010a) 'Messina . . . ovvero quando la rinascita della città inizia dal mare . . .', in M. Savino (ed.), *Waterfront d'Italia. Piani politiche progetti*, Milano: FrancoAngeli, pp. 302–329.

Savino, M. (2010b) 'Città e waterfront tra piani, progetti, politiche ed immancabili retoriche', in M. Savino (ed.), *Waterfront d'Italia. Piani politiche progetti*, Milano: FrancoAngeli, pp. 302–329.

11 Valparaiso, Port, Railway and Industry

A Cultural Landscape Which Generated Modernity in Need of Preservation

Marcela Pizzi Kirschbaum

Historical Background

In Latin America, the genesis, identity and image of port cities in most cases is the result of commercial exchange processes and industrialization which have shaped distinctive cultural landscapes, generally associated with railway and shipping activities. Processes which originated during the nineteenth century, they consolidated during the first decades of the twentieth century and fell into obsolescence after the 1950s, the decade when valuable industrial, railway and port infrastructures, tangible testimonies of the generation of the modern city, suffered abandonment, deterioration or were replaced (Romero 1976).

In Chile, port cities were founded with different characteristics to those inland settlements with predominantly mining and agricultural vocations that had been established during the colonial period. Colonization was carried out mainly inland, conditioned by the topographic characteristics of our coast and the insecure sailing conditions in the South Pacific. In this context, it was not rare for the Spanish Crown to display a lack of interest in forming coastal settlements, except for a few fortified settlements such as Valdivia, San Carlos de Ancud and Valparaiso, destined to protect clippers and ships sailing to Callao, the main port of the Peruvian vice-royalty (Benavides et al. 1994).

From 1811 on, after gaining independence from Spain, Chilean local authorities allowed free commerce, which until then had been restricted to the Spanish Crown's domains, in the coastal settlements. Consequently, this favoured their development to the detriment of the inland cities. In this way, sleepy fishermen's coves achieved greater socio-economic importance, first as delivery and raw material storage areas, before becoming consolidated later as larger urban exchange centres. The increasing flow of shipping and international commerce connecting the Atlantic and the Pacific Oceans positioned our coast as a strategic fuel and goods supply point after crossing the Strait of Magellan.

In this context, Valparaiso, located 33°2' south latitude and 71°38' west longitude, became the major commercial port in the South Pacific, peaking between 1880 and 1914 as a mandatory supply stopover for the merchant routes coming through the Atlantic, reflecting the urban development in plans of the time (Figure 11.1). Later, due to several events such as a destructive earthquake in 1906 that reduced the city to rubble, the effects of World War I and the opening of the Panama Canal in 1914, Valparaiso started to decline, becoming removed from the new commercial sailing routes, a situation which was worsened by the nitrate crisis, due to its replacement by low-cost synthetic products. Nitrate deposits were located in the northern desert territories, in the provinces of Tarapacá and Antofagasta, which were annexed by Chile after winning the War of the Pacific or Nitrate War, which took place between 1879 and 1883 against Peru and Bolivia. As a result, Chile became the main world producer of this component, used as a base in the preparation of gunpowder and as a fertilizer. To these events, we must add the effects of the establishment of a second commercial port, San Antonio, in 1912, mainly for copper and agricultural exports, and those of the 1929 world economic depression, which finally confirmed Santiago (to the detriment of Valparaiso) as the capital city and political and financial centre of the country. In contrast, the slower development of Valparaiso has meant that its exceptional, universal values of a mixed industrial, port and railway heritage still remain as an image of its access to modernity, leading to its declaration by UNESCO in 2003 as a World Heritage City (CMN 2004).

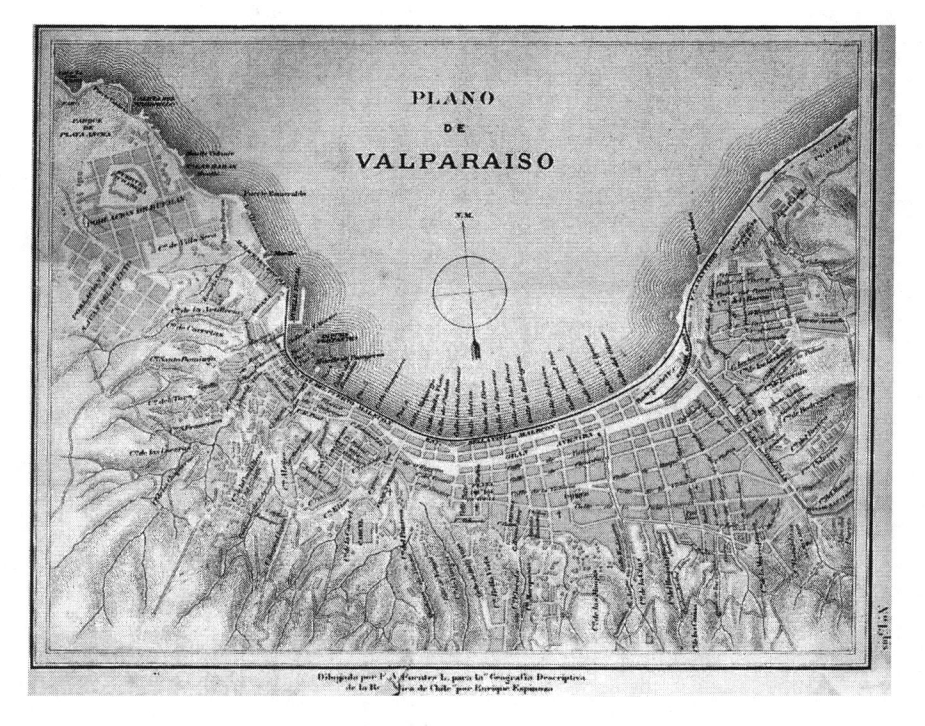

Figure 11.1 Plan of Valparaíso in 1895

Previously, the port of Valparaiso had prevailed over other settlements on the Chilean coast due to its proximity to Santiago, which facilitated the rapid departure of raw materials and at the same time the entrance of abundant foreign imports. During the nineteenth century, a great boost to this commercial exchange process was initiated by wheat exports to California in the United States and also to Australia, due to the gold rush in both destinations, and also by the hectic mining activity, triggering a process to revitalize the city. As a result, the population increased dramatically from around 5,000 inhabitants by the end of the eighteenth century to close to 16,000 in the second decade of the nineteenth century, with a large amount of foreigners, mainly of Anglo-Saxon origin, who generally controlled the commercial and financial sector and integrated neo-European architectural models and technology.

The social changes and urban development carried out in this period of history radically affected a great number of ports in the world, which had to rapidly enter the modern era due to the productive pressures of the time, as a consequence sweeping away valuable industrial and railway heritage structures. Due to these circumstances, few port cities still retain traces of the industrialization era, like Valparaiso, where resulting from the adaptation of new technologies, valuable expressions still remain, with a foreign touch provided by immigrants in their struggle with an adverse geographical context.

The second half of the nineteenth and the first decades of the twentieth centuries formed the golden age of Valparaiso, which then underwent a far-reaching modernization process, with specialized areas, the definition of the port area and the building of important industrial infrastructure. The population continued to increase, reaching 70,000 inhabitants by 1870, 100,000 by 1885 and 160,000 by 1910.

The Former Valparaiso–Santiago Railway

The railway associated with this particular context acquired an important role in the economic process, becoming the main means of transportation of raw materials, products and people in its links with Santiago and the inland cities of the rest of the country, generating a terrestrial network in connection with the navigation system. This means of transportation contributed to the development of Valparaiso as an industrial hub, with its tracks running parallel to the shoreline due to the difficult topographic conditions, on a narrow flat strip crossed by forty-two hills, in a grand amphitheatre setting a few metres away from the sea (Jiménez 2000; Weisberg 2000; Fadda, Cortés, 2007). As a negative consequence, these geographical determinants which conditioned the layout of the railway tracks generated a barrier and consequently the detachment of the inhabitants from the shore, a situation which today needs to be repaired.

To understand the origins of the former Valparaiso–Santiago railway, we must go back to the 1840s, when the US engineer William Wheelwright, who had already been responsible for the first railroad in Chile connecting Copiapó and Caldera, came up with the idea of connecting the port of Valparaiso and Santiago. The railway's layout was designed by the Italian engineer Hilario Pulini and its final version by the American Alan Campbell. The first section (up to Quillota) was built in 1857, and, upon reaching Santiago by 1863, it was concluded by the US engineer Henry Meiggs (Rivera 1963; Thomson 2000; Pizzi 2009).

Associated with the railway, the metalworking industry—an area of technology closely related to the mining industry—developed greatly in Valparaiso, generating a large storage infrastructure in addition to a swarm of towing boats and a forest of cranes.

The industrial and railway heritage still present on the Valparaiso shoreline is mainly located in five distinctive areas.

Area 1: The Plaza Sotomayor area, where significant institutional buildings related to port activities are located, such as the port captaincy, customs administration building and navy command headquarters. The port railway station acts as the beginning and ending point of the railroad connecting the civic centre with the rest of the city and Santiago to the north. Built in 1895 in neoclassical style, it was later replaced in 1937, when the railway tracks were moved closer to the shore, by a rationalist building in reinforced concrete which was designed by the architect Luis Herreros, and recently it has been remodelled again. The station tower together with the buildings across the street form a port access to the city from the sea (Figure 11.2), the only instance where the port actually makes contact with the shoreline (Figure 11.4).

Area 2: The area from Plaza Sotomayor to the north, through the Avenida Errázuriz, reaching the University of Valparaiso Law School, includes two former train stations: Francia and Baron. The latter, which has a tower similar to that of Kings Cross station in London, acted as a terminal station for a decade and was declared a national monument in 1972. The station continued in service until the 1970s, when a great part of its infrastructure was demolished to give way to a new elevated highway, leaving the tower isolated between two roads. The exceptional Bodegas Simon Bolívar (warehouses), (Figure 11.3) probably the largest reinforced concrete structure existing in South America, are located in this area.

Part of the area was redeveloped as a cruise terminal in 2002 and another has been proposed for a future commercial mega-project including a huge mall, which has resulted in strong complaints from the citizens. Other areas have been franchised for cold storage and as warehouses for the Empresa Portuaria de Valparaíso, EPV Valparaíso Port Company. In this area we

Figure 11.2 Port access from the sea

Figure 11.3 Bodegas (warehouses) Simon Bolívar

can find the interesting old Baron Pier, built by the English firm Pearson & Sons Ltd. in 1917. Originally serving for offloading coal used as fuel for the railway and for raw material cargo shipments, today it is used for massive public artistic and sports events (Figure 11.4).

> **Area 3:** This area includes a group of distinctive railway infrastructure buildings across Baron Station, such as the Bodegas; Sudamericana; Agencias Aéreas y Marítimas; the SAAM South American air and sea agency warehouses; the electric train warehouse belonging to the state railway company; the old armoury, used as repair hangar; and the Turntable. The latter is the only protected heritage building although in advanced state of deterioration (Figure 11.4).

> **Area 4:** This area continues north from Baron Station up to the Santa Maria Technical University, which was built in 1931 in neo-Gothic style by Josue Smith Solar and Jose Thomas Smith Miller, evoking the Anglo – American past, although it was built much later (Figure 11.4).

> **Area 5:** Between the University of Santa Maria and the Caleta Portales cove, in this area the Paseo Wheelwright walkway was built in 2006 with the intention of recovering the shore area for the inhabitants' leisure. The walkway includes resting areas, cycle lanes and viewing points. Caleta Portales was built in 1860. Formerly used as a slaughterhouse, it was restored in 1929 and again recently in 2005 for use by fishermen (Pizzi 2010) (Figure 11.4).

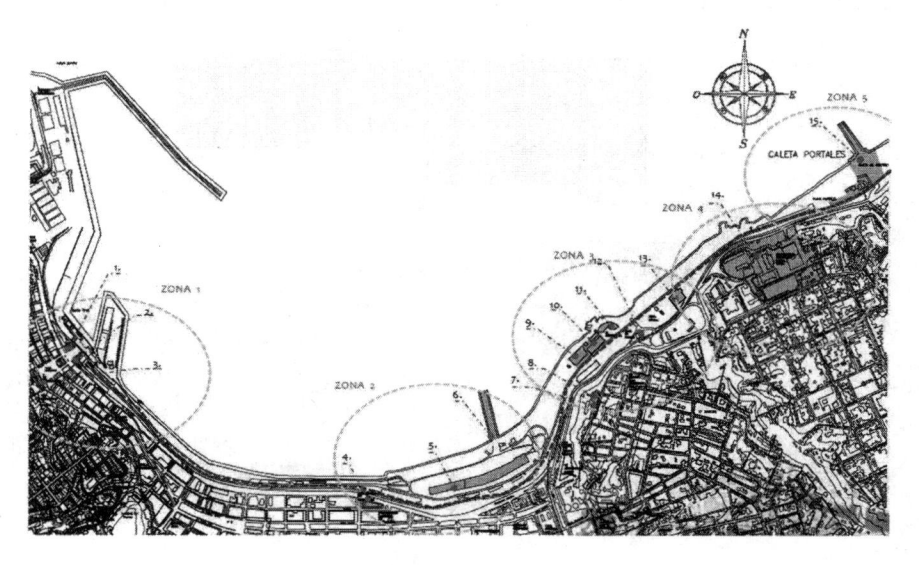

Figure 11.4 Main industrial heritage areas

Revitalization Actions

Valparaiso is more than isolated buildings. Due to the irregular layout conditioned by the topography, Valparaiso is full of unexpected perspectives, winding stairs, corners, diverging streets, irregular squares, plazas and lookouts, mixed in a vernacular architecture with a strong maritime influence in a process of dynamic transformation. Its identity is reflected in a natural amphitheatre with distinctive areas which form part of the inhabitants' collective memory in a language that expresses Valparaiso's historical development in the construction of its social, cultural, economic and urban heritage.

In the 1960s, the Chilean government launched several actions with the intention of revitalizing the Port of Valparaiso. The first relevant milestone was the development of the Plan Intercomunal de Valparaiso (PIV), the intercommunal plan for Valparaiso prepared by the Public Works Ministry (MOP) in 1965, which established the port as a central element of a conurbation including the coastal cities of Viña del Mar, Concon and the interior cities of Quilpué and Villa Alemana. It identified industrial and residential areas, regulated the coastline, and designed highways and a road network between its components. It was an instrument used as a base for later generating a macro-infrastructure including the elevated highway, Avenida España; the La Pólvora–Las Palmas–Ruta 60 ring road; and a new access to the city through Cabritería, in order to expand the port to Yolanda and Caleta Portales. In this context, an elevated highway was designed connecting Valparaiso and the neighbouring city of Viña del Mar in order to mitigate traffic congestion. However, only the first stretches were built due to the effects on the urban landscape and the public reaction, as it was designed without the intervention of architects, generated no connection with the surrounding areas and destroyed important beaches. Some fragments remained abandoned until 2005, being reused to generate lookouts as part of the new Wheelwright Walkway.

Later, the transfer of the National Congress to Valparaiso in 1986 was an important action taken while seeking to decentralize political decisions, which until then had mainly been made in Santiago. The intention and goal was also to trigger economic development—to little effect, however.

After the return to democracy in 1990, the governments of presidents Patricio Aylwin Azócar (March 1990–March 1994) and Eduardo Frei Ruíz Tagle (March 1994–March 1998) designed and implemented major infrastructure projects for the city, such as the Santiago–Quilpué highway; the Troncal Sur main highway; the Ferrocarril Regional Metropolitano regional metropolitan railway, connecting Valparaiso with Viña del Mar and Limache using the former Valparaiso–Santiago railroad layout today known as MERVAL; the Camino La Pólvora, a new access road to Valparaiso; and improvement of the port infrastructure and the generation of Peñuelas, an outer land harbour in Placilla. To achieve this, the PIV was updated, generating a new instrument, the Plan Regulador Metropolitano de Valparaiso (known as the PREMVAL Valparaiso metropolitan regulatory plan), which took close to ten years to be approved by local authorities. This instrument expands the urban area up to Placilla, allowing the development of Curauma, a new satellite city of around 200,000 inhabitants, in the former fields belonging to the Forestal Valparaiso forestry commission.

Most of these projects were consolidated during President Ricardo Lagos's government (March 1998–March 2002), including the nomination of Valparaiso as a World Heritage City by UNESCO in 2003, after being designated as one of the cities to be revitalized for the bicentennial of the republic of Chile in 2010. This denomination allowed access to an international loan for use in the regeneration of the most deteriorated heritage areas. This led to the creation of the Programa de Recuperación y Desarrollo Urbano de Valparaíso, the Valparaiso recovery and urban development programme (PRDUV). Considering interventions on a large and small scale, it was partially implemented, with limitations, during the government of President Michelle Bachelet (March 2006–March 2010). A series of major port city revitalization projects were designed with the intention of regenerating the seashore as a leisure area and transforming port cities into tourist cities, taking the city of Barcelona as a model. In order to achieve this, in the case of Valparaiso, port activities were franchised, highways were built and the MERVAL regional metropolitan train inaugurated in 2005 (MOP 2005). Smaller-scale interventions were focused on the aesthetics, trying to create the image of a cultural city through festivals and events—to little effect, however (Poduje 2009).

UNESCO's declaration of Valparaiso as a World Heritage City sets out a protected area and a buffer zone, in the intention (amongst other objectives) of generating a local conscience regarding the need to preserve this cultural landscape. In this context, several projects arose such as the Lift Recovery Programme and projects for the improvement of public spaces, the preservation of old buildings, the generation of a historical archive at the municipal level and a heritage programme related to the different neighbourhoods. In addition, changes were made to PREMVAL in order to defend views of the bay by refusing permits for high-rise buildings.

The area declared as a World Heritage Site is limited to the Alegre and Concepción hills, the Matriz church, Plaza Sotomayor and its surrounding buildings, Plaza Echaurren and Calle Serrano, Calle Prat, the Cordillera Hill and Márquez Gorge. Around this area, a protective buffer zone extends from the sea border in the north up to Avenida Alemania in the south, and from the San Juan de Dios gorge in the east.

According to UNESCO's conventions, states are given support in their efforts to identify and preserve their heritage through viable proposals, which is the reason why areas and not the whole city are protected. Nevertheless, this declaration did not consider all the significant industrial heritage remains associated with the port activities and the railway on the shoreline. Valparaiso's heritage should be understood in sections, in which the combination of the spontaneous architecture developed in the hills, the commercial buildings of the historic centre and the buildings associated with the port and railway activities, as a whole, make up its value. All the industrial remains should be protected, since these are scarce and in danger. Building conditions in this area are more flexible than in the protected area, which includes the most the city's representative buildings. A second buffer area relates to the former port station which together with the captaincy building and the customs building form a port access from the sea.[1]

In spite of the UNESCO nomination in 2003, and the regeneration actions described, Valparaiso continues to decay, with no significant incentives or investments, in a context with structural problems in which the decision processes are broken up into numerous entities with no global policy, which does not allow revitalization to really succeed. We must add the devastating effects of two more earthquakes—that of 1985 and recently in 2010—and the empowerment of groups of citizens opposing, with or without good reason, various proposed interventions.

The intention to transform Valparaiso into a tourist attraction should respect the different levels of historical strata and create an adequate balance with contemporary architectural expressions in order to preserve its image, character and identity. The concept of 'heritage' needs to be considered in a broader sense, by adding the industrial architecture associated with the port activity and railway, as yet not valued, to the traditional architecture protected by UNESCO (Pizzi 2011).

Port cities are especially important instruments of development, with no more than twenty in South America serving a large extension of territory. Three of them are located in Chile—Antofagasta, Valparaíso and San Antonio—the latter two strategically associated with a terrestrial corridor connecting the Pacific and Atlantic Oceans, with a strong commercial future.

Today the relation between cities and water is becoming an increasingly salient issue in urban studies. In this framework, the recognition, recovery and revitalization of the industrial architectural heritage associated with railways, anthropological 'places' that generated modern cities, is vital in order to preserve the tangible and intangible cultural landscapes of port cities which give meaning to our existence (Norberg-Schulz 1975; Augé 2001).

Note

1   Previously identified by the author as part of the Area 1 industrial and railway heritage.

Bibliography

ARPA, (2010) Red de Archivos Patrimoniales de Valparaíso, www.arpa.ucv.cl/
Augé, M (2001) *Los no lugares: Espacios del Anonimato, Antropología sobre la Modernidad*, Ed. Gedisa, Barcelona, España.

Benavides, J., Pizzi, M. and Valenzuela, M.P. (1994) *Ciudades y Arquitectura Portuaria.' Los puertos mayores del litoral chileno.* Editorial Universitaria, Santiago, Chile.

BID, Banco Interamericano de Desarrollo (2006) *Preparación Programa de Recuperación y Desarrollo Urbanos de Valparaíso*, Santiago, Chile.

Consejo de Monumentos Nacionales, CMN, Ministerio de Educación, Gobierno de Chile (2004) 'Postulación de Valparaíso como Sitio de Patrimonio Mundial UNESCO', *Segunda Serie* No 70, 1ª edición, en Cuadernos CMN Santiago, Chile.

Espinosa, Enrique (1897) *Jeografía descriptiva de la República de Chile: arreglada según las últimas divisiones administrativas, las más recientes esploraciones i en conformidad al censo jeneral de la República levantado el 28 de noviembre de 1895.* Imprenta i Encuadernación Barcelona, Santiago de Chile.

Fadda, G. and Cortés, A. (2007) 'Barrios. En busca de su definición en Valparaíso', *en Revista Urbano* Vol. 10, No 16, Ediciones Universidad de Bío Bío, Concepción, Chile, 50–59.

Jiménez, C. (2000) 'Tradición y Cultura Local. Identificación del Patrimonio Arquitectónico', *en CA* No 101, ediciones Colegio de Arquitectos A.G., Santiago, Chile, 38–41.

Jiménez, C. and Ferrada, M. (2003) 'Los Valores Universales del Patrimonio Arquitectónico y Urbano de Valparaíso', *en Revista Urbano*, Concepción, Chile.

Memoria Chilena, www.memoriachilena.cl/

Ministerio de Obras Públicas, MOP, Gobierno de Chile (2005) *Chile 2010: Visión Ciudad Bicentenario*, Santiago, Chile.

Norberg-Schulz, Ch. (1975) "Existencia, Espacio, Arquitectura", Editorial Blume, Barcelona, España.

Pizzi, M. (2009) 'Marco Histórico de la Ciudad de Valparaíso', *en "Santiago, Rosario, Bordeaux,"* Editorial A&P, Rosario, Argentina, 40–43.

Pizzi, M. (2010) 'Valparaíso, ciudad Patrimonio de la Humanidad, Tensión entre su revitalización y la preservación de su identidad', *en Portus*, No. 19, 86–91.

Pizzi, M. (2011) 'Patrimonio e Industria, Génesis del Paisaje Cultural de la Ciudad Latinoamericana del siglo XX. Una Necesaria Regeneración', *en 'Anales de Investigación'*, Editorial Universidad ORT, Montevideo, Uruguay, 61–70.

Pizzi, M., Valenzuela, M.P., Aguilar, D. and Palma, C. (2008) 'Carácter e Identidad del Borde Costero de Valparaíso: Puesta en Valor del Patrimonio Arquitectónico Ferroviario Industrial', Seminario de Investigación Inédito, dirigido por las Profesoras Marcela Pizzi y María Paz Valenzuela, Facultad de Arquitectura y Urbanismo, Universidad de Chile, Santiago, Chile.

Poduje, Iván (2009) 'Valparaíso a la deriva. Auge y caída de una ciudad de Vanguardia', *en Revista Ciudad y Arquitectura (CA)*, No. 139, abril—mayo, Ediciones Colegio de Arquitectos de Chile, A.G., Morgan Impresores, Santiago, Chile.

Rivera, R. (1963) *Historia del Ferrocarril entre Santiago y Valparaíso*, Universidad Católica de Valparaíso, Chile.

Romero, J.L. (1976) *Latinoamérica, las Ciudades y las Ideas*, Siglo XXI Editores, Buenos Aires, Argentina.

Thomson, I. (2000) *Historia del Ferrocarril en Chile*, Centro de Investigaciones Barros Arana Santiago, Chile.

Waisberg, M. (2000) 'Valparaíso: El Legado Urbanístico y Arquitectónico', *en Revista de Arquitectura*, No 3; Santiago, Chile.

12 Regenerating Urban Waterfronts in China

The Rebirth of the Shanghai Bund

Chen Yu

Introduction

'The Bund is back!' An article adapted from *ForbesLife Magazine* featured the return of luxury and extravagance to this three-quarter-mile-long waterfront in Shanghai, a nostalgic remembrance of her past as 'the Paris of the Orient' (Jones 2011). In the early twentieth century, passengers approaching Shanghai from the Huangpu River (Whampoa River) would not have missed the Shanghai Bund—the grand prospect of this leading treaty port in China. Developed in the Shanghai International Settlement, this stretch of promenade extends from its southern end at the Edward VII Avenue (today's Yan'an Road) to the northern end at the Garden Bridge (today's Waibaidu Bridge). After 1949, the Shanghai Bund kept a low profile up to the point when its first round of large-scale redevelopment was initiated in 1994. An even more astonishing regeneration of the Shanghai Bund in the first decade of the twenty-first century attracted global attention to this waterfront promenade. International and local media's fervent reports on the 'return of the Shanghai Bund' showed the excessive interest in heritages that were created in China's 'semi-colonial and semi-feudal' era.

China's modern history started with the signing of the Nanjing Treaty (1842). The Qing government was forced to open five port cities for foreign trade and settlement, including Shanghai, Ningbo, Fuzhou, Xiamen and Guangzhou. Many more ports were opened in subsequent Sino-foreign treaties. The establishment of the 'rent-in-perpetuity' system (*yongzu zhi*) legalized foreigners' land rights in treaty ports and safeguarded their real estate in China. To avoid conflicts with the locals in developed areas and to ensure access to bodies of water, foreigners would build their settlements outside walled Chinese cities and close to waterways. The waterfronts became central to the economic, social and cultural life of treaty ports, when water traffic was the most important means of transporting people and goods to and fro. Within the Shanghai International Settlement, a towing path along the west bank of Huangpu River was turned into the Bund, known for its exotic architecture and charming waterfront spaces.

After Shanghai's liberation in 1949, the buildings along the Bund were taken over by the newly established Communist Party. Though heavily criticized as a symbol of supremacy of Western powers over the Chinese, these extraordinary, high-quality buildings have been occupied and used by government bodies since the 1950s. The isolation of socialist China from the West slowed the pace of Shanghai's development. Ironically, this situation allowed the Bund to retain its waterfront character, notwithstanding certain undesirable alternations and a lack of maintenance. Since China announced her open-door policy in 1978, Shanghai, the most powerful economic engine in China, has grown at an accelerated pace. The Bund experienced large-scale redevelopment in the 1990s to tackle transportation and flooding problems. However, the widened road and massive levee cut off the physical and visual connections between pedestrian routes and the river. The utilitarian approach to redeveloping the Bund thus proved problematic.

While people were murmuring about the loss of waterfront life along the Bund, the fate of this promenade was changed again, thanks to rising concerns about Shanghai's cultural identity in the post-reform era. In 2002, Shanghai won the bid to host the 2010 Expo. The necessity of renovating the Shanghai Bund was again raised for discussion. An ambitious regeneration plan was proposed and implemented, with committed support from the Shanghai Municipal Government, especially the Huangpu District Office. A double-deck underground tunnel was constructed to reduce traffic at ground level, and a park was expanded from the street level to the top of the levee. As the local government asserted, the regenerated Bund—with a stunning view toward Lujiazui on the east bank of the Huangpu River—was a perfect place to exhibit this city's past, present and future.

Like the Shanghai Bund, the other urban waterfronts in former Chinese treaty ports were shaped with remarkable semi-colonial characteristics and imprinted with controversial connotations. Many of these are undergoing regeneration. For example, the revitalization of the Ningbo Bund was initiated in 2002 and further promoted in 2013, and the Guangzhou (Canton) Bund has been experiencing a transformation since 2010. How do we understand the problems and challenges in the regeneration of urban waterfronts in China? What are the potentials for redeveloping the kinds of historic waterfronts that were created in semi-colonial China? How might the regeneration of these waterfronts contribute to contemporary urban life? Through examining the spatial formation and transformation of the Shanghai Bund, especially its rebirth in the early twenty-first century, this chapter aims to answer these questions in the context of China's changing political climate and economic context.

Building a Grand Promenade in Treaty-Port Shanghai

Shanghai became part of Songjiang County in Suzhou Prefecture in 1264 when commercial activities flourished in Jiangnan (south of the Yangtze River) during the Song Dynasty (960–1279). To protect this region from pirates, a walled town was built in 1553 which became the nucleus of the

City of Shanghai. The changing foreign policies of the Qing led to the establishment of Shanghai as the major trade port in the Yangtze Delta, despite its low administrative level in China's political hierarchy. After the opening of Shanghai as a treaty port in 1842, the British, Americans and French set up their concessions in 1843, 1848 and 1849 respectively. Built along the west bank of the Huangpu River and outside the walled city, these concessions were separated by two water bodies: Yang Jing Bing (Yang-king-pang) and the Suzhou River (Soochow Creek). In 1863, the British and American concessions merged as the Shanghai International Settlement, while the French Concession retained its independence (Figure 12.1).

The boundary of the British Concession was defined in the Shanghai Land Regulations that also served as guidelines for its land development. To ensure the public access to the river, 'a large road along the bank of the river, from the Yang-king-pang Northwards, which was a towing-path for the grain junks, must be repaired and replaced by the renters' (Shanghai Land Regulations 1845: 3). By 1848, this towing path had evolved into a

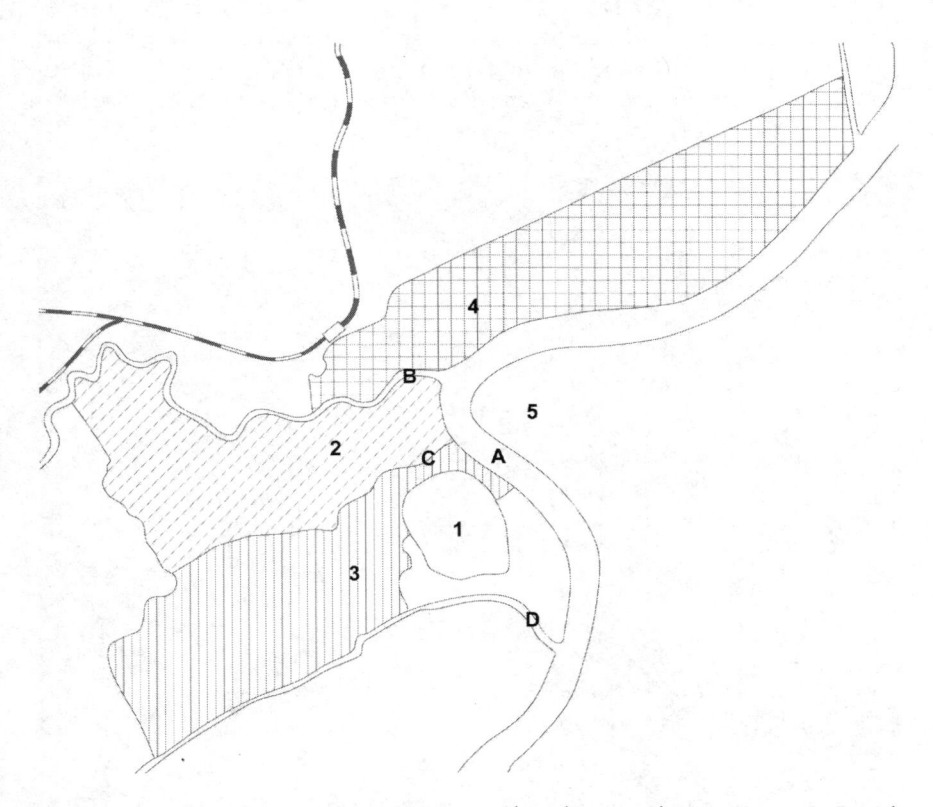

Figure 12.1 Map of foreign concessions in Shanghai. 1. Chinese Town; 2. British Concession; 3. French Concession; 4. American Concession; 5. Pudong; A. Huangpu River; B. Suzhou River; C. Yang Jing Bing; D. Lu Jia Bing

public road with a width of around 9 metres. In the 1850s, more than ten private piers had been constructed in front of their respective factories, and two bridges were built over the Suzhou River and Yang Jing Bing to connect the three concessions. From that point on, the Bund would become the most important north-south artery in Shanghai (Qian 2006). It was lined with large lots containing two-to-three-storey bungalows,[1] which were built by the factories to function as offices-cum-residential estates. The remarkable landscape of the Bund stood out from its desolate surroundings in the 1860s (Figure 12.2).

The Bund's infrastructure gradually improved, due to the prosperity of the foreign concessions. In 1862, the Bund's main road was endowed with the official name of 'Yangtze'. To tackle the problem of silting in the Huangpu River, the Shanghai Municipal Council began to reclaim the Bund in 1864. Expanding eastwards, the Bund grew into a promenade with a motorway of approximately 9 metres and a 2.4-metre pedestrian path in front of the factory buildings. The number of piers along the Bund was increased from ten to twelve. To beautify the Bund, a row of trees was planted and street lamps erected alongside the pedestrian path. The charm of the Bund was further enhanced with the opening of the Bund Park (Huangpu Park) in 1868, which was built on a piece of reclaimed land at the estuary of the

Figure 12.2 The Bund looking north, 1860–1870

Suzhou River. In ten years, a greenbelt took shape to separate the busy piers from the main thoroughfare, which had been progressively surfaced with asphalt since 1887 (Luo 2002). Not only did the broad promenade and the open waterfront spaces attract public attention, the exotic architecture with its consistent setback from the road also caught people's eyes. The old bungalows were replaced by medium-to-high-rise buildings as the Bund became 'the Wall Street of the Orient'.

Despite the frequent turnover of its lots, the Bund's development was controlled by the Road and Jetty Committee from 1846, up to 1865 when the committee was dismissed and replaced by the Shanghai Municipal Council. How to utilize the Bund was always a focus in developing the Shanghai International Settlement. In the late 1860s, a proposal for constructing a new ferry terminal for steamships along the Bund was forwarded, on grounds of economic interest. However, this plan was suspended because of concerns about the pollution that might be caused by any new port facilities. It was believed that the Bund was the only scenic spot in Shanghai where people could breathe in fresh air from the Huangpu River. Thus it was considered that the natural and artificial landscapes of the Bund should be retained to entertain the public and to safeguard the sanitation of this port city. Thanks to this public concern, the Bund was able to evolve from a functional embankment to a pleasurable promenade. In the early twentieth century, the Bund was no doubt the best representative of the accomplishments that foreign communities had achieved on Chinese soil (Figure 12.3).

Figure 12.3 A bird's-eye view of the Bund in the 1930s

As Taylor points out, politically and culturally, the Bund was 'the single most important spatial reminder' of the treaty port system established in China after the First Opium War (Taylor 2002). As such, this controversial symbol of Westerners' supremacy over the Chinese triggered anti-imperialist campaigns in Shanghai. As early as 1878, Chinese elites had protested against a notorious restriction on Chinese visitors to the Bund Park, which had been built with revenues from all groups of people in the Shanghai International Settlement. On 30 May 1925, the Shanghai Municipal Police shot dead thirteen Chinese protesters and wounded many others during a protest march through the Shanghai International Settlement. This incident led to the outbreak of the 30 May Movement across China, which was regarded as 'a defining moment in the development of modern Chinese nationalism' (Bickers 1998). In accounts of China's modern history, the Bund has always been recalled and portrayed as a place where China proved its progress towards modernization, yet one where the Chinese experienced imperialist exploitation. The Chinese love-hate attitude towards the Bund had a strong impact on its development in socialist China.

Transforming the Waterfront in Socialist Shanghai

The liberation of Shanghai in 1949 was followed by the departure of its foreign communities. The exotic buildings along the Bund were taken over by the new authority and gradually taken into use by various government institutions. For instance, within a year of the Hong Kong Shanghai Bank of China (HSBC) leaving Shanghai in 1955, its building at No. 12 on the Bund was taken over by the Shanghai Municipal Government as office space. Along the Bund, building features with the imprints of the semi-colonial era were either demolished or disguised, and the name of the promenade was changed from Yangtze to 'Zhongshan' after Sun Yat-sen (the father of Modern China). During the Cultural Revolution, Shanghai's foreign concessions were condemned as 'the citadel for imperialists who invaded China in the semi-colonial and semi-feudal era' (Du and Jin 1965). The anti-imperialist momentum was strengthened by the tension between socialist China and the capitalist West. The Bund was a supreme setting for the performance of patriotic campaigning. In the 1950s, five rounds of renovation plans were proposed by the government to increase the transport capability of the Bund. However, none of them was realized, because Shanghai's development at that time was too sluggish. Ironically, the result was that the Bund's waterfront character remained intact, with lush greenery spreading over the whole stretch of the promenade.

After Deng Xiaoping announced the Open-Door Policy in 1978, the urban development of Shanghai sped up. As the former financial centre and then political core of Shanghai, the Bund was targeted to expedite the urbanization of this largest city in China. People believed that the Bund would be changed from a source of shame to a source of pride in Shanghai and even throughout China (Luo 1987). In 1993, the Shanghai Government initiated a project of 'Reconstructing the Bund' (Chongjian Waitan), aiming to resume its financial position in the world. The area around the Bund was designated as Shanghai's Central Business District (CBD). An 'Exchange Plan' (Zhihua Jihua) was approved by the Shanghai Municipal Government on 23 August 1994. According to this Plan, the Bund buildings that had been occupied by government institutions since the 1950s would be vacated and leased to financial institutions and other designated agents. In November 1994, the Shanghai Bund Real Estate Exchange Company was set up by the Shanghai Government to carry out this task. To lead the first step of this Exchange Plan, the Shanghai Municipal Government moved out of the Bund No. 12 (the former HSBC building) on 1 July 1994, which had been used as the Municipal Building (Shifu Dalou) since 1956. After signing the Exchange Agreement in December 1996, Shanghai Pudong Development Bank became the new tenant in this historic building. A two-year renovation project was initiated with the aim of restoring the glory of this grand architectural monument built in 1923. By 1999, nineteen of the buildings along Zhongshan East No. 1 Road had completed the exchange process, and fourteen of them were leased to financial institutions (*Xinmin Evening Newspaper* 2014).

Despite passionate debate over the Exchange Plan, the focus of the Reconstructing the Bund project was indeed about improving its capability in transportation and flood prevention. Thirty-one ferries along the Bund were removed to grant space for the Bund's expansion eastwards for 80 metres. Zhongshan Road, consisting of today's Zhongshan East No. 1 and No. 2 Roads, was altered from a four-lane roadway to an eleven-lane expressway. At its northern end, a concrete bridge (Wusong Road Gate Bridge) was constructed in 1991 to replace the old Waibaidu Bridge as the main traffic road across the Suzhou River. At the junction of Zhongshan Road and Yan'an Road, the exit of the Yan'an elevated expressway was built in 1996 to channel traffic from the old city centre to the Bund. This massive expressway exit obstructed the view towards the Bund, and locals joked that it was 'the No. 1 turn of Asia'. To prevent floods during typhoon seasons, a container-shape levee (3.5 metres higher than street level) was built along the river. This giant levee was designed to be adequate to protect Shanghai from a once-in-a-century flood event.

In contrast with the enthusiasm for preserving the Bund buildings, other original landscape elements of the Bund were discarded in this renovation project. To leave space for road widening, the lush greenery spreading over the promenade was removed, and the Gutzlaff Signal Tower erected in 1907 was moved eastwards by 22.4 metres. Also, the old Bund Park was encroached upon during this project. At the same time, a new layer of landscape imbued with socialist ideology was imposed over the Bund to dilute any semi-colonial echoes. In 1993, the monument to the People's Hero was erected to commemorate those martyrs who had died to liberate Shanghai since the First Opium War. In the plaza where the statue of Sir George Balfour (the first British consul in Shanghai) had stood, a bronze statue was erected of Chen Yi, the first communist mayor of Shanghai. The plaza was officially named after him too. A viewing deck was opened on the top of the levee to remind people of the disappearing waterfront life.

This renovation plan was no doubt an engineering success in terms of resolving Shanghai's traffic problems and securing the Bund against the threat of flooding. However, the utilitarian approach of this project led to some undesirable results. The wider expressway introduced an immense volume of traffic traversing the Bund, which not only increased air and noise pollution in the area, but also cut off the pedestrian flow to the waterfront and negatively impacted the walking experience along the pedestrian routes. The massive levee completely blocked the view towards the river for pedestrians. The sharp drop between the levee and the pedestrian route, as well as the limited space on the levee crown, made it hard for the Bund to accommodate huge crowds during public holidays. The Bund became a place dominated by automobiles, rather than a space for people's enjoyment. The never-ending traffic flow with a backdrop of neon-lit architecture was captured in fanciful images that signified the modernized Bund in socialist China. Shanghai's projection of a modern image was further advanced by the appearance of a cluster of skyscrapers in the Pudong Special Economic Zone that was established in 1993 on the other side of the Huangpu River.

The Shanghai Municipal Government's initiation of the Restructuring the Bund project was no doubt driven by economic interests. The Exchange Plan for the Bund buildings revealed the attempt to utilize heritage for economic development. Socialist ideology was carefully implanted into the Bund's artificial landscapes, because the Bund's semi-colonial origin was never forgotten by the Chinese. Its landscape always remind people of the humiliation that China suffered after the First Opium War. Despite being the most eye-catching constructions in Shanghai since the early twentieth century, the architectural value of the Bund Buildings remained relatively underappreciated until 20 November 1996 when the buildings were inscribed on China's fourth list of national heritage sites. Four years later, Tongji University was engaged by the Shanghai Municipal Development and Reform Commission to conduct research on the conservation and cultural tourism plan of the Bund area. On 25 July 2002, the Conservation Regulations on the Historic Cultural Sites and Excellent Heritage Architectures in Shanghai were ratified. This formalized the conservation of the Bund. However, in the same year, a proposal to nominate the Bund as a UNESCO heritage site triggered heated debate among Shanghai's residents. The opposing party contended that the Bund was 'a symbol of colonial oppression, and the Bund architectures could not truly represent the spirit of Chinese culture' (Tan 2003). How to reinterpret and promulgate the cultural significance of the Bund remained a sensitive topic in its contemporary redevelopment.

Returning the Bund to People in Post-Reform Shanghai

The rise of Shanghai attracted global attention and its city vision changed again in the post-reform era. In 2002, Shanghai won the bid to host the 2010 Expo. The process of organizing this mega-event opened a window for Shanghai to accelerate the regeneration of its old city centre. Significantly, in the 1990s the Exchange Plan contributed to the enthusiastic conservation of the Bund buildings. Despite the high conservation costs, new tenants had no reservations about such an investment and expected high returns from these projects. In November 2002, the Bund No. 18 (the former Shanghai headquarters for the Chartered Bank of India, Australia and China) commenced a two-year-long restoration. Completed in September 2004, this project won the 2006 UNESCO Asia-Pacific Heritage Award of Excellence for Culture Heritage Conservation. This spotlighted accomplishment in architectural conservation set a solid foundation for commercial operations. This building and those like it along the Bund became the venues of choice for international luxury brands seeking to anchor their flagship stores. The culture of the Bund was thus exploited to magnify these brands' influence in China. The exclusiveness of these high-end flagship stores, restaurants, galleries and so on raised a debate about the public nature of the Bund in socialist China. However, the congregation of international brands no doubt boosted the Bund's profile on the world stage, which was vital in re-establishing Shanghai's global image.

In April 2007, the Shanghai Municipal Government approved the integrated renovation project in the Bund area. Within merely one decade, the Bund was undergoing another round of large-scale redevelopment. This time, the Bund's renovation was set within a more ambitious preparation plan for the 2010 Expo. The cultural values of the Bund were highlighted to echo the Shanghai Expo's theme of 'Better City—Better Life'. As the Shanghai Municipal Government asserted, the Bund should be returned to the people. The regeneration of the Bund was planned as the flagship for the holistic plan of revitalizing urban waterfronts in Shanghai. More importantly, it was to be integrated with the other three stretches of waterfronts, which are separated by the Huangpu River and Suzhou River. To gain some of the reflected glory of the Bund, all these neighbouring waterfronts were branded after it, including East Bund (Dong Waitan) along Pudong, North Bund (Bei Waitan) north to Suzhou River, and South Bund (Nan Waitan) from Yan'an Road southwards.

To return the Bund to the people, the first and most important action for the renovation project was to reduce vehicular traffic at ground level. Hence, a double-deck tunnel was constructed under the Bund that accommodated six lanes. This tunnel, with a length of 3.3 kilometres, has its southern end at Old Taiping Lane, follows Zhongshan Road to cross the

Suzhou River, and further extends along Daming East Road and Wusong Road to reach Haining Road. The construction of the Bund Tunnel commenced in July 2007 and was completed in April 2010. It was an incredible engineering triumph to carry out such a complex project within a dense conservation area. The roadway at the ground level of the Bund was reversed from eleven lanes back to four, reserved mainly for the use of public transportation. In 2008, less than two decades after their construction, the exit of the Yan'an Expressway at the Bund and the Wusong Road Gate Bridge were demolished to clear the visual obstructions along the river. This reveals the Shanghai Municipal Government's determination to remedy the mistakes made in the Bund's first round of redevelopment in the 1990s (Figure 12.4).

As a result, a large amount of vehicular traffic crossing the Bund was diverted underground and more space at ground level was released for street activities. This alteration also allowed a smooth transition from the street level to the crown of the giant levee. A series of terraces were created at different levels, connected by ramps with gradients ranging from 3% to 5%. This design solution reduced the massive bulk of the levee and also provided more space for public gatherings. Meanwhile, the pedestrian path in front of the Bund buildings was widened to between

Figure 12.4 The Shanghai Bund, December 2007

10 and 15 metres. This broad sidewalk serves as an amenity belt that hosts street furniture, lamps, signboards, greenery and so on. In addition to existing nodes like the Bund Park and Chen Yi Plaza, the Financial Plaza was created at the junction of Fuzhou Road and the Bund to signify Shanghai's recapture of its financial position in the world. The century-old Waibaidu Bridge was dismantled for repair on 1 March 2008 and restored in February 2009. As the Shanghai Municipal Government has proposed, all these design solutions offer greater lustre to this historic waterfront.

On 28 March 2010, one month prior to the official opening of the 2010 Expo, the Shanghai Bund was reopened to the public after a three-year renovation programme. Zhou Wei, then director of Huangpu District Office, announced that 'this regeneration project was to retrieve the past ambience of the Bund, and to release the Bund from the busy traffic, and to allow visitors and pedestrians to recall the glory of the Bund' (Luo 2009). It is notable that local and international media widely referred to the Shanghai Municipal Government's claim that the Bund had been turned into a global landmark like the Champs Elysées in Paris. As openly promulgated, this renovation project was to restore the landscape of the Bund its condition in the 1930s (Tan 2010: 40). The association of the redevelopment of the Bund with the Champs Elysées in Paris and its great renown in the early twentieth century reveals the desire to position Shanghai as a global city to compete with other metropolises. However, the discourse around the Bund's nomination as a UNESCO heritage site remains arguable, because people still believe that 'the Bund was a result of colonial history, a shame for the Chinese people, and also a representation of the dark era in the History of China' (Yang 2010).

The successful organization of the 2010 Expo, in particular the infrastructure improvements, allowed Shanghai to 'step up a level in internationalization' (Knowledge Wharton 2010). The rebirth of the Shanghai Bund shows that the Chinese attitude towards semi-colonial heritage had changed from masking it to making use of it by turning it into an object of consumption to bolster the city image. The vision of returning the Bund to the people has had a far-sighted influence on the use of waterfront spaces and Bund buildings. The new design of the public spaces attracts numerous visitors and has turned the Bund into the most popular tourist attraction in Shanghai. People now frequent the Bund more for recreational purposes than shopping. Controlling access by private car and surface parking further contributed to a change in the Bund's position on Shanghai's commercial map. As a consequence, luxury international brands started to withdraw from the Bund in 2012 (Zhao 2013). Although it is hard to predict how the Bund buildings could be better utilized in the future, its openness to and integration with public uses are highly anticipated in the name of the People's Bund (Figure 12.5).

Figure 12.5 The Shanghai Bund, October 2010

Conclusion

The formation of the Shanghai Bund proved the significance of waterfronts in China's treaty ports. It was along these linear waterfront spaces that foreign communities started to grow their commercial and social life in China. To ensure public access to the water, a regular setback from the riverbank was granted as a result of the negotiation and compromise between the Chinese government and foreign powers. The Western management established in foreign settlements allowed the Bund to present an orderly and modern outlook that was extraordinary in China at that time. However, the charming public spaces and exotic architecture in these areas have been criticized as a symbol of imperialist triumph on Chinese soil and a reflection of China's weakness after the Opium Wars. The Shanghai Bund and its ilk bore undeniable semi-colonial imprints. Over decades, these urban waterfronts have been remembered as places where China proved progress towards modernization, and yet also as places where the Chinese suffered humiliations imposed by the imperialists. The ambivalent Chinese attitude towards the semi-colonial heritage sites had an intangible yet powerful impact on their redevelopment in socialist China.

After 1978, the pace of urbanization in Chinese cities began to accelerate. Due to their advanced development and pivotal position in the cities, urban waterfronts like the Shanghai Bund faced the challenge of acting as a stimulus to city development. Reclaiming urban waterfronts was one of the most efficient and effective ways of increasing traffic flow in dense city centres. These promenades with linear open spaces could be easily widened into a broad traffic corridor. The renovation of the Shanghai Bund in the 1990s proved a triumph of engineering in resolving transportation and flooding problems. However, it is not surprising to note that the social and cultural values of historic urban waterfronts were often neglected in profit-driven development strategies and utilitarian approaches. The Bund's architecture was adapted to attract financial institutions, and socialist ideology was carefully implanted into the Bund's artificial landscapes to dilute any semi-colonial echoes. The Bund's post-1949 development process indicates that the redevelopment of historic urban waterfronts in China is closely linked to a changing political climate and economic environs. How to define and reinterpret their cultural significance and relevance to China's contemporary image has always been an implicit and critical factor in the regeneration of urban waterfronts that were created in the semi-colonial era.

With the rise of China's political and economic position in the world, Chinese cities were driven to reconfigure their cultural resources to compete with each other and with overseas rivals. The Shanghai Bund's renovation in the twenty-first century indicates a paradigm shift in the Chinese attitude towards semi-colonial heritage and their awareness of place competitiveness in the global context. The social and cultural values of semi-colonial heritage were reinterpreted to strengthen the city's identity. Despite their reluctance to fully address the cultural significance of these semi-colonial heritage sites, local governments realized the importance of employing them to bolster city image and to increase their competitiveness in the global context. The regeneration of the Shanghai Bund and its ilk proves that historic urban waterfronts could contribute to the quality of urban life in many aspects. Their geographical advantages and historical values have great potential to provide a powerful impetus for the economic, social and cultural development of the cities.

Note

1   The word *bungalow* in an Asian context widely refers to a detached house built during the colonial/semi-colonial era.

Bibliography

Bickers, R. (1998) 'Shanghailanders: The Formation and Identity of the British Settler Community in Shanghai, 1843–1937', *The Past and Present Society*, 159: 161–211.

Crow, D.G. (1999) *Historic Photographs of Shanghai, Hong Kong & Macao*, Hong Kong: Pressroom Printer & Designer.

Du, Y. and Y. Jin (1965) 'Jiu Zhongguo Shanghai Gonggong Zujie Jiebei, Daoqi he Waitan Gongyuan Ruyuan Guize: Meiying Diguo Zhuyi de Qinghua Zuizheng

[The Boundary Stele of the Shanghai International Settlement in Old China, Daoqi and Entry Regulations for the Bund Park: The Criminal Evidences of the American and British Imperialism]', *Wenwu [Cultural Relics]*, 4: 51–55.

Jones, F.-O. (2011) 'The Bund Is Back', Adapted from *ForbesLife Magazine*, 24 October 2011. Available at: www.forbes.com/forbes-life-magazine/2011/1107/escapes-bund-waterfront-shanghai-road-trip-finn-olaf-jones.html.

Knowledge Wharton (2010) 'Expo 2010's Legacy: What Did Shanghai Gain?' 24 November 2010. Available at: www.knowledgeatwharton.com.cn/index.cfm?fa=viewArticle&articleID=2336&languageid=1.

Luo, J. (2009) 'Shanghai Waitan Tongdao yu Dixia Kongjian Zongti Sheji [Shanghai Bund Tunnel and Master Plan of Underground Spaces]', *Shanghai Jianshe Keji [Shanghai Construction Science and Technology]*, 2: 4–8.

Luo, K. and W. Yan. (1987) 'Waitan, Shanghai de Chuangkou [The Bund: The Window of Shanghai]', *Liaowang [Outlook Weekly]*, 37: 17–19.

Luo, S. (2002) 'Waitan: Jindai Shanghai de Yanjing [The Bund: The Eyes of Modern Shanghai]', *Shiliao Yanjiu [Archives and History]*, 4: 32–38.

The Political Consultative Committees of Shanghai, Tianjin, Liaoning Province, Qingdao, Guangdong Province, Xiamen, Wuhan, and Guangzhou (compiled) (1992) *Lieqiang zai Zhongguo de Zujie [The Imperialists' Concessions in China]*, Beijing: Zhongguo Wenshi Press, 2.

Qian, Z. (2006) 'Shanghai Waitan: Dongya Zuifu Shengming de Guoji Gonggong Kongjian [The Shanghai Bund: The Most Famous International Public Space in East Asia]', *Tongji Daxue Xuebao Sehhui Kexue Ban [Tongji University Journal Social Science Section]*, 17(1): 34–39.

Shanghai Land Regulations (1845) From the Shanghai Land Regulations (Original and Present Codes) and Sundry Documents Relating There to, published by order of the Municipal Council for 1861; and Reprinted, with an Index, by order of the Municipal Council of 1868–69, Shanghai: North-China Herald Office.

Shanghai Municipal Archives (undated) *The Bund: Old Shanghai in Postcards*, Shanghai.

Tan, T. (2003) 'The Shanghai Bund: Heritage Site or Symbol of Colonialism?' 3 August 2003. Available at: http://202.157.165.165/Cities/DL/Aug0203Heritage.html.

Tan, Z. (ed.) (2010) 'Shanghai Waitan Shibo qian Chongsheng [The Rebirth of the Shanghai Bund before the Opening of the Expo]', *Duiwai Chuanbo [International Communications]*, 5: 40.

Taylor, J. E. (2002) 'The Bund: Littoral Space of Empire in the Treaty Ports of East Asia', *Social History*, 27(2): 125–42.

Xinmin Evening Newspaper (2014) 'Waitan Wanguo Jianzhu Ershi Nian Xiushan Jishi [A Record of 20-year Renovation of the Bund Architectures]', 6 January 2014. Available at: http://collection.sina.com.cn/cqyw/20140106/0829139237.shtml.

Yang, H. (2010) 'Shanghai Waitan Shenbao Shijie Wenhua Yichan de Kexingxing Fenxi [Feasibility Analysis of the Shanghai Bund's Application for UNESCO Cultural Heritages]', *Jingji Yanjiu Daokan [Economic Research Guide]*, 35(199): 74–75.

Zhao, Y. (2013) 'Yizhong Shechi Pinpai Cheli Waitan: Yeji Xiahua, Zhuanzhan Ersanxian Shichang [The Luxury Brands withdraw from the Bund: The Performance Declined and Shifting to the Second/Third Tier Markets]', *Time Weekly*, 240, 4 July 2013. Available at: http://time-weekly.com/story/2013–07–04/130175.html

13 The Landscape of Tokyo as a City on the Water—Past and Present

Hidenobu Jinnai

'City on the Water' From Edo to Modern Tokyo

Under the Tokugawa Shogunate, the city of Edo flourished greatly in practice both politically and economically as the main city of Japan. With the arrival of the Meiji Restoration (1867–68), the emperor moved to Edo from Kyoto. Edo became the capital of a modern nation and it changed its name to Tokyo.

Edo, the predecessor of Tokyo, had the unique personality of a 'city on the water'. In 1590, Tokugawa Ieyasu, who had moved to Edo, built a huge castle around the small medieval castle in Dokan Ota by utilizing the uneven topography at the protrusion of Musashino, a sprawling swamp that looks east out to the sea. As a defence system, an inner moat and outer moat encircled the castle (Jinnai 1990). Furthermore, to transport the materials necessary to construct the castle (such as a large amount of rocks) and also salt, foods and other such daily sustenance, the natural flow of the river was modified and several man-made canals were constructed, thus creating the urban grid of the 'city on the water' encircled by water channels in a mesh-like manner (Suzuki 1978).

In Edo, the area that developed on the hills to the west of the castle was called 'Yamanote' and was a lush green residential zone where the large residences of mainly ruling-class warriors stretched out. The lowland area to the east of the castle, resulting from the mesh-like formation of the water channels, was called 'Shitamachi' (downtown). It set the stage for the economic activities of merchants and craftsmen who were engaged in commerce and production (Seidensticker 1983).

The large amount of goods that arrived by large vessels from all over Japan were transferred onto small vessels offshore from the island of Tsukudajima, situated at the mouth of the River Sumida. These small vessels then travelled on the canal to transport the goods to the warehouses along the riverbanks (Yoshida 2015).

It is clear just by looking at the old maps that canals played an important role right from the early formation of Edo (Suzuki 2003). In fact, the maps show a much greater emphasis on the canal network than on roads.

Indeed, water had diverse functions and roles in Edo. In addition to ship transport/logistic activities and water-reliant production activities, the large number of fishing villages along the seashore of the city also played an important role. Shrines and temples were built in this community, while famed spots and places of amusement that enhanced the waterfront developed in the surroundings. In Japan, where people did not dominate but rather lived alongside nature, there was a sense of the sacred significance of water, and the sea and rivers played the role of purifying the soul (Jinnai 1990).

Edo was a city of wooden architecture. To protect itself from fire, empty lots (*hirokoji*) were retained at the foot of each bridge as fire prevention zones. Ordinarily, these lots were used as amusement districts, dotted with rows of makeshift teahouses and playhouses. Leading examples are Ryogoku Hirokoji and Edobashi Hirokoji (Takeuchi 2000). The development of a lively waterside plaza at the foot of each bridge, a key source of urban mobility, was one of the characteristics of Edo.

Playhouses that were approved by the Shogunate were built close to the canals and rivers, and the upper class travelled by boat to reach these amusement spots. In such a way, water was deeply connected with urban culture. Another characteristic of Edo is the many landscape paintings of the urban waterfront. Edo was a true 'city on the water'.

With the arrival of the Meiji era came modernization. A railway, horse-drawn railway and streetcars were introduced and Tokyo gradually evolved into a land city. Edo's characteristic as a 'city on the water' continued to be passed on, as many important buildings and facilities representative of the era of civilization and enlightenment emerged along the waterfront, rivers and canals. Until the Great Kanto Earthquake (1923), rows of traditional Japanese restaurants dotted the waterfront. However, by the latter part of the Meiji era, these establishments along the River Sumida and Tokyo Bay waterfront had been replaced by factories and large warehouses that relied on ship transport as the area developed into a modern economy support zone.

The Great Kanto Earthquake of 1923 totally eradicated the Edo sentiments along the waterfront. Instead, during the early days of the Showa era, the period of restoration, modern architecture of splendid design and modern bridges emerged, cultivating a new kind of waterfront beauty. In particular, the many beautiful modern steel bridges that characterized the River Sumida were said to be like a bridge exposition (Jinnai 1993).

With heavy traffic on the rivers and canals, ship transport inside the city remained active even after the earthquake. We are fortunate to have the dynamic visual record of cargo being unloaded by a crane that was installed on the roof of the Mitsubishi warehouse building. This building, facing the River Nihonbashi that runs through central Tokyo, was completed in 1930.

From the Loss of the Waterfront to Its Revival

In such a way, from the Edo period until right after the Second World War, the waterfront space was for some time the key player in various urban activities and landscapes of Tokyo (Pernice 2006). But by about 1960, during the period of high economic growth, it became the major victim of modern urban development. In particular, to realize the 1964 Tokyo Olympics, the canals and the riverfront that had been kept as open spaces became the first targets of the major urban infrastructural overhaul, making way for a highway network.

Water pollution is said to have been at its worst at about the time of the 1964 Tokyo Olympics. It was a time of true ordeal for the Tokyo waterfront. People who were raised in the downtown area tell me that they remember that the River Sumida and canals in central Tokyo were like a dead river. Some even commented that the river looked as though coal tar had been dumped there.

Fortunately, by the 1970s, the situation had gradually improved and newspapers optimistically reported that fish had returned to the River Sumida. After the 1973 oil shock, however, Japan entered a low growth period. There was self-reflection over the industrial development–only attitude that had destroyed the natural environment. History, environment, traditional culture, and everyday life were reconsidered and examined. The 'preservation' of landscapes, amenities and historical districts came to be a term used occasionally even in the field of urban planning.

With the extension of the underground sewerage system, citizens and public entities began to profess a greater interest in water. Against this background, sewerage regulations became stricter and water quality improved. By the late 1970s, there was a revival of the fireworks and regattas that had adorned the urban culture of Edo-Tokyo, the eternal city on the water, along with that of pleasure boats where banquets were held on the water. The waterfront revival rapidly spread to Tokyo Bay (Jinnai 1989). Youths discovered the charm of the Odaiba Marine Park and it garnered popularity as a windsurfing mecca. The dynamic waterscape of the view over the central Tokyo skyline was an impressive sight. This marked the first stage in the reinstatement of Tokyo's waterfront and it can be interpreted as the recovery of nature and the movement to revive recreational space (Figure 13.1).

There was also the birth of a movement to rediscover the value of the rivers that encircled the centre of Tokyo, the city on the water that had evolved from Edo. In 1979, the Kanda YMCA launched a civic boating activity along the Kanda, Nihonbashi and Sumida rivers to observe the city from the water.

Upon my return to Japan from my urban research methodology studies in Italy between 1973 and 1976, I began teaching at Hosei University. Since 1977, I have been working with the students at the Hosei University

Figure 13.1 View of central Tokyo from Odaiba Marine Park, early 1980s

Figure 13.2 Boat-survey of the city from the water, undertaken by Jinnai study group, 1980

Department of Architecture to reassess the historical urban space of Tokyo. Having realized the importance of Tokyo as a 'city on the water', in 1980 I also launched research to study Tokyo from a boat, as observed from the waterside (Figure 13.2).

While travelling on the water channels by boat to observe Tokyo from the water, one notes the successive emergence of numerous stone walls that were used to build canals during the Edo era, the remains of the castle gate, the old stone Tokiwa Bridge from the Meiji era, the Nihonbashi Bridge and other modern bridges from the early Showa era, and finally the numerous kinds of modern architecture that were built along the waterfront. All reveal the compressed history of Edo-Tokyo that has passed along the rivers and canals (Jinnai 1990). Gradually, the awareness of Edo, the predecessor of Tokyo, as a city on the water has come to be instilled amongst its citizens.

Turning Point in Land Usage and Waterfront Restoration

In the 1970s, the industrial and economic structure in the bay area of Tokyo in fact reached a major turning point. During the premodern era, the shallow waters of the Tokyo Bay had originally been the perfect fishing spot: along the coastline, in places like Fukagawa, Tsukudajima, Shinagawa, Omori, Haneda and so on, there were many fishing towns that formed a traditional community. Famed locations and amusement areas developed among the temples and shrines and their remains surface clearly in local surveys. Although canals remained during the modern era for vessel transport and drainage purposes, land reclamation from the shallow waters was pursued to expand the factory and port space. This led to the physical distancing of the sea at the hands of humans. This was further accelerated by seawater pollution caused by urbanization and industrialization.

However, with the arrival of the 1970s and the end of the age of industrialization, the factories, now deemed to be inefficient use of land, began to withdraw from the seashores close to central Tokyo. Furthermore, the innovation of port functions led to the collapse of the existing system of transferring cargo onto small vessels and transporting it into warehouses along the canal. In the new system, large container ships docked at the wharf where the cargo was unloaded and transported by truck. Warehouses were no longer necessary. With these changes over time, converting the use of the factory and port-function sites became focal issues here in Tokyo, in the same way as in Western cities. This happened in the early 1980s.

In such a way, the second stage of waterfront restoration saw the birth of the movement to construct residential buildings on the waterfront land. With the expansion of residential areas into the suburbs and use of central urban space for business purposes, the central Tokyo wards rapidly lost their night-time population. In the late 1970s, discussions took place to use the sites of the ex-factories and logistic facilities to supply homes, thus returning central Tokyo to the people. The Okawabata Project was one such plan to develop the area along the mouth of the River Sumida in the Chuo ward. Based on the project concept, River City 21 was realized on the former site of the Ishikawajima-Harima Heavy Industries Co. Ltd shipbuilding yard. Rows of many high-rise residential buildings formed a new skyline. Taking advantage of this occasion, the Tokyo Metropolitan Government created the so-called Super Embankment. This system resuscitated the waterfront in Okawabata. Unlike the tall, ugly concrete embankment that was built in the 1960s to protect the city from water disasters such as typhoons, this was a mildly sloped embankment that resembled a greenery-filled park. Now, pedestrians were able to approach the River Sumida and the edge of the waterfront.

At about the same time came the third stage, the so-called loft culture movement, in the early 1980s. With the changes in the logistics system, container ships became the main means of ship cargo transport. Cities were commonly inclined to move the wharfs to the area outside the existing old ports where the water was deeper and the space larger. At the same time, warehouses in the vicinity of old ports lost their goods warehousing function, affording the possibility of land usage in a new and contemporary way. The creative movement that had been bred by artists who lived on the top floors of warehouses (lofts) in the Soho district of New York spread to Tokyo. In the early 1980s, there were enthusiastic movements to convert empty warehouses into galleries, live venues, restaurants, event spaces, discos, etc. in the bay areas such as Okawabashi, Fukagawa, Shibaura, Shinagawa, and they won popularity among the young people (Jinnai 1989).

In such a way, from the late 1970s to the mid 1980s, the waterfront in Tokyo brimmed with the joy of having been returned to the hands of the people (Jinnai 1993).

Lights and Shadows of Waterfront Development

However, the fourth stage during the late 1980s coincided with the bubble economy period, completely overturning the situation. The demand for high-rise office buildings shot up as Tokyo, the sophisticated tech society, became known as the leading global centre of finance. Low-density lands in the bay area became the perfect targets for this development. As sophistication and efficient land usage came to be sought, one after another the warehouses that had gained popularity in the loft culture disappeared, to be replaced by high-rises, or so-called intelligent buildings. With skyrocketing land prices, it became difficult to supply housing. Thereafter, bay area development projects stopped and by the peak of the bubble economy era, business space supply became the focus. It seems that there was once again a return to uninhabited urban space planning.

Looking at overseas cases, it seems that there, appropriate waterfront functions and roles—as residential, cultural and artistic activity hubs, for example—continued to be properly planned and deep rooted even after the

1980s, leading to the realization of complex and charming bay areas. This was the main difference from Japan.

At the International Waterfront Conference that was held in Venice in 1991, a presentation was made of the Tokyo metropolitan government's urban development plan for the Tokyo Waterfront City on the man-made reclaimed land (lot no. 13). Criticism was voiced over the tight scheduling of this business function–focused, large-scale development planning that was due to be executed. This direction of development was actually abandoned with the cancellation of the Tokyo Expo during Governor Aoshima's administration. However, the recreational functions around the Odaiba Marine Park, and the event and cultural functions of the Tokyo Waterfront City around the Big Site convention centre have been successful.

Nature is recovering in the small bay where a man-made beach has been created. Another interesting sight offshore is the fortress (the fort on which the canon was installed that was hastily constructed as protection against attacks from Western combat fleets during the end of the Edo era). Regattas, beach volleyball games and other such events are held here. The scene of banquets held on the pleasure boats that congregate on the water offers a new kind of waterfront landscape, typical of contemporary Tokyo.

At the aforementioned International Waterfront Conference in Venice, the residents of the community of Tsukudajima, the former fishermen's village that is situated at the mouth of the River Sumida, united under their powerful community leaders to safeguard their lands and homes from the economic waves of the development deluge, including the mass development of River City 21 on adjacent land. These fishermen were highly commended by the mayor of Venice for preserving their traditional community and old wooden houses. The commemorative trophy that was made by the maestro of Murano decorates the Sumiyoshi shrine office.

During the fifth stage, after the bursting of the bubble economy in the 1990s, the character and image of the Tokyo Waterfront City changed. Establishments that had gained popularity in the loft culture were gone and people's interest in the waterfront, the image of a business space with rows of high-rise offices, receded like an ebb tide. Consequently, the reclaimed lands have never been inhabited, and no one has shown any attachment to them.

But this can also be described as the arrival of a new situation. With the decline in land prices, Japanese society had entered the sixth stage—maturity—and this strengthened the phenomenon of the return to central Tokyo. Within this flow, the number of high-rise apartments in central Tokyo increased at an accelerated pace, with reclaimed areas proving to be perfect building sites. This time, we saw the successive construction at the hands of developers of high-rise apartment buildings in place of bubble-era offices.

Since the abandonment of the Tokyo Waterfront City planning, the public sector in Tokyo has remained in the shadows and has refrained from taking a strong initiative in urban planning. Instead, development has been pursued at the hands of private developers. This situation is somewhat different from that in Western cities where the public sector has taken the lead in calling upon the private sector to strategically and dynamically pursue waterfront development.

In any case, in this space that saw the successive emergence of high-rise residences, we see a changing definition of the waterfront. During the loft culture period, we sensed the joy of the waterfront being returned to the hands of the people, and there was a feeling that people were seeking cultural stimulation in this space that was detached from everyday life. Yet, at this point, this was changing as it came to be defined as an everyday space inhabited by many people.

At the same time, during the splendid waterfront boom of the uninhabited Tokyo Waterfront City in the 1980s, there was a steady expansion of movements by civilians and residents to preserve the natural environment of the many riverfront areas of Tokyo, including the Sumida, Kanda, Meguro, Tama and Nogawa rivers. In places like Hino City, 30km to the west of central Tokyo, movements to preserve the water quality of the Tama region's agricultural water channels became active. It is symbolic that the River Nogawa in Musashino was so polluted that it was nicknamed the 'Waste River'. Yet, thanks to the efforts of civilians and public entities, this same river has been restored as a beautiful waterfront environment where marine creatures can survive (Jinnai 2013).

Movements to preserve, restore and utilize the various water spaces that shape Tokyo's ecosystem have increased steadily, after coming into being right after the urban waterfront boom had subsided from the Tokyo Waterfront City like a low tide. The aforementioned water spaces include inland rivers that have a long history and have been a familiar part of people's everyday lives, canals, drinking water tanks, agricultural water channels, springs that dot the cliff lines, and lakes created around the springs. It is possible to reassess Tokyo as a 'city on the water' from an all-round perspective, not just from the downtown area, the eastern lowland where canals and rivers pass which we saw earlier, but also from the west that covers the hills of Yamanote, suburbs and countryside.

In this direction, the extension of the underground sewerage system and construction of anti-flood underground water tanks played a big role in the restoration of Tokyo's water space. In consideration of all the aspects of the rivers—such as flood control, water utilization and environment—amendments were made to the River Act (2007) to introduce a river maintenance planning system reflective of local opinions. It also needs to be pointed out that this resulted in a heightened movement to restore the waterfront environment.

Waterfront Movements in Central Tokyo in Recent Years

Many of the rivers in Japan have swift currents. Floods from heavy, concentrated rain and typhoons are problems. The rivers are also exposed to the dangers of high sea tides. As a result, by the modern era, there were stringent flood prevention measures. The area surrounding the dykes and inland space are under strict public control by the national government or public entities. The mooring of boats is not permitted and various activities by private citizens have been banned. As controls have become stricter, the distancing of the people from the waters has also increased.

However, since the mid 1970s, the values of the time have changed sharply. Among citizens, there has been a rapidly growing interest in rivers and the waterfront. Water quality has improved and today there is an increased interest in the needs of the waterfront, bringing back the waterfront to the hands of the people and utilizing these water spaces effectively for different purposes.

Against this background, a movement to relax waterside space usage regulations has taken off in Tokyo Waterfront City. Under the name 'Canal Renaissance', in limited regions the port authority of Metropolitan Tokyo began relaxing water area usage regulations for canals and suchlike. As a result, based on talks at the local community meetings, floating restaurants, on-board cafes etc. have been realized in Shinagawaura, the Tennozu districts and Toyosu district, among others. This is how liveliness has returned to the waterfront.

In recent years, in addition to the Tokyo municipal government, ward offices for the districts of Chuo, Koto and Sumida (home to many water channels, rivers and canals amongst others) have begun to focus on urban planning that utilizes the waterside and also on the development of cultural tourism. Thanks to the favourable winds brought by the birth of the Tokyo Sky Tree (634m), the new symbol of Tokyo, there has been a stronger movement to connect the wider Tokyo area by water transport and to restore Tokyo to a 'city on the water'. The Chuo ward has built a boat landing site at the foot of the Nihonbashi Bridge which has proved successful; the main player there is the small 'Kawasemi' (kingfisher) water bus that is run by the Tokyo municipal park association. Thanks to community trials on pleasure boating, the plans to use inland rivers in the Koto and Sumida wards are on track. Soon, it will be possible to enjoy the boat ride to the Tokyo Sky Tree neighbourhood along the Nihonbashi, Sumida, Onagi (passing through the Ogibashi lock gate), Yokojukken and Kitajukken river route.

Partly due to the effects of the aforementioned Canal Renaissance, in 2011 Metropolitan Tokyo took the initiative to call upon four wards—Chuo, Taito, Koto and Sumida—that face the River Sumida to embark on the 'Sumida River Renaissance'. Today, that term is spreading inside Tokyo. Last May, an impressive illuminations event was organized called 'Tokyo Fireflies'. The numerous participants released LED light bulbs on the water; the bulbs lit up like fireflies to create a flow of lights. It created an illusionary world where tradition and modernity merged splendidly. Of all the rivers, the citizens of Edo-Tokyo have the strongest attachment to the River Sumida. Historical memories are everywhere, there are many shrines and famed spots, and in the surrounding areas, there are many neighbourhoods that are fun to stroll through.

With the heightening of interest in the eastern area of Tokyo around the River Sumida, the Taito ward took advantage of the recent movements by the Ministry of Land, Infrastructure, Transport and Tourism to relax regulations. It will soon open two open-air cafes in the controlled area of the riverfront inside the Sumida river park. These will be Tokyo's first open-air cafes, perfectly located for enjoying the riverfront landscape. Much expectation is also being held out for the deliberation of a project to use lighting effects to enhance the allure of the Sumida riverfront.

The Future Direction that Tokyo Should Aim For

In Europe, cities like London, Amsterdam, Hamburg and so on, have experienced many cases of the splendid success of large-scale public waterfront restoration and redevelopment projects. In all, the ports and industrial zones that were built during the modern age of industrialization were matched with contemporary needs and their uses converted according to a plan, resulting in a splendid restoration. Tokyo, however, has many market economy–based development projects that have been implemented at the hands of private developers. But unfortunately, there are only a handful of cases of large-scale public urban restoration that are based on a particular vision and implemented according to a well-planned process like in Europe.

Yet, within this historical experience, Tokyo has built a city on the water with diverse topographical and natural conditions, and a rich array of functions and uses that have taken advantage of the aforementioned situations. Thus, from the perspective of the waterfront landscape, a new kind of modern theme, it seems that Tokyo has much greater potential than other cities worldwide.

Unlike a European city, historically Tokyo did not have fortresses, and the boundaries between the city and countryside were also vague. It has built an environment of abundantly incorporated natural elements such as water and greenery within the urban grid. From here the unique sensitivities of its landscape have emerged. The slopes of the land, forests on the hills, greenery along the cliffs, presence of springs, and the many rivers that meander through the uneven topography and varying coastline have determined the direction taken by the urban space. Tokyo has shown its diverse faces as the 'city on the water', by being more than just a port space that faces the bay or a waterfront of the river or canal.

If we look to the bay area, we note that lands which have been reclaimed from shallow waters and are surrounded by canals in certain ways form an archipelago (group of islands) together with the man-made islands floating on the water. The bay area has the potential to create an attractive waterfront landscape and a new kind of urban environment by nurturing the characteristic of each island.

Since the Meiji Restoration in the late nineteenth century, Japan has pursued modernization and Westernization. Achieving high growth in the post-war period, it created an affluent society. We have been in the maturity stage for a long time and we are now preparing for a rapidly ageing and declining population. Our Japanese society has repeatedly expanded and developed its cities by sacrificing its history and nature; today, it is approaching a true turning point.

Amongst its citizens, there have been movements to reassess the richness of the topography unique to Tokyo and the value of the urban culture bred by the water and greenery; these movements have fortunately become quite strong in recent years. In different regions, we see civilian activities to resuscitate and in many ways utilize the waterfront space that had been either lost or damaged by modern industrialization.

The key water route that encircles central Tokyo—the Sumida, Kanda and Nihonbashi rivers—narrates the history of Edo-Tokyo as it still lies dormant today with very little ship traffic. However, much expectation is being held out for the restoration and utilization of this dynamic and rich water space, which Tokyo can boast to the world. Since 2005, there has been serious consideration on ways to demolish the highways that were forcibly built above Nihonbashi in the lead-up to the Tokyo Olympics. If that materializes in the near future, a true 'city on the water' will be resuscitated in central Tokyo.

Today, the Sumida River Renaissance is being looked to for further development so that a grand design can be created for Tokyo, the 'city on the water'. I have repeatedly said that Tokyo is blessed with a rich topography and a variety of water spaces such as rivers, water channels, springs, ponds, moats, canals and the sea (Jinnai 2013). The future possibilities for the waterfront are bound to be great. Now is the time to re-examine the basis of the major significance and value of the landscape of Tokyo, the 'city on the water'.

Bibliography

Jinnai, H. (ed.) (1989) *Mizube Toshi—Edo-Tokyo no Waterfront Tanken (Water City: Adventure of Waterfront of Edo-Tokyo)*, Tokyo: Asahi Shinbunsha.

Jinnai, H. (1990) 'The Spatial Structure of Edo,' in *Tokugawa Japan: The Social and Economic Antecedents of Modern Japan*, Tokyo: University of Tokyo Press. pp. 124–146.

Jinnai, H. (ed.) (1993) *Misu no Tokyo (Tokyo as a Water City)*, Tokyo: Iwanami shoten.

Jinnai, H. (1995) *Tokyo, a Spatial Anthropology*, Berkley: University California Press.

Jinnai, H. (ed.) (2013) *Mizu no Toshi Edo-Tokyo (Water City Edo-Tokyo)*, Tokyo: Kodansha.

Pernice, R. (2006) 'The Transformation of Tokyo During the 1950s and Early 1960s Projects Between City Planning and Urban Utopia', *Journal of Asian Architecture and Building Engineering*, 5(2): 253–260.

Pernice, R. (2007) 'The Issue of Tokyo Bay's Reclaimed Lands as the Origin of Urban Utopias in Modern Japanese Architecture', *AIJ-Journal of Architecture and Planning*, 267(March): 259–266.

Sacchi, L. (2004) *Tokyo City and Architecture*, Milano: Íkira Editore

Seidensticker, E.G. (1983) *Low City, High City*, New York: Knopf.

Suzuki, M. (1978) *Edo no Kawa, Tokyo no Kawa (Rivers in Edo, Rivers in Tokyo)*, Tokyo: Nihon Hoso Shuppan Kyokai.

Suzuki, M. (ed.) (2003) *Zusetsu Edo-Tokyo no Kawa to Mizube no Jiten (Encyclopedia of Rivers of Edo-Tokyo and Waterfronts)*, Tokyo: Kashiwa shobo.

Takeuchi, M. (2000) *Edo no Sakariba-ko (Bustling places in Edo)*, Tokyo: Kyoiku shuppan.

Waley, P. (2013) 'Placing Tokyo in Time and Space', *Journal of Urban History*, 39: 331–335.

Yoshida, N. (2015) *Toshi Edo ni ikiru (Live in a City Edo)*, Tokyo: Iwanami shoten.

New Redevelopment Strategies

14 The Transformation of North-western European Urban Waterfronts—Divergence and Convergence of Redevelopment Strategies

Dirk Schubert

Introduction

First of all, the term *north-western Europe* needs defining. The geographical definition of north-western Europe includes the states of Scandinavia, the Baltic States, Ireland and the northern parts of Great Britain and Germany. It is comprised of cities of various population sizes and economic significance on the Baltic and the North Sea. This article does not examine examples in former Eastern bloc countries such as Gdansk (Lorens 2001), Gdynia, Szczin, St Petersburg (Figure 14.1), Kaliningrad, Klaipeda, Riga and Tallinn, because of their difficult post-socialist political and economic situations. In Eastern Europe developments in sea ports have transformed many waterfronts, which were—usually for military reasons—cut off from the city and inaccessible. Many ambitious projects were delayed there, had to be altered and their scale reduced. Conflicts between investors and planners with long, varied experience from Western countries and the agenda of newcomers in the field with post-socialist leanings seem to be inevitable. Any literature on the subject is also scarce. However, a comparative study of these projects would be a worthwhile endeavour.

North-western European seaports and waterfront transformations have more characteristics in common with each other than with their counterparts worldwide. Examples and projects like Swansea, Cardiff, Belfast (Titanic Quarter), Glasgow (Glasgow Harbour), Edinburgh (Leith and Granton Waterfront), Hull, Gateshead, Newcastle, Portsmouth, Koge, Aalborg, Helsingborg (Northern Harbour H99), Stavanger, Rotterdam (Kop van Zuid), Amsterdam (Eastern Docklands) and Bremen (Überseestadt) could not be evaluated due to lack of space. The question arises whether there is a specific north-western European tradition and planning culture that typifies these projects and goes beyond a response to weather conditions alone.

Figure 14.1 St Petersburg: apartments and unfinished, speculative investments along Malaya Neva

How do these projects differ from those in southern Europe, the Mediterranean region, North America or Asia?

For several decades now, port cities worldwide have been restructuring former derelict docks and waterfronts in their inner cities. Relocation of ship building to Asia, containerization of cargo handling and significant contraction in job opportunities had already led to the transformation of inner city waterfronts in North America in the 1960s. San Francisco, Baltimore and Boston have been the most important examples to demonstrate how derelict waterfronts can be revitalized, revaluated and reintegrated into the urban fabric. The abandonment and subsequent reclamation of the waterfront can be understood only in the context of worldwide restructuring, changes in dock labour and the spatial framework of city and port. Differences in cause, procedure, results and planning traditions must be taken into account. Transformation and reclamation is not simply a matter of architectural design but also depends on a complex set of planning, institutional, political, client-related, economic, ecological, legal and financial issues. For this reason comparative case studies help to identify characteristic local features that may provide opportunities for port and city, water and land, history, the present day and the future to merge into a new symbiosis.

What dimensions would be available for a comparison of projects and plans to allow classification of types, 'success stories' and 'best practices'? First of all, it seems obvious to consider the temporal perspective (Schubert 2011a: 62). Start, implementation and completion of projects allow conclusions to be drawn about the various guiding principles that relate to planning. For this reason it seems appropriate to categorize 'generations' of waterfront regeneration projects. However, in many cases it is not so easy to put a date to the start of the planning and construction process, and even more difficult to identify the 'end' of a project. Many projects were extended after the start of planning, changed or (repeatedly) converted. Gothenburg (Norra Älvstranden) is one example of a project that has been 'in progress' for the past thirty years.

Another way of approaching categorization by type is to look at the overriding objectives for a transformation, which are linked to the individual urban and regional context of the housing and office market (Schubert 2011b: 78). The reason for a project is often driven by a specific goal. Projects in Copenhagen and Helsinki can be seen as housing led, even though they also include other uses. Typical examples for office-led development are the London Docklands and the Isle of Dogs, while Bilbao could be analyzed as culture led and Genova as tourism led.

However, the authors Newman and Thornley (1996: 29) have taken diverse planning cultures as the starting point for their differentiation. They distinguish between Scandinavian and Eastern European, Napoleonic, British and Mediterranean planning cultures. Each one is derived from a mix of historic, political and planning law framework conditions.

Seaports clearly share structural similarities, developed in response to common dynamics. Yet, in a way, no two seaports are alike, and no seaport in the world is like another. Each has its own face, special character and individual history. Their geographical conditions, technical possibilities, historical development, constellation of stakeholders and transport connections to the hinterland are different (Schubert 2011a: 54). As a rule, the cycle of transformations is always quite similar. The starting point is always the withdrawal and/or relocation of the port or the navy. This results in underused areas, many close to the city centre, that become available for new uses. Planners and architects produce ideas—often utopian at first—which develop into proposals. In a step-by-step process they are transferred into concrete master plans or local plans and are detailed further in construction projects. In most cases, special competent bodies and development corporations are specifically constituted for this purpose. In due course, this is followed by an incremental implementation of plans and leads to the eventual revitalization of the port and waterfront, which are once again made accessible to the public. Large-scale waterfront transformations are important features for the marketing of cities that seek to create a new post-industrial image.

Scandinavian Examples

However, the local conditions of these examples remain extremely diverse. The transformation of the waterfront near Copenhagen's city centre, where regeneration started nearly two decades ago, is nearing completion. The harbour area became one of the trendiest spots. New uses have been introduced on the waterfront, ranging from an opera house, housing and office developments to floating swimming baths as well as a 12-kilometre promenade that already is a popular destination. Sydhavn, Teglholmen and Sluseholmen are new residential areas of approximately 120 hectares with nearly 5,000 residential units, crisscrossed by canals with houseboats. More than thirty architects were involved and have contributed to the diverse design proposals for the neighbourhood. Following the Dutch example, all areas are pedestrian and bicycle friendly.

Plans for the Nordhavn project rely on artificial landfill to create attractive waterfront sites. The implementation of proposals for homes for approximately 40,000 citizens and the same number of jobs is anticipated to take the next thirty to forty years. Realization has just begun and the target is to create 'an area of opportunity' that is distinctive, authentic, diverse and complex. Ferries and water buses connect the northern and southern waterfront areas of Copenhagen. The Öresund Bridge, opened in 2000, has allowed the two cities of Copenhagen and Malmö to coalesce. This was achieved through a kind of division of labour: Copenhagen has a ferry port, cruise ship terminal and airport, while most transhipment was relocated to Malmö. A dual-state company, Copenhagen Malmö Ports (CMP), is responsible for port development plans.

In Malmö, Västra Hamnen (130 hectares), an area created by landfill next to the city centre, was occupied by a shipyard (Kockum) and later by a car factory (SAAB). The bridge crossing the Öresund has linked Malmö and South Sweden to the rest of the European mainland, offering opportunities for new business activities and jobs and creating demand for housing. Heavy industries are being replaced by other businesses. Former industrial areas of Malmö became sites for Malmö University buildings as well as high-tech and IT firms and service industries. The city has bought a lot of the land since 1996 and owns most of the Västra Hamnen redevelopment area. In 2001, there was an attempt to catalyze further investment with the 'BoO1' European Housing Fair, but it went bankrupt. The Turning Torso high-rise (architect: Santiago Calatrava) is the highest residential building in Sweden (190 metres) and a landmark building within the mixed-use areas of Flagghusen, Dockan, Fullriggaren, Masthusen and Varvsparken, comprising around 2,500 students' apartments (2008: 294). The residential areas open up towards the water, with parks and plazas offering views to the Öresund Bridge. The mix of uses provides a diverse character, although residential use dominates. Västra Hamnen has become a showpiece for sustainable urban redevelopment in the Malmö area, designed to prevent urban sprawl and support sustainable, denser development. This large-scale redevelopment process, in a city with only about 280,000 inhabitants, involved a change of identity, which was achieved by the concept of 'planning in dialogue'.

The examples of waterfront redevelopment in Stockholm also illustrate the Swedish proactive, plan-led welfare state approach. Hammarby Sjöstad is a model project for sustainable housing that was implemented on a former industrial waterfront site. When planning work began in the 1980s, it was seen as a unique opportunity to expand the inner city. Hammarby Sjöstad ('lake/water-city') is located on the south-east side of the central Söderalm Island. Once completed (by around 2018), the new 160-hectare city neighbourhood will have approximately 13,000 apartments for more than 28,000 residents and a total of 36,000 people who will live and work in this area. Today nearly 80% of Hammarby Sjöstad—Stockholm's largest and most popular urban development project—has been built. The location within the urban district provides a 'natural' extension of the city centre, which was an important factor influencing the design of the urban fabric, infrastructure and architecture.

The implementation of Hammarby Sjöstad adds a new 'growth ring' to the urban areas of Stockholm. The architecture can be described as modern, semi-open blocks—a combination of modernistic and open typologies and closed, traditional urban elements. Inner city street dimensions, block sizes, building heights, density and mix of functionality are integrated with a new openness, waterfront views, parks and sunlight. The modernistic architecture focuses on sustainable and even contemporary materials such as glass, wood, steel and stone. Each building block was designed and detailed by a different team of architects. This system was criticized for its 'copy-paste architecture', with three to six buildings of the same style in a row, especially at the waterfront.

The construction of Hammarby Sjöstad is based on strict environmental requirements. Therefore, a special programme was devised to cut the environmental footprint by half, as compared to an area built in the early 1990s. This required completely new environmental solutions, which led to the 'Hammarby model'. The Hammarby model describes the new neighbourhood's own eco-cycle, offering environmental solutions for energy, waste, water and sewage.

Another transformation project that has been placed on the agenda recently is Royal Seaport, Sweden's largest city district. This is to be developed over the next two decades, around 3.2 kilometers from the city centre of Stockholm. It stretches from Hjorthagen in the north, through the port area, to Loudden in the south. The project is being built at Värtahamnen, Stockholm's largest port, which will be reconstructed and extended further into the bay. Today the port serves only the extensive ferry traffic to Finland and Estonia, while huge parts are vacant and free for other uses. Planning of the Royal Seaport project started in early 2000. Building work on the Värtahamnen Port extension started in 2008 and the first residential buildings were completed by 2011. In 2013, a new passenger terminal was opened. The former commercial and industrial site, comprising around 240 hectares, is to provide 12,000 dwellings for 350 residents, as well as workplaces. Partial completion is planned for 2020 and the whole project is expected to be fully developed by 2030. The project is based on the experience of Hammarby Sjöstad—especially its environmental programme—with the target to create a sustainable urban district in central Stockholm. The development of the Royal Seaport will focus on efficient building processes and sustainable transport solutions as well as energy conservation and efficiency. To achieve this goal, three overall environmental targets were defined:

- by 2020, carbon emissions to be lower than 1.5 tonnes per person and year,
- by 2030, Stockholm Royal Seaport to be free of fossil fuels,
- Stockholm Royal Seaport is to adapt to future climate change.

A third transformation project is the redevelopment of Kvarnholmen (Mill Island), a peninsula located east of Stockholm's inner city at the border to the archipelago. Most of the historic industrial buildings will be renewed and transformed into apartments and some offices. The master plan also includes the construction of several new modernistic apartment buildings at the waterfront for high-income earners. Construction of 2,500 dwellings for 5,000 people started around 2010. The target group for the new residential area is families, a fact that is proven by the proposal for a new primary school for 700 pupils and several other facilities for small children. The Kvarnholmen project is expected to be completed by 2022.

In Helsinki ('Daughter of the Baltic Sea') transhipment of cargo was completely relocated to the new city of Vuosaari, while passenger terminals remained. Since the early 1980s, the city has been considering ideas for converting the industrial waterfront to housing. The port near the city centre serves only ferries and cruise ships (South Harbour: Eteläsatama; West Terminal: Länsiterminaali). Jätkäsaari is still the home port for ferries from Helsinki to Tallinn; more than 5 million passengers travel from the terminals each year. Former ports and dockyards are being developed into new housing areas at Ruoholahti and Jätkäsaari that are near to completion (Figure 14.2). An underground line connects Ruoholahti to the city centre. Advertising slogans proclaim it to be 'the Amsterdam of the Baltic Sea'. According to a new strategic plan (2009), approximately 16,000 people will live in an area of 100 hectares and around 6,000 jobs will be provided (Othengrafen 2012: 143). The construction has required massive landfill and the clean-up of contaminated soil.

Altogether 20 kilometres of new public promenades have been built in these areas. Pedestrian and cycle routes offer a network of safe and pleasant connections. The archipelago along the shoreline of Helsinki comprises around 300 islands, most owned by the state and the city but assigned for

Figure 14.2 Helsinki: ferries, shipyards and new residential buildings along the waterfront

use by the defence forces. It is intended to develop the archipelago for the use of citizens in the future. As the city of Helsinki owns about 70% of the land, a plan-led approach could be implemented.

Oslo is a city in stormy transition, rapidly expanding and anticipating that its population will grow from around 630,000 inhabitants today to around 800,000 in a decade. The region has a population of approximately 1.8 million, which is more than one third of the country's total population. The former port facilities have been relocated, and Oslo Fjord offers space for Oslo's booming expansion. The conversion of the port and dockyards in the city centre began with the Aker Brygge project, where 380 apartments were built, plus office space, shops and restaurants. Meanwhile, relocated on Tjuvholmen ('Island of Thieves'), the Astrup Fearnley Museum of Contemporary Arts (architect: Renzo Piano) has become a new highlight. The idyllic canals of Tjuvholmen provide attractive gathering points along the waterfront and attract more than 6 million visitors per year.

Discussion revolved around the question of whether the new development would be on the right scale for the existing urban fabric, and critics spoke of a new Hong Kong rising up on Oslo Fjord. While work on the western part of the 225-hectare site was started in 1982, the eastern part of the transformation did not begin until 2000. The ensuing controversy was focused on development that would take place in either Harbour City or Fjord City. It was decided in favour of Fjord City because this development provided approximately 9,000 residential units and new jobs on the waterfront. A charette was held to involve participation of locals as well as national and international experts. In tandem with improvements to the transport infrastructure, the Oslo Opera flagship project in Bjorvika (architects: Snohetta) and the Edvard Munch Museum (architects: Einar Myklebust and Gunnar Fougner) ensured that Fjord City was running 'on course'. The culture-led Bilbao effect may have played only a minor role here, although culture is an important catalyst. Plans for the transformation of Norway's prosperous oil capital Stavanger (Urban Sjofront) are still in their early stage.

Irish and British Examples of Waterfront Transformation

In Dublin, plans for the transformation of the Custom House Docks (11 hectares) and the International Finance Service Centre (IFSC) began in the 1980s with the relocation of the port to the mouth of the Liffey (Figure 14.3). In the 1970s, the neglected docklands developed a reputation as being one of Dublin's most notorious 'no-go-areas' (Wonneberger

Figure 14.3 Dublin: different scale of buildings along the Liffey

2011: 54). Accompanied by selective out-migration of the population as well as industries, the inner city and especially the docklands declined. The changing economic situation under the Urban Renewal Act set the path for transformation in the port area. The provision of tax incentives, which was not common at the time, made the project a big success. Deriving from the East Asian Tiger economies, the name 'Celtic Tiger' refers to a period of rapid economic growth in Ireland, and especially in booming Dublin.

The city needed to become more competitive and so adopted a proactive approach. The IFSC was developed as a mono-structure comprising offices, financial service providers, banks and insurance companies, with only a few apartments. Foreign investments were attracted and created many new jobs. However, next to Dublin's most successful business district lay one of its poorest and most disadvantaged communities. During the implementation of the IFSC, central government played an important role by giving financial incentives. Later, the city and Dublin Docklands Development Authority (DDDA) took over more responsibility (Moore 2008: 101) to guarantee greater democratic control, participation and a change from property-led regeneration to a more inclusive perspective. The notorious flats at Sheriff Street were demolished and some of the long-stay residents were relocated in the immediate locality. Critics complain about a significant social polarization to keep yuppies apart from the poorer community by means of a 'Berlin Wall' and a park that serves as a buffer zone between Sheriff Street and the IFSC.

The redevelopment area was extended and now comprises 520 hectares, including the existing housing areas around it. At first, the planners sought to exploit the experience of Baltimore and later on that of the London Docklands to build a 'world-class city quarter'. The DDDA was granted similar powers to the London Docklands Development Corporation (LDDC). The regeneration of the historic docklands has changed the 'mental map' of Dublin City, and based on the 1997 master plan, housing as well as cultural facilities such as a new college and performing arts venue were built. The National Conference Centre at Spencer Dock/Royal Canal is another prestigious project; the neighbouring apartment buildings heated up the discussion about high-rise development. The DDDA was founded to secure social and economic regeneration on a sustainable basis. The surrounding communities, where 'everybody knows everybody else', had also been taken into consideration through education and training programmes. A tramway (LUAS) provides good access to the city centre. About 20% of the more than 3,500 new homes was specifically reserved for social and affordable housing, in the context of the national Social Inclusion Agenda.

New lifestyles and work patterns began to take hold in the former docklands. Young professional residents wanted launderettes, dry cleaners, convenience stores, restaurants and cafés. The new-found café culture in Dublin's urban society is signalling the increasing internationalization of consumer demand. After decades of deterioration, unemployment and social problems, the five dockland communities generally embraced the ongoing changes and job opportunities in the financial or IT sector. But the significant changes brought a widespread debate about high-rise buildings (which were absolutely new in Dublin) and living in flats as opposed to the traditional way of living. Many of the old structures were demolished and much of the area's cultural heritage lost. While the old communities are rooted in a specific local urban port territory, the new residents, living in gated apartments, tend to have a more nomadic lifestyle. Another form of inner-city living began to emerge in Dublin as a result of regeneration.

Dublin's docklands were promoted as a dynamic, futuristic place to work and live by re-branding and re-imagining Dublin as a boomtown, although the Celtic Tiger boom has reinforced inequality. However, the rapid realization of projects in Dublin was caught up in the maelstrom of the financial and housing crisis and an over-heated market. An updated master plan (2012–2040) was prepared which relates to the Dublin City Development Plan. In 2013 the DDDA was abolished and its responsibilities were assumed by the City Council. Meanwhile a 'critical mass' is being built that may attract further inward investment and mitigate the worst excesses of a purely 'market-led' approach with the aim of achieving more sustainable development.

While waterfronts in Great Britain are mostly discussed through the example of the market-led London Docklands redevelopment, another approach was started in Liverpool. The redevelopment was launched in the 1980s by the Merseyside Development Corporation (MDC), a quango (quasi autonomous non-governmental organization) installed by the Thatcher government and Michael Heseltine. One of Liverpool's flagship projects was Albert Dock, which re-opened as a tourist attraction in 1988. In a period when Liverpool pursued radical left-wing policies in opposition to the ideas of the central government, it became difficult to gain access to subsidies and to attract new businesses. Port facilities and shipyards on both sides of the Mersey were closed down and unemployment was mounting, resulting in political unrest and the deterioration of housing stock in many areas. The population decreased from 885,500 in 1930 to 436,000 inhabitants in 2006. Liverpool found it difficult to adjust to new global challenges. The docks had always been separated from residential areas by a dock wall, with a few openings for controlling dockers and cargo. Access to the docks was by the famous Liverpool Overhead Railway ('the dockers' umbrella'), which was closed in 1956. Much of Liverpool's wealth and heritage are a result of its position as the 'Second City of the Empire', built on world sea trading, which peaked at the turn of the nineteenth century.

The Liverpool One mixed-use development (formerly the Paradise Project) opened in 2008, when Liverpool was the European Capital of Culture (Figure 14.4). It reversed the decline, soon becoming a big success and a turning point for Liverpool. This was followed by UNESCO world heritage status being granted to the Maritime Mercantile City on Liverpool's

Figure 14.4 Liverpool One, view from Royal Albert Dock

waterfront and the adjoining six areas (Liverpool City Council 2003), including a buffer zone at Pier Head, the Three Graces (Royal Liver Building, Cunard Building and the Port of Liverpool Building), Albert Dock to the south and Stanley Dock (the largest brick warehouse in the world) to the north. It is 'the supreme example of a commercial port at the time of Britain's greatest global influence. . . . The biggest and most complete system of docks in the world' (Hinchcliffe 2008: 1).

Meanwhile two large-scale redevelopment projects are under way. Liverpool Waters is a flagship project north of the city centre, on the western side of the Mersey. It is proposed to regenerate 60 hectares of mostly derelict and redundant former docks including open water spaces. The land is now owned by Peel Land and Property (Ports) Ltd. Group (Peel Holdings), while the Stanley Dock Tobacco North Warehouse is being redeveloped into a hotel and conference centre by another company (Harcourt Developments). In 2012, planning permission for the development was granted. Liverpool Waters is a 5.5 billion–pound investment that will extend over the next thirty to fifty years. The project will support substantial growth for Liverpool's economy and draw on the heritage and unique identity of the former port facilities. It will provide 9,000 apartments, offices, hotels, bars and a cruise ship terminal as well as the 55-storey Shanghai Tower and other skyscrapers.

As the large-scale redevelopment project could have a potentially damaging impact on the Outstanding Universal Value of the World Heritage Site, Liverpool was placed on the 'in danger' list in 2012. It is feared that the Three Graces would play only 'second violin' to such a leviathan. The World Heritage Management Plan seeks to ensure that the conservation of cities can be used as a positive driving force in the regeneration process.

Liverpool Water's sister project (Wirral Waters) is situated on the other shore of the Mersey, in the Birkenhead dockland area. Although even larger in scale, there is no debate about its world heritage status. Wirral Waters is a 4.5 billion–pound project in an area with unused docks and former industrial sites. About 15,000 apartments are to be combined with office space for 27,000 permanent jobs, retail and cultural facilities. In 2010, the project obtained full approval; this will lead to one of Britain's biggest and most visionary redevelopment schemes over the next decade.

The redevelopment of both sides of the Mersey will mean a radical transformation for all Liverpudlians. Of course, the obvious question is: how can the demand for this number of homes and offices be generated? Unlike the other regeneration projects discussed in this chapter, Liverpool Waters was initiated by a private developer. Having learned from other projects, it seems to be proactive, plan-led and includes a variety of uses. Spatial sequences and design principles that reflect the past are proposed. Land use plans will create specific neighbourhoods, distinguished by variations in use, population density and structure and heritage as well as assets. If the participation and local interests of all stakeholders were secured, it could become a great opportunity for Liverpool. The development would help the region—which has suffered for almost three decades from deindustrialization, job losses, a shrinking population and a negative image—to re-establish connections to the European and global economy, last but not least by new port facilities (Liverpool 2) for post-Panamax vessels. HafenCity in Hamburg is an apt precedent for Liverpool Waters.

High Expectations: HafenCity Hamburg

Hamburg's specific topography is shaped by the confluence of the River Alster and its tributaries into the Elbe. Most of the port is owned by the City of Hamburg and is governed by the Hamburg Port Authority (HPA). The waterfront along the northern shore of the River Elbe in Altona, with splendid views towards the shipyards and ocean liners, plays a special role in Hamburg. Like in other seaport cities, the oldest facilities and infrastructures from the mid-nineteenth century near the city centre became vacant or underused in the 1980s and the port moved seawards where new container terminals were built. When its port-related activities declined, public attention became increasingly focused on new uses. In the early 1980s, the northern shore of the Elbe comprised a heterogeneous mix of land uses, with buildings from the mid-nineteenth century to the post-war period.

A catchy name was found for the zone: 'String of Pearls'. It was assumed that applying a coherent strategy for the whole area would be difficult, but that a string of spectacular projects based on a market-led approach would generate enough interest—and, consequently, higher land values—to upgrade the area. Since then, a number of new buildings and conversions of older warehouses have significantly gentrified the area along the northern Elbe bank by means of a short-term, project-based approach. The implementation of projects was not strictly governed by planning requirements, but by the availability of plots and developers' interests as well as investment considerations that originated from different periods and planning contexts. The metaphor of the 'String of Pearls' suggests that there had been an urban planning concept, but it was not coined until the project was already under way.

HafenCity is more ambitious, a giant step that differs from the String of Pearls in that it is the most important urban redevelopment project in Hamburg and one of the largest projects of its kind in Europe. HafenCity re-establishes the connection between the River Elbe and the city centre, giving Hamburg a new direction for growth: down to and alongside the river. It extends from the Speicherstadt (Warehouse District), to the Elbbrücken, the bridges across the river. For the first time, a large area is being taken from the port and put to other uses. The existing site covers approximately 155 hectares of both old and new operational port facilities. It is surrounded by several older, partly neglected housing estates, a wholesale market, industry, port facilities and railway lines.

HafenCity started at the end of the 1990s. Hamburg has adopted a plan-led, mixed-use approach for the redevelopment. Following a competition for a master plan, specific districts were designed with a focus on offices, housing, shopping and recreation. In a way, HafenCity is a latecomer project, where planners tried to avoid the mistakes of other waterfront revitalization projects, such as mono-structures and delays in public transport connections. Approximately 5,500 apartments for 10,000 to 12,000 inhabitants were planned, with projections for required social infrastructure such as schools and community centres based on these figures. The area is within the Elbe flood plain, making built and organizational solutions for the protection of people and buildings indispensable.

The master plan specifies the phased implementation of developments in sub-districts. It lays down the principal development sequence from west to east, avoiding uncontrolled construction activities throughout the development area. A zoning plan for HafenCity's first phase was drawn up in 2000, and land sales started in 2001. A development agency was devised in 2002 and the first buildings completed by 2004. The newly founded GHS (Gesellschaft für Hafen- und Stadtentwicklung GmbH, later HafenCity Hamburg GmbH) is responsible for the area and the implementation of its projects. A typical quango was set up in order to hasten development; it soon owned most of the land.

In 2008, a maritime museum was opened in Speicher B, an old brick warehouse. Hamburg has applied for the Warehouse District (Speicherstadt) and the office district (Kontorhaus Viertel, with the famous Chilehaus), both next to the HafenCity, to be inscribed on the World Heritage List. Plans for the future centre (Überseequartier) were finalized in 2006. Construction of the proposed characteristic mixed-use development began in 2007, starting with a new metro line. In 2004, a temporary cruise terminal received its first passengers at Hamburg. However, the world financial crisis caused some delays and vacancies of office space in the Überseequartier. While the northern part has been realized in the meantime, the southern part was still a big hole in the ground in 2013, awaiting development. It is being discussed whether perhaps another developer should be involved and the concept for the district changed. The most spectacular project in the area is a concert hall (Elbphilharmonie) on top of Speicher A (Warehouse A) on the western edge of HafenCity (architects: Herzog & de Meuron), which will be finally opened in 2017. The landmark project has attracted a good deal of international attention, not only because of its spectacular architecture but also because of rapidly increasing costs and delays in construction works. Already in its planning and construction phase, it has become a distinctive new international landmark for the city.

An updated master plan for the eastern part of HafenCity was decided in 2010. Three districts with a variety of uses are in the pipeline. The Baakenhafen neighbourhood will comprise different types of housing and recreation. Oberhafen will be transformed into a creative and cultural district, where existing older warehouses are to be reused and sport facilities provided right on the waterfront. The most eastern district, the Elbbrücken neighbourhood, will mark the entrance to the city with high-rise buildings and a mix of offices, residential and shopping facilities. An extension of the new metro line (U4) for this area is already under construction.

HafenCity implied an intended jump in scale and a more complex implementation strategy that was formulated with the city as developer and as a project embedded in urban perspectives of inner-city expansion. It is based on a more plan-led and proactive approach, which also allows for improvements and updates of the plan to accommodate changes in the office and housing market. The implementation phase was predicted to last about twenty-five years.

The 'Leap across the River Elbe', in contrast, was initiated in 2004 and reorganized the urban perspectives for the entire city, with a focus on Wilhelmsburg, the largest river island in Europe. Using architectural projects, the geographical centre of Hamburg will be moved from the periphery into a new centre by means of a diverse range of projects and plans that are part of a long-term strategy. The International Building Exhibition and the International Garden Show, both held in 2013, and the relocation of the Ministry of Urban Development and Environment, focused attention on Wilhelmsburg. The upgrading of Wilhelmsburg will take many decades and must be embedded in a process that balances demands for growth and new housing with the requirements of local inhabitants for affordable housing and possible dangers of gentrification.

Conclusion

All of these projects have in common an attractive waterfront location, which is met with high demand for housing and offices and the hope of corresponding returns for developers. Very often contamination from previous uses has to be removed from the site and high infrastructure and construction costs (piles, flood control etc.) result in higher expenditure. Furthermore, fragmented authorities and long planning and implementation phases with cyclical fluctuations in the housing and office markets hamper the implementation of projects. However, obstructions between port and city authorities in northern European cities have in general been successfully overcome. Port authorities are actively involved in restructuring measures and have installed robust conflict resolution tools.

The projects and plans illustrate paradigm shifts in urban planning in many seaport cities. Shortage of funding and deficits in the budget make untargeted subsidies impossible, which in turn requires more flexible plans and concentration on projects with the greatest anticipated impact. It is important for revitalization of waterfront areas to maintain the 'otherness' and special identity of waterfront areas, including their culture, ethic and economic and visual dimensions. Wrong decisions regarding these assets may lead to devitalization, whereas historic waterfronts can act as catalysts for economic regeneration. While most of the academic literature on waterfront transformations is descriptive and concerned with ex post facto evaluations of 'successful' transfers, it now makes more sense to look at the 'secrets of success' (Peck and Theodore 2010: 169).

While the projects in north-west Europe described in this chapter benefited from a 'late-comer advantage', there are a number of trends that point in different directions.[1]

Structural change and (image) improvements, re-inventing and re-branding are often explicitly intended, and there is a will for experimentation that is manifested in open and unbiased proposals. However, an increasing convergence is noted that is related to the appointment of quangos and the professional promotion of projects through web presence, newsletters, info centres and property fairs. Lighthouse projects and buildings designed by 'star architects' are used as identity anchors against a backdrop of development for tourism, global marketing and competitive (symbolic) urban growth-oriented politics. The waterfront projects serve as a catalyst for further investments (Doucet 2013: 2038). Often the issue at stake is to establish new planning cultures and more flexible planning processes. Whether the 'Mediterranean lifestyle' portrayed across advertisements—showing beautiful people drinking cappuccino in the sunshine on the quays all year round, or enjoying their sunny (but often windy and cold) balcony—is entirely convincing for north-west European projects remains doubtful.

Note

1   For further projects in northern Europe, see also *Portus 25*, the online magazine of RETE, June 2013, www.portusonline.org/en/category/this_issue/report.

Bibliography

Doucet, B. (2013) 'Variations of the Entrepreneurial City: Goals, Roles and visions in Rotterdam's Kop van Zuid and Glasgow Harbour Megaprojects', *International Journal of Urban and Regional Research*, 376(November): 2035–54.

Hinchcliffe, J. (2008) 'The Conversation of Port Heritage: Lessons from Liverpool, English Heritage', in *On the Waterfront. Cultural, Heritage and Regeneration of Port Cities*, Liverpool: English Heritage, Chapter 5, 1–8.

Jamison, A. (2008) 'Greening the City: Urban Environmentalism from Mumford to Malmö', in M. Hard and Th. J. Misa (eds.), *Urban Machinery. Inside Modern European Cities*, London: The MIT Press, 281–298.

Liverpool City Council (2003) *Maritime Mercantile City Liverpool, Nomination of Liverpool—Maritime Mercantile City for Inscription on the World Heritage List*, Liverpool: Liverpool University Press.

Lorens, P. (2001) 'A Brief History of Development and Planning Efforts', in P. Lorens (ed.), *Large Scale Urban Developments*, Gdansk: Gdansk University of Technology Press, 209–220.

Moore, N. (2008) *Dublin Docklands Reinvented. The Post-Industrial Regeneration of a European City Quarter*, Dublin: Four Courts Press.

Newman, P. and Thornley, A. (1996) *Urban Planning in Europe*, London: Routledge.

Othengrafen, F. (2012) *Uncovering the Unconscious Dimensions of Planning: Using Culture as a Tool to Analyse Spatial Planning Practices*, Farnham: Ashgate.

Peck, J. and Theodore, N. (2010) 'Mobilizing Policy: Models, Methods, and Mutations', *Geoforum*, 4: 169–174.

Schubert, D. (2011a) 'Seaport Cities: Phases of Spatial Restructuring and Types and Dimensions of Redevelopment', in C. Hein (ed.), *Port Cities. Dynamic Landscapes and Global Networks*, London and New York: Routledge, 54–69.

Schubert, D. (2011b) 'Waterfront Revitalizations: From a Local to a Regional Perspective in London, Barcelona, Rotterdam, and Hamburg', in G. Desfor, J. Laidley and D. Schubert (eds.), *Transforming Urban Waterfronts, Fixity and Flow*, New York, London: Routledge, 74–97.

Wonneberger, A. (2011) 'Dockland Regeneration, Community, and Social Organization in Dublin', in G. Desfor, J. Laidley and D. Schubert (eds.), *Transforming Urban Waterfronts, Fixity and Flow*, New York, London: Routledge, 54–72.

15 The Internationalization of the Marseille Waterfront
An Integrated Approach

Oriana Giovinazzi

The natural configuration of the site makes Marseille look like a large amphitheatre—overlooking the sea and surrounded by rocky hills—in which two different urban centres, represented by a rich north and a poor south, are physically separated by the Canebière, the main urban axis.

Characterized by a close relationship with the port area, which has always been the basis of the city's different evolutionary processes, Marseille has long had a leading role in the trade system and has suffered, particularly following the emergence of new economic realities in the Far East, from the industrial crisis and the decline of its role as a Mediterranean city.

The port of Marseille—one of the most important in France, the fifth largest in Europe and among the 50 largest ports in the world—extends over 10,000 hectares of land in different geographical areas: the Bassins Est, next to the city centre, also known as the 'Vieux Port', mainly dedicated to passenger traffic (ferries and cruises) and different cargo on short distances and oriented towards the Mediterranean; and the Bassins Ouest, extended over the municipalities of Fos, Martigues, Port de Bouc and Port Saint Louis du Rhone, located approximately 50 kilometres from the city and known as 'Port de Fos', a port-industrial complex which includes refineries, storage areas and manufacturing activities (Figure 15.1).

The relationship between the city and its 'two ports' has always been complex and constantly evolving, characterized by positive large-scale impacts and negative, rather localized impacts, as well as by development dynamics strongly determined by trends of population growth, the expansion of port areas, industrial innovation, space conflicts, and the removal or partial reintegration of the port and urban functions.

The transfer of a large part of port activities—as has happened to many ancient ports in direct contact with the historic fabric—has led to the loss of the relationship and integration between the urban and maritime city that had developed over the centuries. In many cases, at the European as well as other levels, the choice has been to recover these areas while respecting the historical memory and the changing landscape of ferries, cranes and containers that have always characterized the same areas, with the purpose of preserving and representing the vocation and maritime identity of the city.

Figure 15.1 A view of the urban waterfront and port area in Marseille. The integration between Vieux Port and the contemporary city

That is also what has happened to Marseille, where in recent decades the port has been rediscovered as a place with great potential. Hence, transformation operations have been carried out, initially to improve the quality of urban life and to recover the maritime identity, and then—with the city's candidacy as a European Capital of Culture—to promote a new image of Marseille, that of an international port city.

It is in particular the Bassins Est, the Vieux Port with its rich architectural heritage, that was affected by the earliest regeneration interventions, starting in the 1990s. It provides the particular focus for the Euroméditerranée programme, a vast operation of national interest destined to become the great 'opportunity' for Marseille, also following its candidacy and designation as European Capital of Culture for 2013.

Totally immersed in the historic fabric of the city, the ancient port has an urban character and is able to accommodate numerous public and private activities on its piers (theatre, hotels, locations for entertainment and leisure, harbour, direct connections to the historic centre); it is a site that is particularly representative of the entire metropolitan area and is experiencing a progressive increase in dynamism.

Many of the large structures serving the metropolitan area, architectural icons and new urban activities have been built on the docks and integrated with the port functions; the Bassins Est has been made accessible again and its functions visible to the community. The port is back to being a part of everyday life for residents and tourists, after for years having been the source of many conflicts.

Urban Dynamics and Strategic Planning for the Territory

The planning of the port city is made particularly complex and articulated owing to the urban dynamics that have been affecting Marseille since the 1970s. Over time the process of urban renewal has been accompanied by a planning system in constant evolution (albeit with some limitations), thanks to some flexibility of action under the initiative and responsibility of the municipality. Several planning tools have been developed for the purpose of responding to concrete problems encountered on the territory.

The planning legislation and master plans are of great methodological interest. Interpreted not as constraints and limitations to development, rather they are seen as operational guarantees in order to create regional synergies and public-private partnerships.

The Plan d'Occupation de Sols—POS (Land Use Plan) of 1981 from the outset has emphasized the need to manage the excessive population growth recorded around the 1970s, acting in particular on the demand for services and infrastructure and limiting property speculation as much as possible.

The two subsequent revisions of the POS, in 1993 and 2000, were significant in the definition of the Euroméditerranée project (described in detail in this chapter), by providing some interventions within the Zones d'Amenagement Concerté—ZAC (Joint Management Zones), in particular in three port areas: Joliette, Saint-Charles and Cité de la Méditerranée.

With regard to operations on the existing urban fabric, Opérations Programmées d'Améliorement de l'Habitat—OPAH (Programmed Housing Improvement Operations) have been privileged. This is the case, for example, of the redevelopment of Rue de la République and the recovery of approximately 5,000 housing units spread along the urban axis. While the former tool (the POS) allows the creation or identification of ways to implement programmes at the urban scale, the latter provides specific financial contributions with the purpose of encouraging the different property owners to redevelop their properties.

The Plan Local d'Urbanisme—PLU (Local Development Plan) and the Schéma de Cohérence Territorial—SCOT (Territorial Coherence Scheme), which are new plans introduced by the law of Solidarité et Renouvellement Urbain—SRU (Solidarity and Urban Renewal), instead represent a coherent and more closely linked response to territorial governance.

Specifically, the PLU covers strategic planning in a widespread manner and makes it possible to respond to more structured and complex dynamics, in particular the challenges related to urban regeneration in Marseille posed by the real estate and private markets in general.

The SCOT aims to present a planning strategy at the conurbation scale, setting common goals concerning transport, infrastructure and urban renewal; the plan thus concerns operations management in a medium radius, with the purpose of intervening in central areas of the urban reality, like for example Euroméditerranée. For more distant areas, or outside the city at least, the reference is the Grand Project Urbain—GPU (Great Urban Project).

Long-term planning with regard to the port is expressed through strategic visions that allow the identification of new guidelines for development and priorities investment. These become effective when they get translated into operational plans.

The strategic vision for the port of Marseille is detailed in the Projet Stratégique 2009–2013 (Strategic Project 2009–2013), a document that provides an in-depth analysis of the challenges which the port is facing, as well as strategic development goals divided into five different sectors: containers, energy, dry bulk, ro-ro and passenger traffic.

In addition to this strategic plan, a long-term vision has recently been developed for the Bassins Est area of the port. Drawn up by the Commission Cousque at the request of the Conseil de Surveillance du Port de Marseille-Fos, it proposes the division of the waterfront into three areas: a first site centred around the Euroméditerranée area and city-port interface, strongly linked to tertiary sector development; a second site dedicated to cargo handling, industrial and logistic development; and a third site related to leisure and recreation (beaches, nautical centre, marina, etc.). These strategic orientations are made operational through the Charte Ville-Port, or City-Port Charter.

However, most of the strategic documents of the city and the Marseille conurbation not only support the port's development, but at the same time express its ambition to become a leading centre in terms of services and commercial activities.

The Marseille Provence Métropole (MPM) economic development strategy (2008–2014) considers the port and logistics activities as one of the economic drivers of the metropolis, capable of stimulating a culture of enterprise and business based on the knowledge economy.

In the document *Métropole euroméditerranéenne des échanges et de la connaissance* (Euro-Mediterranean Metropolis of Trade and Knowledge), the port and port-related industries are the key elements in making Marseille a trade metropolis of southern Europe and ensuring a top place in the tourism economy.

In the strategic document for the city of Marseille, *Marseille Attractive 2012–2020*, the three principal strategies are to become a leading trade platform for the south of Europe, to become a city of knowledge and creativity, and to become a 'destination' city. These strategies also define the role assigned to the port and the related sectors, in the first place making it one of the drivers of trading ambitions and in the second facilitating the positioning of Marseille as an attractive destination. These strategic guidelines are used to develop a concrete action plan from an international perspective.

Euroméditerranée and the Vision of the Port City in 2020

The recovery of the ancient Docks de la Joliette as new functional destinations has implemented an ambitious project, known as 'Euroméditerranée', launched in 1995 under the initiative and with the financial support of the state and local authorities (state 50%, Ville de Marseille 25%, Région Provence Alpes Cote d'Azur 10%, Conseil Général des Bouches du Rhone 10% and Communauté Urbaine Marseille Provence Métropole 5%) in collaboration with the Marseille-Fos Port Authority. Euroméditerranée is part of a vast Opération d'Intérêt National—OIN (Operation of National Interest), developed by the European Union and widespread in the Mediterranean region, which mainly concerns the countries of the south. This intervention affects the city of Marseille and its urban agglomeration with the establishment of the Établissement Public d'Aménagement Euroméditerranée (EPAEM)—a public participation company for development which includes professionals, state and local representatives, and numerous institutional actors—and which, with its 480 hectares, is the largest project of urban planning and economic-cultural development in Europe.

The activity of EPAEM can be summarized as follows:

- to perform a strategic task that consists of analyzing the urban area's resources, searching for business sectors to attract to the area, defining the priority lines of development, and drafting the required plan of action to implement the policies and to plan the interventions;

- to coordinate strategies and priority actions for the different partners;
- to mobilize the funds needed to complete the operation;
- to direct the design and manage interventions in collaboration with the various stakeholders involved in the programme;
- to promote and market the Euroméditerranée project.

The agency therefore has large margins of operation, from defining the interventions programme to the possibility of managing the construction of infrastructure, public spaces and services; from buildings and areas acquisition, also through expropriation procedures, to the task of creating and managing the supply of land within or outside the existing planning instruments.

The intervention programme refers to the long term, with a vision to 2020 which aims to rebuild the local economy through a large urban renewal project and which provides for reviving the port area's close contact with the city and the regeneration of large abandoned industrial areas, as well as their architectural and historical heritage, mainly for tourism, culture and recreation purposes (Figure 15.2). The purpose of the project is the same as most of the interventions undertaken in the last decades on the waterfront, with the intent of regaining the relationship with the water and the Mediterranean Sea, while respecting the maritime identity of the territory, keeping some port activities and integrating them with the recovery of the city centre, and strengthening some metropolitan functions through the development of

Figure 15.2 A waterfront view from Hangar J1 after completion of the redevelopment process

synergies and innovative solutions. However, Marseille, already the capital of southern France, is pursuing a further, no less important objective: to return to being one of the largest cities in the Mediterranean and Europe, while also increasing its international competitiveness as European Capital of Culture 2013.

Euroméditerranée sets out an excellent combination of urbanity and development, not only economically and politically, but also and in particular strategically, with impacts on different territorial scales. This is an exemplary case of large-scale mobilization that has given rise to forms of consultation and participation through dialogue between public and private stakeholders, and has integrated different urban realities.

Euroméditerranée has contributed significantly to the economic dynamics by rebuilding a market with high growth potential and sectoral diversification, and by enhancing in particular four supply chains of excellence: financial services, maritime industry and international trade, telecommunications, and tourism and cruises.

The Urban Transformation Project for the Vieux Port

The perimeter affected by the Euroméditerranée project—originally planned for 310 hectares and expanded in 2007 by an additional 180 hectares—is located in the heart of Marseille just 15 minutes from the international airport, between the commercial harbour, the Vieux Port and the TGV railway station, in the city area behind the port—a particularly rich and easily accessible area thanks to an efficient highway system. In recent years, this area (which at the same time includes a part of the Port Autonome, the old, mostly abandoned industrial areas and some nineteenth-century residential quarters) has experienced a gradual process of renewal and construction that, in an overall strategy for improving urban and environmental quality, has also affected adjacent sectors.

The project implementation has involved five urban areas to date, in particular: the waterfront and the area comprised in the Cité de la Méditerranée project; the new Joliette business and residential centre with the works of internationally renowned architects (Zaha Hadid, Jean Nouvel, Massimiliano Fuksas and Stefano Boeri); the Belle de Mai cultural centre and tertiary sectors, achieved through the structural and functional regeneration of existing industrial buildings; the centre of Saint-Charles, which houses the new railway station and the neighbouring environment; and finally Rue de la République, the central axis that connects Place de la Joliette with the Vieux Port and Canabière.

The first phase of Euroméditerranée has contributed significantly to the redefinition of the land-sea relationship and the enhancement of Marseille's maritime identity, as well as to the improvement and diversification of the urban economy and its employment base. The sharp increase in property values in the city centre and in the outskirts of the metropolis is one of the most interesting effects of the not only urban but also social and economic transformation activated by the interventions.

The objectives pursued at the urban scale are also intended to have an impact at the metropolitan level:

- reorganization of urban planning, construction of new infrastructure and redevelopment of the great urban arteries;
- reconstitution of a new central core, in particular in the area north of the city, with the aim of bridging the historical and social separation with the south;
- improvement of the accessibility of the areas affected by the interventions, mobility and public transport;
- creation of great public spaces, cultural complexes and places dedicated to leisure;
- conferment to the city of a specific business and trade vocation through the strengthening of the port functions and the presence of high-level companies, international organizations and university research activities.

The City-Port Integration Process

The urban dynamics that have characterized the Euroméditerranée project respond to the complexity of the city-port interface context. The timing of the project development and the intervention implementation methods have resulted in the Schéma de Référence (Scheme of Reference), which illustrates the entire operation and its objectives, driving its evolution in the respect of an overall consistency.

Marseille stands as an example of integration between the urban context and the port area, in which it has been chosen to maintain a certain harmony between the historic and the contemporary city.

The dynamism of the Marseille city-port is guaranteed by a project which provides a long-term global vision, in which a balance can be seen between the old and new (regeneration interventions and innovative buildings by great names in architecture), between the port and urban areas (old harbour docks that coexist with the city centre), and between the local and metropolitan (urban renewal of roads, rehabilitation of residential buildings and construction of major infrastructure).

The New Urban Polarities Serving the Metropolis

The project is part of a historic context overlooking the water, which makes the most of the exceptional resources of the site and strengthens the fabric of public spaces and green areas. In order to ensure continuity, the principal axes and the entrances to the city have been reconfigured, the waterfront reassembled and some urban polarities consolidated or created around the major settlements to enhance the metropolitan appeal.

The Cité de la Méditerranée

The Cité de la Méditerranée is the symbol of the transformation of Marseille: the site regeneration project is an 'original' programme which complements and addresses the relationship between the city and the port through the insertion in functional or abandoned port areas of cultural, educational, scientific, recreational and tertiary activities that testify to Marseille's role as a major metropolis for economic and cultural exchanges between Europe and the Mediterranean.

Located between the entrance of the Vieux Port and Arenc, the Cité de la Méditerranée (60 hectares) is one of the most ambitious and representative programmes of Euroméditerranée, fitting into the framework of actions undertaken to reopen the city to the sea and construct new relations between city and port. The restitution of 3 kilometres of waterfront for the public enjoyment of residents and tourists involves the reconstruction or creation of new connections between the two territories and the definition of forms of integration that combine the rehabilitation of historic buildings with new pieces of architecture, also generating new economic dynamics.

The Joliette Business District

Located on the seafront, the Joliette has many resources and much potential, in particular a strategic position between the port and the city centre, remarkable accessibility (international airport, TGV railway station, highway system and trunk lines) that render this a privileged place for the establishment of businesses. The neighbourhood has quickly turned into an attractive and dynamic district at the international level—specializing in services, trade and telecommunications—as a result of the Les Docks restoration project (1992–2002) and the Place de la Joliette redevelopment intervention (completed in 1998).

The outcome of the recovery of the old port areas has in fact started a remarkable regeneration process, converting them into very dynamic business districts that have attracted a lot of investment for the construction of residential and quality public spaces, facilities not only for the local community but also for the metropolis (libraries, hospitals, sports facilities, cultural centres, exhibition spaces, etc.). The quality of the areas has further increased with the realization of new public transport services, such as the metro and tram, with the recovery of major road infrastructure, such as the Boulevard de Dunkerque, and the rearrangement of numerous public squares and gardens, such as Place de la Méditerranée.

The Pole of Saint-Charles (ZAC) and the Port d'Aix

The renewal programme undertaken in this territorial area, extending over 16 hectares, concerns in particular the two entrances to the city: the Gare de Saint-Charles with regard to rail transport and the Port d'Aix as regards the highway system.

The neighbourhood hosting the Saint-Charles station has become the subject of some significant urban transformations with the arrival of the TGV Méditerranée high-speed train, becoming a pole of multimodal interchange between rail, highway terminals, urban lines of public transport (bus, metro, tramway) and private traffic.

With regard to the Port d'Aix, the biggest change is the interment of the A7 motorway, which has made it possible to free the area from traffic and improve the urban quality of the neighbourhood, also with the realization of student residences, commercial spaces, public facilities and services, green areas and the like.

The Gare Maritime de la Major

During the renovation of the Joliette, the Grand Port de Marseille reconfigured the J3 and J2 piers in order to install a new international maritime terminal dedicated to passenger traffic (Corsica, and Algeria and Tunisia in North Africa). The Gare Maritime de la Major, spread over 6,700 square metres of land and completed in 2006 with a total investment of approximately 25,000 euros, is a multipurpose facility intended for the use of tourists and residents that not only hosts the service dedicated to cruises and ferries but also spaces and facilities for cultural and leisure activities (Figure 15.3)

The Renewed Rue de la République

Inaugurated in 1864 to connect the Vieux Port with the port district of the Joliette, Rue de la République has for decades been one of Marseille' most

Figure 15.3 Gare Maritime de la Major, the new international cruise terminal on piers J3 and J2

important trade paths; abandoned and in a state of degradation, it has been the subject of a recent renovation process that has transformed the road into a wide boulevard overlooked by residences in Haussmann style running through the historic centre of the city up to the sea. The Euroméditerranée project has permitted painstaking work to be carried out for the recovery of the buildings and façades in the respect of their historical and commercial character, the reduction of road traffic through the construction of the new Blancarde-Euroméditerranée Gantes tram line (completed in 2007), the extension of the sidewalks, the insertion of rich vegetation and the installation of new street furniture.

The planning and policy choices of the different actors involved in the project have proposed a rich and diverse use of the areas in terms of space and time, and have given priority to the existing urban fabric, by recovering, enhancing and strengthening the place's identity as a port.

The Public Space and Green Areas

One of the main aspects that characterizes Euroméditerranée is the provision of green areas and public spaces, which currently occupy 27,600 square metres of land (45,000 square metres at the end of the operation), and, through reorganization of their different uses, boost the quality of urban life and give a renewed image of Marseille; squares, boulevards, parks and interchange nodes which consolidate the connections between the city centre and surrounding suburbs return accessibility to the port and enhance the waterfront views (Esplanade de la Major, Place de la Joliette, Place de la Méditerranée, Boulevard du Littoral, etc.).

The Recovery of the Historic and Architectural Heritage, between Maritime Culture and Tourism

While promoting sustainable development, Euroméditerranée has accompanied the urban regeneration process with actions aimed at the recovery or enhancement of existing sites and heritage, with the aim of protecting the historic character and the identity of the city as a port, without forgetting the outcome that the city has experienced in recent years in terms of attracting tourists (more than 4 million visitors, including 700,000 cruise passengers). Of particular concern have been military, cultural and industrial buildings, including Fort Saint-Jean, the Cathédrale de la Major, Les Docks on the Quais de la Joliette, the Silo d'Arenc and the Belle de Mai. Not only public property, but entire residential neighbourhoods have been valorized by OPAH and numerous political choices have been aimed at enhancing tourist appeal and welcoming visitors (convention centre, maritime terminal, hotels and residences, commercial facilities, cultural complex, etc.).

Figure 15.4 Musée des Civilisations de l'Europe et de la Méditerranée (MuCEM) and Centre Régional de la Méditerranée (CRM) in the Robert Laffont Promenade or Esplanade du J4

The Waterfront and Great Names in Architecture

The design of a new city image for Marseille has been accomplished through redevelopment of the waterfront and the creation of new relations between city and port, mainly linked to the Cité de la Méditerranée project and public enjoyment by residents and tourists. However, it is in particular the big names in architecture (Zaha Hadid, Jean Nouvel, Massimiliano Fuksas, Rudy Ricciotti, etc.) that have contributed on one hand to the metamorphosis of the areas affected by the Euroméditerranée project, creating a skyline along the seafront marked by contemporary and ambitious architecture (the CMA-CGM Tower, the MuCEM—Musée des Civilisations de l'Europe et de la Méditerranée, the CRM—Centre Régional de la Méditerranée, the Quais d'Arenc, the Terraces du Port, the Euromed Center, etc.) that integrates with the historical and maritime heritage, and on the other hand that have confirmed the territory's attractiveness and strengthened Marseille' position in the Mediterranean and European context, also helping to promote it at an international level (Figure 15.4).

The Extension of the Euroméditerranée Perimeter: The Euromed Project

In 2007 it was decided to extend the OIN northwards to confirm the role of Marseille as an Euro-Mediterranean capital and base of operations for the European Union's future with regard to the Mediterranean.

The extension project, known as 'Euromed', covers an area of 170 hectares, bound by Cap Pinède and Les Arnavaux to the north, the village of Canet to the east and the CMA tower to the south, and characterized by a diverse topography and numerous urban fractures mainly attributable to the presence of infrastructure.

The programme involves the construction of 14,000 residences, 500,000 square metres of office space and 200,000 square metres of retail and cultural space in the framework of an agreement between the EPAEM, Ville de Marseille, the region and the state for the financing of the planned works. In addition to EPAEM, the operation involves the participation of several stakeholders, including the Réseau Ferré de France, Grand Port Maritime de Marseille (GPMM), Société Nationale des Chemins de fer Français (SNCF), Établissement Public Foncier (PACA) and Agence d'Urbanisme de l'Agglomération Marseillaise (AgAM).

The aim is to point to a new form of development that does not result in further land consumption and that ensures a better connection between the city centre and nearby suburbs. In particular, the objective is to provide the city with a business district of international size and new infrastructure; facilitate the development of emerging sectors with high growth potential (tourism and cruises); and increase employment at the metropolitan level, especially in the knowledge economy and port logistics industry: in summary, to start an exemplary operation in terms of sustainable development (economic development, social cohesion and environmental protection).

Marseille, European Capital of Culture and New International City-Port

Over the last decades Marseille has been the subject of policies, strategies and actions that have generated profound changes and produced interesting effects on the territory, a development process that has allowed the metropolitan city to acquire a new ability to address its challenges using a systemic approach.

In this process, the choice of shared planning and integrated management has proved strategic—in the awareness of resources and area needs, opportunities and critical issues—and it has been possible to put together a multiplicity of policies and action in different sectors, generating innovative solutions aimed at achieving important results and objectives, shared both at different levels and by stakeholders involved in various capacities.

The mix of tools and strategies used to enhance and strengthen the city's role at regional and national level was also fielded to project and affirm the image of the city of Marseille at the international level.

The programme proposed for the candidacy of Marseille as the European Capital of Culture for 2013 has integrated the Euroméditerranée vision to increase the city's role as a place of exchange between the southern Mediterranean area and continental Europe, and to project its image at an international level. It gave a detailed argument for the forms and ways in which the material landscape and the cultural proposals present in the areas affected by the redevelopment and regeneration process, already in place, could take a central role in the great event.

The orientation of the plan is aimed to encourage urban porosity and functional relationships between the port and the city; to reaffirm the vocation of the Bassins Est as an industrial, commercial and logistics centre; and to increase the attractiveness of the city centre to tourists and cruises in respect of sustainable development.

Immediately after the appointment of Marseille as European Capital of Culture for 2013, a large survey was conducted on the territory to identify the suitable places to host various happenings related to the event. Full of history, the port of Marseille was chosen as the heart of the event, specifically in relation to the availability of space in what is one of the landscapes that most characterizes the city of Marseille. This work saw collaboration between the Marseille Provence 2013 association and GPMM, which has assumed the burden of some major interventions required to make the places located in the Vieux Port available for public enjoyment.

The transformation of the urban waterfront, as well as the status of Marseille Province as a European Capital of Culture in 2013, have left a glimpse of the new possibilities of enhancing the positive image and visibility of the port city. As part of the Euroméditerranée redevelopment project, the relationship between the city and the port is revisited through interventions on the old port facilities for a partial transformation to public use, for the identification of urban functions, and for the creation of new connections, both physical and not, between the city and its maritime heritage.

The candidacy for European Capital of Culture for 2013 resulted in a great chance for land development, as well as a valuable tool to strengthen existing relationships (institutions, local authorities, trade associations, chambers of commerce, etc.) and create new networks with public and private stakeholders (universities, research centres, businesses, financial institutions, etc.) with a view towards international promotion.

The event marketing has aimed to increase the territory's competitiveness and restore a positive image of the port for the local community, by implementing effective communication tools, promoting and boosting the leading sectors in order to increase and diversify employment, intensify network cooperation, invest in skills and areas with high potential appeal, enhance the port's heritage and maritime identity, attract flows of people (business, leisure, congress, etc.) and financial capitals, major events, highly qualified human resources, cultural tourism and the like.

The integrated management of the different phases of Euromediterranée project and the events related to the European Capital of Culture for 2013, combined with a strategic plan for the development and promotion of the metropolitan city, where tourism and culture have been identified as drivers of primary growth, have proven to be the keystone in the process of urban renewal and economic regeneration of the metropolitan area that has projected Marseille into the international context.

Bibliography

Berry-Chikhaoui, I. and Deboulet, A. (2007), 'Restructurations urbaines à Marseille l'heure de l'internationalisation', in Berry-Chikhaou, I., Deboulet, A., Roulleau-Berger, L. (eds.), *Villes Internationales*, La Découverte Editions, Paris, 139-168.

Bertoncello, B. and Dubois, J. (2010), *Marseille Euroméditerranée accélérateur de métropole*, Editions Parenthèses, Marseille.

Bertoncello, B. and Rodrigues-Malta, R. (2001), 'Euroméditerranée: les échelles d'un grand projet de régénération urbaine', in Donzel, A. (ed.), *Métropolisation, gouvernance et citoyenneté dans la région urbaine marseillaise*, Maison-Neuve et Larose, Paris, 405–420.

Bertoncello, B. and Rodrigues-Malta, R. (2003), 'Marseille versus Euroméditerranée', *Annales de Géographie*, n. 632, Editions Armand Colin, Paris, 424–436.

Borruey, R. (2008), 'Réapprendre à voir le port. Retour sur une histoire urbaine et architecturale du port de Marseille', in Gasnault, F (ed.), *Une Aventure portuaire. Les archives du Service maritime des Bouches-du-Rhône, aménageur des ports de Marseille, 19e–20e siècles*, Archives départementales des Bouches-du-Rhône, Marseille.

Bulle, C. (2012), 'Marseille, ville méditerranéenne?', *Rives méditerranéennes*, n. 42, UMR TELEMME, Aix-en-Provence.

Euromediterranée (2000), *Schéma de référence actualisé: une méthode pour un projet de renouvellement urbain*, Euroméditerranée, Marseille.

Giovinazzi, O. (2010), 'Waterfront urbano-portuali in Europa. Tendenze in atto', in Savino, M. (ed.), *Waterfront d'Italia. Piani Politiche Progetti*, Franco Angeli Publisher, Milano, 372–380.

Giovinazzi, O. (2015a), 'Le aree portuali dismesse: interazioni con la città', *Trasporti & Cultura*, Monographic Issue "Porti e Città", Year XV, n. 41, Laura Facchinelli Publisher, Venezia, 6–13.

Giovinazzi, O. (2015b), 'Re-imagining public spaces. New development opportunities on the water', *PORTUS—Port City Relationship and Urban Waterfront Redevelopment*, Year XV, n. 29, RETE Publisher, Venezia. Available at:portusonline.org/en/re-imagining-public-spaces-new-development-opportunities-on-the-water/

Giovinazzi, O. (2015c), 'Rethinking the harbor landscape. Interpretations and contemporary visions' *PORTUS—Port City Relationship and Urban Waterfront Redevelopment*, Year XV, n. 30, RETE Publisher, Venezia. Available at: portusonline.org/en/rethinking-the-port-landscape-interpretations-and-contemporary-visions/

Giovinazzi, O. and Moretti, M. (2010), 'Port Cities and Urban Waterfront: Transformations and Opportunities', in *Special Issue TEMA—Journal of Land Use, Mobility and Environment*, vol. 3, Selected Paper 2009, DiPiST, "Federico II" University, Naples.

Grésillon, B. (2011), *Un enjeu capitale: Marseille Provence 2013*, Editions de l'Aube, Paris, 171.

Grésillon, B. (2013), 'Marseille-Provence 2013, avant, pendant et après?', *Revue Urbanisme*, n. 389, Paris, 26–31.

Langevin, P. and Juan, J.C. (2007), *Marseille, une métropole entre Europe et Méditerranée*, La Documentation Française, Paris, 224.

Morel, B. (1999), *Marseille: naissance d'une métropole*, Métropoles 2000, L'Harmattan, Paris, 221.

Morel, B. (2010), 'Marseille-Provence 2013, capitale européenne de la culture: la vision de l'urbaniste et du politique', in Grésillon, B. (ed.), 'Villes culturelles en Méditerranée', *Revue géographique des Pays Méditerranéens*, n. 114, Presses Universitaires de Provence, Aix-en-Provence, 31–34.

Ronai, S. (2009), 'Marseille: une métropole en mutation', *Hérodote*, vol. 4, n. 135, Editions La Découverte, Paris, 128–147.

16 The Missing Link

Redevelopment of the Urban Waterfront as a Function of Cruise Ship Tourism

Carola Hein and Felicitas Hillmann

Introduction

Port cities have played a key role in the socio-economic and cultural development of many regions since antiquity (Braudel 1982). They are nodes for the mobility of goods, people and money, and have long served as places of social and technological innovation (Hein 2011, 2013). They are places of cosmopolitan culture, reaching beyond national boundaries, integrating migrants and migratory flows into everyday life, places where changes in global shipping, transport and the division of labour generate new social and spatial structures and where financial speculation allows for experiments in built form (Hillmann 2011). Trade inserts the needs of (port) economics into port-related sections of the city, creating, using, and reusing diverse urban spaces; it introduces its own temporality into the development of the city as a whole (Hein 2015). As port industries change radically and cities evolve, cities become places where the logics of maritime flows (commodities, capital and people) become most visible (Sassen 2002), where new social conditions emerge and where architectural and urban trends start.

After centuries of change, the relationship between port and city has taken another new turn in the past decade: port cities' post-industrial revitalization of historic centres and existing ports, which (along with existing migration-related infrastructure) has fostered the recent boom in cruise ship tourism, with its migrant crews and mobile tourists (Hein 2013). Specifically, urban elites in port cities around the world have revitalized urban spaces with the help of urban planners by musealizing their historical port facilities and nearby urban centres and constructing new developments on their waterfronts (Breen and Rigby 1996; Meyer 2003). The current boom in cruise tourism takes advantage of such local changes in some port cities, while operating on a global scale and often beyond national environmental restrictions or labour laws. In turn, cruise tourism is an accentuated form of short-term mobility that shapes urban planning decision-making, pushing port cities to prioritize consumer-oriented spaces and places, and enticing them to turn themselves into a cliché of the post-industrial city, rather than enabling them to honour or extend their traditionally heterogeneous and cosmopolitan character. Politicians, planners and publicists often promote redevelopment and urban regeneration both for short-term cruise visitors and, more broadly, for tourism in general as a way to reconnect the city with its waterfront and thus benefit the city. But such transformations cater to elite groups, displacing other citizens and largely ignoring the needs of the workers and migrants who literally support the new development, thereby contributing to social and spatial fragmentation within these cities. Up to now only few studies have tackled this complex relationship empirically (Mah 2014).

Cruise-ship passengers often encounter a very partial narrative of modern port cities, whether or not they know it. For them, the revitalized waterfronts showcase only a very select and carefully curated part of the more complex urban structure. This narrative continues on the ships themselves. These immense structures, with room for several thousand passengers plus crew, function as gated communities focused on fun and consumption. They fulfil the postmodern dream of a well-organized, safe society, being 'non-places', transitory and consumer-oriented (Augé 1995)—an endless party; at the same time, this image of cruise ships conceals the workers of the industry, for whom the vessels are places of 'real life.'

Cruise ship travel is not a recent invention. Pleasure travel has long been part of port activities, and modern cruise ship activity dates back at least a century. We argue that the current rise in cruise tourism, as a privileged form of mobility, intersects with a period of infrastructural transformation of port cities, and that it reflects changing social relations within post-industrial societies. This chapter provides, first, a brief history of the development of cruise ship travel from a pastime for the wealthy into a mass phenomenon, in each case offering the tourist the opportunity to travel in a secluded and sheltered setting while enjoying glimpses of foreign places. It then reflects on the transformation of ports, waterfronts and port cities since the 1980s as related to this shift from elite to mass consumption, arguing that new spatial and socio-economic patterns have emerged in port cities around the world. To illustrate these findings, the chapter discusses two examples in detail: Hamburg and Genova. The conclusion highlights the ambiguous role of cruise tourism in urban redevelopment and regeneration, and points towards the need for further research that discusses the spatial and social transformation of the port in this context and puts emphasis on the new narratives and images as produced by planners and city marketing.

History: Port Cities and Pleasure Travel for the Wealthy

From its very beginnings, cruise shipping entailed socio-economic disparity and disturbances that were beyond national frameworks of climate and culture, of laws, regulations, and policies. When steamships replaced sailing ships in the late nineteenth century, the wealthy bourgeoisie took advantage of the new possibilities they offered for travelling, while shipping companies started to offer cruises as a way to fill liners that would otherwise be empty in the winter months (Schäfer 1998: 48–49). In many port cities, local enterprises offered services to voyagers and started to build both their own extravagant ships and terminals for ships visiting from other ports. The Hamburg-based Hapag shipping company had led the transatlantic migration business before World War I, conveying millions of immigrants from Europe to the US. We can consider its director, Albert Ballin, to be one of the inventors of cruise shipping, as under him the company was the first to custom-build a cruise ship. The *Prinzessin Victoria Luise* followed the highest technological standards of pleasure travel for the wealthy.

Launched in 1900, the *Prinzessin Victoria Luise* offered 119 first-class cabins—each including sleeping and living quarters as well as a bathroom—for passengers on trips to the West Indies, the Black Sea, the Mediterranean Sea and the North Sea. The vessel carried businessmen between Europe and the US and ferried numerous US tourists to and from the Caribbean (*New York Times* 1901a). Unlike other vessels, the *Prinzessin Victoria Luise* did not have room for cargo or mail. Instead, she offered passengers a range of amenities, including a library, a gymnasium, space for 'parlour entertainment' and even a darkroom for amateur photography (*New York Times* 1901b). High-level events on board included a reception for the then-president of Venezuela, Cipriano Castro (*New York Times* 1904a). The *New York Times* announced the names of eminent cruise passengers and published accounts of their well-being (*New York Times* 1904), also reporting when, for example, a ship accidentally ran aground off the coast of Jamaica (*New York Times* 1906). Many other companies entered what seems to have been a profitable business, and by 1909 Frank C. Clark was organizing tours across the globe for US tourists with the Hapag liner *Cleveland* (*New York Times* 1911a).

By 1912, Hapag had retired the original *Prinzessin Victoria Luise*. The company refurbished another ship, the *Deutschland*, and renamed it *Victoria Luise* (*New York Times* 1911a). Now the largest and finest cruising ship, it featured an uninterrupted promenade deck a quarter of a mile long, giving passengers the opportunity to enjoy the warm weather of the southern seas; it also provided passengers with large private cabins and public rooms, such as writing and smoking rooms, dining rooms, a gymnasium, and even a palm garden (*New York Times* 1911). During a visit to the Kiel Week regatta, a major annual sailing event in Germany, the ship (at that time primarily used by Ballin and his guests) hosted the German emperor and a number of American visitors (*New York Times* 1912). Indeed, cruise ships appeared to have offered a unique level of seclusion for the entertainment of wealthy leaders. A report from 1913 highlights other ways in which cruise ships functioned outside of national contexts and helped to skew socio-economic differences. In 1913, when local serving staff called a strike at the (US government–owned) Tivoli Hotel, Panama, where passengers were headed, the officers of the second *Victoria Luise* arranged for the ship's waiters to step in and staff the hotel instead (*New York Times* 1913). Working conditions on board went unscrutinized. When a sailor died while shifting a lifeboat in the dark, the story briefly caught the attention of the media but went largely unexplained (*New York Times* 1914).

After the stunning success of the *Victoria Luise*, Ballin developed another ship, the *Meteor*, for less-affluent tourists. This and other new ships allowed Hapag to become the leading cruise shipping company (Schulz 2012).

Cruise ship travel appears to have expanded steadily in the first decades of the twentieth century. After World War I, the shipping company Hamburg-Süd used the *Cap Polonio* for cruise ship purposes, but also offered space for second-class and steerage passengers; that is, it expand service to a larger group of passengers and took a first step towards low-budget cruises. Cruise ships regularly attracted the attention of the *New York Times* between 1923 and 1935, and the number of articles published on cruise shipping is used as an index of cruise ship popularity.[1] Even the Nazi government picked up on the concept; the Hamburg shipyards Blohm & Voss constructed a vessel, the *Wilhelm Gustloff*, for the pleasure trips of the 'Strength through Joy' organization, offering affordable trips for some German workers belonging to the *Arbeiterfront*, a Nazi association. On these ships the daily routines of the passengers were strictly regulated, from getting up at 6:20 in the morning until retiring for the night at midnight. But these trips were part of the Nazi propaganda campaign, and tourists who did not follow these rules risked losing their jobs back on land (Schallenberg 2005: 10, 30).

World War II meant a suspension of such activities, but Americans quickly returned to cruise ships after the end of the war and people from other nations followed. On 29 June 1946, the Norwegian-owned *Stella Polaris* left for the Caribbean with 180 passengers (*New York Times* 1946); famous for having been captured by Germany during the war, she had been refurbished after recapture. A second peak of reporting on cruise ships occurred between 1960 and 1969 with 14,413 records (as counted by ProQuest).[2] By 1967 the *New York Times* was reporting that 315,000 Americans took cruises in the 1966–1967 winter season, but the newspaper also noted that the industry had not sustained its formerly steady growth figure of 5% per year (Bamberger 1967). This ebb in business seems to coincide—if not correlate—with developments in the wider tourism industry, including the increasing availability of air travel to a growing number of tourist destinations.

Cruise Ship Tourism: Becoming a Mass Phenomenon

Since the 1980s, celebrated designs for waterfront revitalization schemes, the architecture of cruise ships, and the largely unknown spaces of the migrant workers map the social and spatial divisions of post-industrial society. In the 1980s, a major change tied together seemingly separate developments—the redevelopment of former inner-city waterfronts and the growth of cruise shipping—to effectively create new spatial and social patterns. As port administrators moved harbour functions to the outskirts of port cities to create container ports and facilitate the storage and transfer of goods onto road and rail, shipping abandoned traditional urban harbours. These former hives of activity on the waterfront were now quiet, and often brownfields, but soon became the site of revitalization schemes. At precisely the same time, cruise ships, traditionally a means of exclusive transportation to faraway destinations for a small elite, found a new customer base (the middle class) and new destinations (urban ports). Smaller than the new industrial ships, cruise ships could take passengers right into the historical heart of port cities. However, these ships did not stay small and would rapidly put new demands on their host cities. By 1985, the largest cruise ship, the *Carnival Holiday* had the same tonnage (46,000 tonnes) as the *Titanic*—although, at 221 m, it was shorter than the older ship (at about 270 m).

The construction of the *Queen Mary II* in 2003 ushered in a new age of truly gigantic cruise ships, including the *Royal Caribbean Oasis* and its sister ship the *Allure*, at 225,000 tonnes and 362 metres these cruise ships are more akin to tankers and container ships than to the pleasure ships of the past (Mouawad 2013). The *Allure* can host nearly 6,300 passengers and a staff of almost 2,400 crew members, and it offers amenities from a shopping mall to a water park, from a zip line to Broadway-style shows (Mouawad 2013). Over the last decade, the number of cruise ship tourists has risen steadily. Cruise tourism has developed into a form of mass tourism. In 2012, US cruise ships carried some 17 million passengers on fully catered vacations and tours to exotic locations (Mouawad 2013).

This impressive growth attests to the shipping companies' ability to find new customers. One strategy has been to provide themed experiences for people of a similar profile: busy executives, families, even fans of heavy-metal music (organized by TUI in 2013). A cruise for single parents offered by MSC in 2010-2011 offered special reductions to single parents with their children, showing the cruise industry adapting to the needs of non-traditional families such as single parenthood. Another strategy to attract customers is to offer them new attractions beyond the activities scheduled on board. Shipping companies organize visits in port cities on the cruise route and tailor programmes for the clientele on the ship. The companies often hire sub-contractors in the port cities who organize the tours for short-term visitors and hence secure a steady flow of visitors for museums and other local attractions.

There are still many ships of smaller dimensions to allow for elite experiences or to fit into smaller ports. The Italian cruise ship company Costa (at one point British-American, but acquired in 2000 by the global Carnival Cruise Company) launched ten German-based cruise ships, such as the *AIDAsol* in 2011. All were built by Meyer Werft, a traditional shipbuilding company on the River Ems in Germany, specializing in luxury passenger ships. The *AIDAsol* has 1,100 cabins and can carry 2,580 passengers and a crew of 611 persons. A larger *AIDA* cruise ship, the *AIDAprima*, is to enter the market in 2015 and offer an eighty-six-day cruise as a grand opening deal, traveling from Yokohama, Japan, where it was built by Mitsubishi, through the Suez Canal and on to Hamburg. Later, the ship will offer seven-day trips.

While the experience of cruise ship passengers is celebrated and extensively promoted, not all of these tours have fairy-tale endings, and the failures of the industry have also made good press. The *Costa Concordia* ran aground off the coast of Italy, near Giglio, in 2012, and more than thirty people died; the following year, the *Carnival Triumph* drifted for several days in the Gulf of Mexico, much to the discomfort of its passengers, until being towed into the port at Mobile, Alabama (Brown *et al.* 2013). Many of these ships are registered in countries with weak regulatory regimes, so the owners are effectively free of oversight in international waters, subject only to the safety and operation regulations of the International Maritime Organization (part of the UN). These and other socio-economic and labour implications of cruise shipping have yet to be fully studied. Similarly, the impact of cruise ships, and their diverse passengers and workers, on post-industrial port cities and waterfronts merits further research.

Port cities have since the 1990s have transformed their urban waterfronts and ports into tourist hubs and the loci of festivals aiming to reconnect the port and the city. Public and private promoters, often in public-private partnerships, collectively created a new vision of urbanism that favoured festivalization (Häußermann and Siebel 1998). With the European Capital of Culture programme and other large-scale events, many port cities have started to turn that vision into a reality. Even before the growth of cruise shipping, they redeveloped former industrial areas, port-related facilities and warehouses into historic monuments that host consumption and leisure activities, such as the architectural lighthouse projects in Baltimore and Osaka, and the aquarium in Genova. Museums and historical buildings flourished as cities developed them into important infrastructure for tourism. In the last decade, this urban redevelopment has attracted additional tourists who reach the city from the water and give new life to old waterfronts. Cities appreciate the revenue that passengers bring, an average of 85 euros per visit in a harbour and 194 euros when including a hotel stay (*Freizeit und Touristik* 2012). Multiplied by the growing number of tourists, this adds up to an important economic incentive. Cruise tourists have little time to spend and the goods available have to fit the taste and expectations of the short-term visitors. There is no time to rethink a decision to buy, and little time for individualized consultancy or slow consumption.

Cruise ships, effectively floating horizontal skyscrapers and movable small cities in their own right, have attracted onlookers to the waterfronts (Figure 16.1). Together, the new multifunctional districts, innovative public spaces, diverse maritime events and increased cruise ship travel, have created a synergy for local revitalization celebrated by local politicians, corporations, design professionals and the press. As with earlier celebrations of cruise ship travel, this story leaves out other more complex urban developments that are related to the growing cruise ship industry, such as informal economies and the people related to them.

Shipping companies often use sites that once served as embarkation points for thousands of migrants: for example, such historic terminals serve as cruise ship hubs for the passengers of MSN cruise ships in Venice and Genova. In other locations, new terminals stand as symbols of the recent growth in cruise ship tourism. These new, mostly centrally located terminals come in a variety of shapes, and many include a range of different functions such as stores, hotel, or public events, making the buildings usable even out of season. The terminal in Vancouver, Canada Place, was among the first to adopt this kind of mall approach.[3] More and more cities have constructed new terminals, resulting in what we can call a new architectural type, and one that attracts leading designers. Both local and foreign visitors are attracted by themed exhibitions and shops celebrating transportation, leisure and consumption. Here urban regeneration strategies are tourism led and serve an external clientele that makes uses of the new infrastructures.

Many of the new terminals are in Asia, attesting to the growing importance of that region as a destination for cruise ships and also illustrating the

Figure 16.1 A cruise ship anchoring in the old harbour of Genova, 2012

importance of these buildings as architectural beacons that create new narratives and attractions for their host cities. Among the first of the terminals custom-designed in Asia is the Osanbashi International Passenger Terminal in Yokohama, which allows tourists to disembark near to the Japanese capital, only 65 kilometres away. The terminal is the result of an international design competition held in 1995, won by Alejandro Zaera-Polo and Farshid Moussavi from the UK. Another more recent example of new terminals in Asia has just opened in the area of the former Hong Kong airport, which was known for its approach over the densely built inner-city Kowloon neighbourhood. Opened in 2013, the new terminal, designed by Norman Foster, provides facilities for the largest vessels, as well as a roof-top garden offering a 360-degree view of the city (Wassener 2013). A new cruise terminal just opened in Singapore, and Chinese port cities that have been expanding their port activities rapidly are racing to build new facilities (Wassener 2013). Other port cities in Asia, such as Manila, are focusing on middle-class tourists and have also started to develop their waterfronts (Van Naerssen 2013).

The increase of cruise ship traffic, passengers and terminals is a further step in the interface between port and city. Now new migratory streams (consisting of tourists, rather than sailors or emigrants, and of elite and middle-class passengers, rather than the working class or impecunious) are taking advantage of existing, often historic ports, updated or new terminals and waterfronts. Cruise ship tourists are often brought in by plane from far-away locations to avoid long-distance sea travel. Migration patterns for many people in the industrialized world have switched from work-related to leisure-related travel. In response, cruise ship tourism links the waterfront and its revitalization with the consumer. But work has not disappeared, for tourism depends on migrant labour. The importance of migrant crews and labourers to the cruise industry and the kinds of spaces these workers must occupy indicate that cruise tourism perpetuates historical class divisions, creating 'cities within cities' (Figure 16.2). Already in 1987, Shannon Wall, president of the National Maritime Union of America, pointed to the exploitation of the crews on cruise ships, as well as issues with sanitation and immigration (Wall 1987).

The rapid growth of this global industry has continued to threaten workers' rights, particularly since it seems to operate between regulatory spheres (Mouawad 2013). The conditions for workers on these ships are extremely bad (Terry 2009). This growth also damages the environment. Activists criticize this industry's environmentally disastrous use of heavy oil and unfiltered sulphurous gasoline, both dangerous to the health of urban inhabitants (De Luca 2013). Several bills have been brought before the US senate to enact national standards, requiring that waste water generated by cruise ships be treated; that 'treated blackwater' be 'avoided in ports, close to bathing beaches or water bodies with restricted circulation, flushing or inflow'; and furthermore, that 'blackwater not be discharged within 4 nautical miles of shellfish beds, coral reefs, or other sensitive habitats'

Figure 16.2 Migrants at the revitalized waterfront, Genova, 2012

(US Government 2013). The 2013 proposal is the fifth such bill proposed since 2004, and spells out the dangers of untreated wastewater specifically:

> (9) In just 1 week, a 3,000-passenger cruise ship generates approximately 200,000 gallons of human sewage, more than 1,000,000 gallons of water from showers and sinks and dishwashing water (commonly known as 'graywater'), more than 8 tons of solid waste, and toxic wastes from dry cleaning and photo-processing laboratories;
>
> (10) In an Environmental Protection Agency survey of 29 ships traveling in Alaskan waters, reported sewage generation rates ranged from 1,000 to 74,000 gallons per day per vessel, with the average volume of sewage generated being 21,000 gallons per day per vessel;
>
> (11) those frequently untreated cruise ship discharges deliver nutrients, hazardous substances, pharmaceuticals, and human pathogens, including viruses and bacteria, directly into the marine environment.
>
> (US Government 2013)

None of these bills have actually been passed. Nonetheless, catering to the cruise ship industry and ignoring climate change may backfire in the long run. For example, the loss of ice in Hudson Bay might curtail cruise shipping. Many tourists are taking cruise ships to the bay to look for ice-based wildlife. If the ice retreats (because of climate change caused in part by the ships themselves) the wildlife may move further north and cruise ships may ignore the port (Stewart *et al.* 2009).

The cruise industry's direct and indirect impact on localities, through its requests for new facilities or through urban redevelopment induced by strong economic incentives, can be very substantial. At the same time, the industry is a very fragile element within complex local economies. In Charleston, South Carolina, citizens are battling a proposal for a new cruise terminal (Severson 2013), in part because they know that the cruise ship industry left Mobile, Alabama altogether when port did not attract enough business (Severson 2013).

In short, the rebuilding of port waterfronts since the 1980s is entangled with a recent boom of cruise ship tourism and has resulted in the creation of new urban structures and social relations. To underscore our argument and point to a new line of research, the following section discusses two geographically, historically, spatially divergent European port cities: Genova, on the Mediterranean, and Hamburg, linked to the North Sea. These port cities exemplify the innovative reuse of existing port infrastructures and the significant recent shifts into post-industrial urban waterfront development and cruise ship development.

Local (Re)actions: Hamburg and Genova

Hamburg and Genova were departure points for international migrants in the late nineteenth century, playing a decisive role in transatlantic migration in particular; the infrastructure of both port cities was suitable for that role. Both cities have become highly diverse in their population and have a strong local urban identity. In recent years, they have shifted their working ports away from the centre, redeveloped their urban waterfronts and promoted themselves as nodes for global cruise ships. The recent boom in the cruise ship industry has affected tourism and the infrastructure for migrant workers in both cities. The shipping business has shaped these cities, and each boasts a major shipping company's headquarters: Hapag, once the global shipping company Hapag-Lloyd, on the Alster in Hamburg; and Costa on Via de Marini in Genova.

Hamburg began to reconstruct its waterfront after the fall of the Iron Curtain and thus before the rapid growth of the cruise ship industry. In 1985, after ten years of planning and the purchase of buildings and land in the area that did not belong to the city, the Hamburg senate founded the GHS (Gesellschaft für Hafen-und Standortentwicklung) as a subsidiary of the city-owned company in charge of the harbour and logistics (Hamburger

Hafen und Lagerhausgesellschaft—today HHLA) to build a project on a 157 hectares waterfront area near the city centre. Various events and festivals have since aimed to bring further funding and people to the area. As part of a seven-year International Building Exhibition (IBA), which came to an end in 2013, the city also promoted sustainable urban development and redeveloped traditional working-class residential areas close to the harbour that have been home to immigrants from many different countries.

The renewal of Hamburg's waterfront has been intimately tied to the city's encouragement of the cruise ship industry. Hamburg registered a half million passengers in 2014, the highest ever number. Two new cruise centres, designed by the Hamburg office of Renner Hainke Wirth, bracket the area of waterfront revitalization. The Elbe River separates these terminal areas from the working harbour. The temporary structure of the Hamburg Cruise Centre is close to the historic centre, adjacent to the recently redeveloped former warehouse district, now an area for leisure and education, and in the new multifunctional HafenCity. The second cruise ship terminal, the Hamburg Cruise Centre Altona, opened in 2011 in the lively western area near the well-attended weekly fish market, popular with tourists. Its roof, accessible to the public, affords broad views of the ships and the river. Other leisure amenities appear along the river, as well as new architectural highlights like the Elbphilharmonie (by the internationally recognized office of Herzog & de Meuron). The new multifunctional waterfront development depends on the continuous presence of tourists, not just locals. Events such as the biennial Cruise Days, held since 2008, woo tourists with extravagant events (Figure 16.3). In 2012, seven cruise ships, including two *AIDA* ships and the *Queen Mary II*, paraded down the Elbe River in front of the city's skyline, illuminated by thousands of blue lights, while fireworks exploded in the sky and a giant street festival brought together citizens and tourists along the waterfront, exemplifying the combination of waterfront renewal and cruise ship tourism in a new spatial paradigm. The growth of cruise ship tourism and the emergence of new migration patterns both for tourists and for workers has already led to debate about constructing a third cruise ship terminal. The city hopes that such a building would not only help meet the current demand but also further increase the numbers of cruise ship tourists. What this development means for citizens and cruise ship workers remains to be seen.

Genova funded the reincorporation of formerly separated waterfront areas into the city through exhibitions and events, including the Capital of Culture event in 2004. In the 1990s, when the old port was abandoned and the working port moved to Voltri, about 10 kilometres to the west, the municipality initiated the reconstruction of the historical centre. The city restored the old town, which had been the place of residence for many migrants from developing countries who worked as staff to support the large population of older people. Cheap housing in the old centre had also attracted students, who came through international mobility programs like

Figure 16.3 Cruise ship and fireworks at the old Elbtunnel during Cruise Days in Hamburg, 2012

ERASMUS. With the restoration of the old centre, new people and investments moved in. Many of the old town palaces are now open to the public and UNESCO declared the Renaissance-period ensemble of Strada Nova (today, Via Garibaldi) a World Heritage Site. The revitalization of the Genova harbour combined historic preservation and restructuring, reinforcing the historic character of the harbour promenade and the historic palaces, in concert with building new structures under the leadership of the global star architect Renzo Piano. Between 1999 and 2007, the city renovated the historic terminal Stazione Marittima—from where mass emigration to the US had taken place—as part of urban development programmes and for the G8 summit (Figure 16.4). When it reopened, it served ferry boats and, increasingly, cruise ships. The new facility provides passengers with easy access to both the centre of the old city and to the waterfront, with its numerous new tourist attractions such as the aquarium, the biosphere and the Bigo (a sculpture resembling a shipyard crane, designed by Piano). For the 1992 Columbus festivities, Genova modernized a former cotton warehouse in Porta del Molo and reopened it to the public. Since then, the number of cruise tourists here has doubled, from 471,245 to nearly 800,000 in 2012. Genoese Mayor Marco Doria welcomes this new tourism as essential for the economy, and the city has already approved projects to continue this transformation. The Affresco plan, again by Piano, aims to integrate the new harbour at Voltri with the old harbour. It includes proposals to update and

Figure 16.4 Stazione Marittima and cruise ship in Genova

expand highway and rail route links between the harbour, the hinterland and the airport located on the sea. This large architectural project, even if accepted, has yet to be implemented (Hillmann 2011).

Parts of this newly built environment are also connected to cruise tourism: Costa Cruise is running the aquarium as a so-called edutainment experience. This is just one example of the contemporary management structure of the waterfront, and the increased entanglement of architecture and space with politics, business and the narration of urban development and mobility.

Conclusions: New Mobilities in Old Migration Architecture

Port cities such as Genova and Hamburg register emerging trade patterns in their spatial and social organization, as we can see in the recent renewal and transformation of historic waterfronts in conjunction with growing mass cruise ship development. The current spatial transformation goes hand in hand with socio-economic restructuring and polarization that is connected to increasingly globalized labour markets. These allow for cheap labour in branches that serve the cruise industry, a phenomenon that needs to be studied more closely. On the cruise vessel, a migrant crew, paid by the shipping company where the ship is registered, works for well-off tourists who experience sea-borne mobility without borders. The port cities themselves have evolved a new economy to provide food, souvenirs and diverse other services to short-term tourists. This economy partly depends on migrant and day labourers. In Hamburg, migrant and day labourers seek work in the harbour, receiving minimal rewards and no job security (TAZ 2011); in Genova, irregular migrants work within the informal economy serving the port and the tourist industry, especially in the food sector. Transnational networks of migrants and money guarantee (through remittances and the exchange of information) a steady flow of workers parallel to the flow of tourists. Most migrants seem to work in labour-intensive, tourist-tied industries; some clean ships; others work in travel agencies or as city guides. Urban studies literature emphasizes the extensive physical changes that the industry creates; the social dimensions of this urban transformation are less reported and analyzed. There is also little research on the different types of linkages, symbolic and material, that drive the transformation of port cities through the cruise industry and that are linked to waterfront regeneration policies.

To sum up: shipping companies and city governments alike have sought to bring big ships back to the city centre and to showcase historic urban centres and urban redevelopment projects on the waterfront. Where huge working ships once sailed into the heart of the city to deliver goods and take other products away, now these giant horizontal skyscrapers of tourists cruise in to revitalize old ports. In place of old patterns of work and leisure, the cruise industry is establishing new migratory corridors and networks. Cruise ships thus help to economically revitalize urban ports that had been abandoned following the containerization of global shipping.

At times, these changes challenge the structure of the entire city, at least in the opinion of some citizens. That is, while politicians, planners and entrepreneurs are in favour of these changes and seek to encourage them, the ordinary inhabitants of cities such as Venice are often moved to organize protests against them. In Venice, the feeling against cruises is so strong that citizens throw themselves into the water, hoping to obstruct passage of the nine or so vessels that, each day, sail through the Canale Giudecca and past San Marco (Corriere del Veneto 2013). The anti-cruise organizations No Grandi Navi and No Global argue that the vibration from the ships damages the historic structures of Venice and that the huge ships displace so much water that they raise the water level in this island city (Pichler 2012). Their protests, and Pichler's documentary on the changing living conditions in Venice, signal that many inhabitants of port cities feel excluded from urban policies (Pichler 2012). They fear that planners ignore their concerns about the quality of urban life in favour of the temporary desires of affluent visitors.

Despite such protests, the ongoing and planned increase of cruise ship tourism is likely to continue to be an integral part of urban waterfront transformations. As cities have reclaimed and redefined their waterfronts to make them more accessible to tourists and (some) local citizens, they have turned them into global brands. But local governments will have to figure out how to integrate the new migratory streams to the benefit of both locals and tourists. Cruise ship traffic thus raises new questions and revives old ones about the historical divides between different population groups, cities within cities, and the multiple migratory streams that touch them. As the physical environment changes, in part because of the cruise industry itself, there is a shift in the narratives and representations of the waterfront and the port city. Local and global leaders, politicians, shipping companies or built-environment professionals are using the advent of the cruise ships as an incentive to further transform the waterfront and the city for the changing demands of cruise travellers, rewriting urban spaces and the living and working conditions of citizens and working-class migrants.

Notes

1　The database ProQuest Historical Newspapers shows two spikes in the number of articles published that include the search term 'cruise ship'. The highest spike occurs in the years 1930 to 1939 with 12,852 articles published in this period and the peak of publications in 1935.
2　The database ProQuest Historical Newspapers shows another spike between 1960 and 1969 with 14,413 articles. The term 'cruise ship' is then used less and less for the period from 2000 to 2009, showing only about 5,037 records.
3　See www.canadaplace.ca.

Bibliography

Augé, M. (1995) *Non-Places: Introduction to an Anthropology of Supermodernity*, Brooklyn, NY: Verso.

Bamberger, W. (1967) 'Cruise Ship Lines Disappointed by Winter Season: Big Increase Not Expected', *New York Times*, 2 April.

Braudel, F. (1982) *The Wheels of Commerce: Civilization and Capitalism 15th–18th Century*, New York: Harper & Row.

Breen, A. and Rigby, D. (1996) *The New Waterfront*, London: Thames and Hudson.

Brown, R., Severson, K., Meier, B. (2013) 'Cruise Line's Woes Are Far from over as Ship Makes Port', *New York Times* 14 February: 14.

Corriere del Veneto (2013) 'Grandi navi, tensione in laguna e i No Global si buttano in acqua', 21 September. Available at: http://corrieredelveneto.corriere.it/veneto/notizie/cronaca/2013/21-settembre-2013/grandi-navi-striscioni-spray-blitz-no-global-aeroporto-2223222791787.shtml. (Accessed on 15 January 2015).

De Luca, D. (2013) 'La questione delle grande navi a Venezia'. Available at: www.ilpost.it/davidedeluca/2013/08/22/la-questione-delle-grandi-navi-a-venezia/ (Accessed on 26 December 2014).

Freizeit und Touristik (2012) 'Genua—Erträge durch Kreuzfahrtschiffe', Newsletter Kreuzfahrt 48, 4 (20 June): 1. Available at: www.kreuzfahrt-forschung.de. (Accessed on 26 December 2014).

Häußermann, H. and Siebel, W. (1998) 'Festivalisierung der Stadtentwicklung', *Werk, Bauen + Wohnen*, June: 20–29.

Hein, C. (ed.) (2011) *Port Cities*, London: Routledge.

Hein, C. (2013) 'Modern Cities: Interactions: Port Cities', in P. Clark (ed.), *Oxford Handbook of Cities in World History*, Oxford and New York: Oxford University Press, 809–827.

Hein, C. (2015) 'Temporalities of the Port, the Waterfront and the Port City', in, *Portus*, Venice: RETE, 29. Available at: www.portusonline.org/temporalities-of-the-port-the-waterfront-and-the-port-city/.

Hein, C. and Hillmann, F. (2013) 'The Missing Link: Redevelopment of the Urban Waterfront as a Function of Cruise Ship Tourism', in, *Portus*, Venice: RETE, 26. Available at: www.portusonline.org/category/this_issue/26/opinions-this_issue/.

Hillmann, F. (2011) *Grosse Schiffe am Horizont und Fragmentierung zuhause. Stadtentwicklung in Genua*, Leipzig: Leipzig Institut für Länderkunde.

Mah, A. (2014) Port cities and global legacies, London: Palgrave Macmillan.

Meyer, H. (1993) *City and Port*, Rotterdam: 010 Publishers.

Mouawad, J. (2013) 'Too Big to Sail? Cruise Ships Face Scrutiny', *New York Times*, 27 October.

New York Times (1901a) 'Henry C. Payne Here', 10 August.

New York Times (1901b) 'New Cruising Yacht', 18 January.

New York Times (1904a) 'Cruise of the Prinzessin Victoria Luise', 24 January.

New York Times (1904b) 'The Victoria Luise at Jamaica', 24 January.

New York Times (1906) 'Victoria Luise Wreck Tale', 29 December.

New York Times (1911a) 'Rival World Cruises', 1 June.

New York Times (1911b) 'Old Deutschland in Port', 3 October.

New York Times (1912) 'Joys of Kiel Week Lure Americans', 23 June.

New York Times (1913) 'Took Ship's Waiters Ashore', 9 March.

New York Times (1914) 'Sailor Killed on Liner', 10 January.

New York Times (1946) 'Luxury Ship off on Cruise Today' 29 June.

Pichler, A. (2012) 'Das Venedig-Prinzip', documentary film. Available at: http://venedigprinzip.de/?lang=en. (Accessed on 15 January 2015).

Sassen, S. (ed.) (2002) *Global Networks, Linked Cities*, New York: Routledge.

Schäfer, C. (1998) *Kreuzfahrten: die touristische Eroberung der Ozeane*, Dissertation, Nürnberg.

Schallenberg, C. (2005) *KdF—Kraft durch Freude*, Bremen: Universität.

Schulz, A. (ed.) (2012) *Verkehr Und Tourismus: Ein Studienbuch in Fallbeispielen*, Munich: Oldenbourg Wissenschaftsverlag.

Severson, K. (2013) 'This Charleston Harbor Battle Is Over Cruise Ships', *New York Times*, 19 February.

Stewart, E.J., Tivy, A., Howell, S.E.L., Dawson, J. and Draper, D. (2009) 'Cruise Tourism and Sea Ice in Canada's Hudson Bay Region', *Arctic*, 63: 57–66.

TAZ (2011) 'Hire und Fire im Hafen. Der Gesamthafenbetrieb hat über Jahre hinweg Tagelöhner beschäftigt', 20 September. Available at: www.taz.de/!77996/. (Accessed 15 January 2015).

Terry, W.C. (2009) 'Working on the Water: On Legal Space and Seafarer Protection in the Cruise Industry', *Economic Geography*, 85: 463–482.

US Government (2013). 'Clean Cruise Ship Act of 2013', 113th Congress, 2013–2015. Available at: www.govtrack.us/congress/bills/113/s1359/text.

Van Naerssen, T. (2013) 'Urban.Development and Globalization: The Case of the Cebu International Port in Central Philippines'. Paper presented at the session: 'Big ships on the horizon and social and spatial fragmentation at home—port cities as emblematic places of urban transformation', RC21- conference, Berlin, 29 August 2013.

Wall, S.J. (1987) 'Letter to the Editor: For the Crew of a Cruise Ship, It's Anything but a "Love Boat" ', *New York Times*, 24 October.

Wassener, B. (2013) 'Hong Kong's Old Airport Reopens', *New York Times*, 11 June. Available at www.nytimes.com/2013/06/12/business/global/hong-kongs-old-airport-reopens-as-a-cruise-ship-terminal.html?_r=0.

Index

Note: figures and tables are denoted with italicized page numbers; end note information is denoted with an n following the page number.